CRITICAL RESEARCH METHODOLOGIES

Studies in Critical Social Sciences Book Series

Haymarket Books is proud to be working with Brill Academic Publishers (www.brill.nl) to republish the *Studies in Critical Social Sciences* book series in paperback editions. This peer-reviewed book series offers insights into our current reality by exploring the content and consequences of power relationships under capitalism, and by considering the spaces of opposition and resistance to these changes that have been defining our new age. Our full catalog of *SCSS* volumes can be viewed at https://www.haymarketbooks .org/series_collections/4-studies-in-critical-social-sciences.

CRITICAL RESEARCH METHODOLOGIES

Ethics and Responsibilities

EDITED BY

ROSE ANN TORRES
DIONISIO NYAGA

Haymarket Books
Chicago, IL

First published in 2021 by Brill Academic Publishers, The Netherlands
© 2021 Koninklijke Brill NV, Leiden, The Netherlands

Published in paperback in 2022 by
Haymarket Books
P.O. Box 180165
Chicago, IL 60618
773-583-7884
www.haymarketbooks.org

ISBN: 978-1-64259-768-4

Distributed to the trade in the US through Consortium Book Sales and
Distribution (www.cbsd.com) and internationally through Ingram Publisher
Services International (www.ingramcontent.com).

This book was published with the generous support of Lannan Foundation and
Wallace Action Fund.

Special discounts are available for bulk purchases by organizations and
institutions. Please call 773-583-7884 or email info@haymarketbooks.org for more
information.

Cover design by Jamie Kerry and Ragina Johnson.

Printed in the United States.

10 9 8 7 6 5 4 3 2 1

Library of Congress Cataloging-in-Publication data is available.

Contents

Acknowledgements

We would like to thank God for seeing us through the making of this book. We also want to thank all the contributors who participated in this journey of examining research methods from a critical perspective. And last but the least, we thank the series editor, David Fasenfest, and Jason Prevost and Jennifer Obdam from Brill Publishing for all the support and guidance.

Notes on Contributors

Katie Bannon
is a recent MEd graduate from the Social Justice Education (sJE) program at the
Ontario Institute for Studies in Education. Bannon teaches Business Software
courses at a post-secondary institution in Toronto, where they focus on integrating community-based action and applying an anti-oppressive and equity-
based lens into pedagogy. Bannon also participates in grassroots community-
based solidarity groups that are dedicated to actioning towards futures that
align with Indigenous sovereignty and Black liberation.

Elizabeth Charles
is a Social Justice Advocate, Educator & Writer and senior People & Culture
Leader who is completing her doctoral studies in Social Justice Education
at the Ontario Institute for Studies in Education (OISE) at The University of
Toronto. Her research focuses on intersectionality and leadership and centres the ontological and epistemological experiences of Black and non-Black
women senior leaders in Canadian workplaces. As Founder of EHC Solutions
Inc., Charles partners with communities of business leaders, students and educators to build inclusive intelligence for global leadership.

Khulood Agha Khan
is currently an elementary school teacher at the Halton District School Board
and a student for a Doctorate of Social Justice in Education at the University
of Toronto. She is a recipient of Bigger Hedges Technology Integration in
Curriculum Award 2018 from the University of Toronto during her Masters
of Teaching. She identifies herself as a Muslim Immigrant woman in Canada.
Her research focuses on Math anxiety in elementary teachers and social justice barriers faced by the immigrant Muslim women in Canada. Her passion to
improve educational pedagogy through research has guided her to be sensitive
to the needs of families and students and has prompted her to focus on equity,
diversity, and inclusion in the school community.

Dionisio Nyaga
earned his Ph.D. at Social Justice Education-OISE/ University of Toronto. He
has master's and bachelor's degrees from Ryerson University's School of Social
Work. He is currently a Lecturer at Ryerson University, School of Social Work,
teaching both undergraduate and graduate courses. His Doctoral research is
focused on uncoupling Black masculinity through the narratives of Kenyan

men in Toronto. His teaching, research and practice interests are in the areas of critical anti-oppression, community development and engagement, anti-Blackness, masculinity studies, diaspora and transnational studies, cultural studies, men and masculinities, social justice, Indigenous and spirituality studies.

Fritz Pino
is an Assistant Professor at the Faculty of Social Work, University of Regina. She completed a PhD in Social Justice Education and a Masters in Social Work from the University of Toronto. Pino's research focuses on the lives and experiences of historically marginalized communities, particularly those who identify as LGBTQ+, racialized immigrant, and older adult. Pino is interested in examining how racialized LGBTQ navigate the complexities and contradictions of everyday life in the margins as reflected through their bodily performances, affect and emotions, and personal desires. Her empirical and community work has been informed by critical intersectionality approaches, particularly from a queer diasporic lens, which pays significant attention to the impact of transnational migration, nation-state of belonging, and normative discourses.

Rose Ann Torres
is an Assistant Professor of Sociology within the Department of Social Science at the University of New Brunswick in Saint John. Torres has published articles and books on gendered citizenship, politics of culture, health, healing, work, Indigenous epistemologies, community development, critical research methodologies, Asian Canada is burning, and identity formation. Her research interest includes post-structural theory, ethical dilemmas and responsibilities, community health and wellness, community development and engagement, economic security, social wellness, and women and gender issues.

Introduction

Critical Research Methodologies

Rose Ann Torres and Dionisio Nyaga

Research methodologies are among the main courses/topics in undergraduate courses in the Social Sciences and Humanities. Students are taught how to collect data and the epistemologies of producing knowledges. This edited collection broaches the question of 'how' of collecting data from a critical deconstructive perspective? To be "critical" ties to the question of considering the power relations between the researcher and the participant. We also include the questions of ethics and positionality to inscribe the art of implicating the self to the modalities of social production of knowledge. Such critical perspectives to research are important since they place research as a political process of aesthetic production of the self and others. This book is an edited collection about research methodologies. It aims to bring out new ways of conceptualizing research methodologies beyond the current liberal and progressive ways. The book is informed by post-structural, anti-colonial, post-colonial, feminist, anti-oppressive, Marxist, ant-racist, anti-Black, anti-Native, anti-Asian, reflexive theories. The contributors of these chapters will use their own research projects to showcase a critical research methodology and ways of visualizing research process. This way students will not only learn the theoretical part on how to critic a research methodology but the art of producing knowledge beyond the present positivist means.

The editors teach research method in social work and sociology department. We (editors) expect that the edited book will be used by the undergraduate and graduate level in Social Sciences and Humanities. Our book is for a wider audience who does not only engage from a critical anti-oppressive lens. This is the reason why our contributors will not only use anti-oppressive approach but, also other theories that will be accessible to the undergraduate and graduate students in the Social Sciences and Humanities. Their research expertise is in the areas of transformative education, Social Work, Queer studies, feminism, anti-oppressive, reflexive, anti-Black studies, disability, and among others. We are not only re-imagining research but also critiquing Euro-centric liberal research and offer a new direction on how to conduct research.

Chapter 1 examines "Critical Research Methodologies: Positionality, Ethics, Power" by Dionisio Nyaga. He identified some specific point in research where colonial erasure of community is supervised by qualitative process in ways that consistently mark other ways of producing knowledge as broken and unimprovable. With that in mind, the chapter calls for the return of subjugated knowledges as an ethical and political process of questioning the whiteness impended in knowledge production.

Chapter 2 focuses on "Research Methodologies: Histories, Issues, Tensions" by Rose Ann Torres. Torres focuses on how such research methods are used from a critical perspective. Torres argues that one of the ways of doing so is to look at the histories, tensions, and issues in research. Research is not just about numbers but also about different praxis and methods used by Indigenous and racialized peoples. It answers the questions of how we know, what we know, and how we know what we know.

Chapter 3 explores "Torn Apart: Racialized Feelings and the Ethics of Doing Research with One's Own Community" by Fritz Pino. Pino reveals how research itself becomes a marker of privilege, including how it reinforces a dominant discourse, which impacts the sense of self of a racialized researcher, as well as their community relationships and solidarity. Ultimately, the analyses encourage us to continue to reflect on the significant role of race and racialization – its discursive and affective impact - in the conduct of academic research.

Chapter 4 examines "Critical Ethnography: Discussions of Ethics and Principles" by Rose Ann Torres. This chapter adopts critical ethnography as a public health qualitative research design in relation to ethics and principles. The central question addressed in this chapter is: What does critical ethnography as a public health qualitative research methodology look like from an ethical perspective?

Chapter 5 explores "My Blackness Is African: Looking at Kenyan Man through Black/Afrocentric Methodologies" by Dionisio Nyaga. This chapter is based on a research that was done among Kenyan men living in Toronto. The main focus of the study was to understand how accent was affecting their lives in terms of access to education, employment and the process of immigration. The result of the study identified the fact that accent made it impossible for them to survive in the classroom and subsequently rendered them unemployed or underemployed.

Chapter 6 focuses on "Storytelling: A Critical Narrative Approach" by Rose Ann Torres. Torres states that storytelling is part of our everyday lives and is used in everything that we do. She adds that storytelling is also about expressing the things that we experience in our dreams, in our visions, and in our different encounters with the universe. In other words, storytelling is the stories we tell from pain, suffering, and joy. It this chapter, Torres discusses storytelling as a critical narrative approach.

Chapter 7 talks about "Research as an Inconsolable Mourning: Reimagining Pedestrian Research" by Rose Ann Torres and Dionisio Nyaga. This chapter engages imagination of ourselves beyond our current place of being. It looks at the return to the "original" place as a traumatic and political reflexive process that plays a great role in developing new ideas and possibilities. Torres and Nyaga argue that such mourning is ongoing, which allows an unending form of grievability to inform research. This will give voice to those voices that have continued to be marginalized. This chapter was written at a time when Black and Asian bodies continue to lose their lives under an environment of COVID-19.

Chapter 8 focuses on "A Black Woman's Perspective on Leadership and Risk-Taking: Exploring Research Methodologies That Can Transcend the Discourse of Mainstream Leadership Thought" by Elizabeth Charles. Sharing her personal experiences with leadership and risk-taking, Charles will demonstrate how when researchers of leadership theories employ methods associated with critical intersectional epistemology, critical ethnography and personal narrative that centre the experiences, epistemologies and standpoint of Black women, they can unveil effective leadership practices of marginalized Black women who have led successfully and transcend those hegemonic elite White patriarchal discourses that all too often get positioned prominently in mainstream leadership thought.

Chapter 9 focuses on "Assessing Math Anxiety in Male Elementary Teachers as Learners and as Teachers" by Khulood Agha Khan. This chapter reports data from a qualitative study that explored and investigated the male elementary teacher's perspective on math anxiety as a student and as a teacher. This study analyzed the relationships among math anxiety, math self-concept, teachers' pedagogy and student performance. Specifically, this study presents data and discussion regarding some of the challenges faced by students and the resiliency to face those challenges.

Chapter 10 explores "Connecting the "Here and Now" with "What Could Be": A Critical Analysis of Imagination as Method Engaging Queer Futurities" by Katie Bannon. This chapter provides a critical analysis of the qualitative research method "Imagination as Method" through engaging a critique that centres knowledge from Black, Indigenous and Queer of Colour theorists.

Chapter 11 focuses on "Black Afrocentric Methodologies: Beyond Colour-Coated Investigation" by Dionisio Nyaga. This chapter looks at the ways in which ethics can precede knowledge so that production of knowledge can be a praxis of being human. The chapter looks at how Black Afrocentric research can help produce knowledge in ways that verb Blackness.

An Afterword concludes the book with comments on "Using Critical Research Methodologies: The Significance of Reflexivity, Resistance, and Response". Torres and Nyaga state that this book engages with the ways in which research has and continues to be implicated in policing and taking life from communities. This volume showcases contributors' understanding of research from different vantage points. It centers the contributors' ways of looking at research and how they use these approaches from a critical perspective. The volume has a mix of different research vantage points that help reimagine research as beyond and between rationality and emotionality. This book identifies critical reflexivity as necessary in the re-evaluation of research.

PART 1

Overview of Critical Research Methodologies

∴

CHAPTER 1

Critical Research Methodologies

Positionality, Ethics, Power

Dionisio Nyaga

1 Introduction

> In the history of ideas, of thought and of the sciences, the same mutation has brought about the opposite effect; it has broken up the long series formed by the progress of consciousness, or the teleology of reason, or the evolution of human thought; it has questioned the themes of convergence and culmination; it has doubted the possibility of creating totalities. It has led to the individualization of different series, which are juxtaposed to one another, follow one another, overlap and intersect, without one being able to reduce them to a linear schema. Thus, in place of the continuous chronology of reason, which was invariably traced back to some inaccessible origin, there have appeared scales that are sometimes very brief, distinct from one another, irreducible to a single law, scales that bear a type of history peculiar to each one, and which cannot be reduced to the general model of a consciousness that acquires, progresses, and remembers.
>
> (FOUCAULT, 2002, p. 8)

> The passage from quality to quantity reveals at the heart of an ontological problem, a political problem. The stakes are quite high. It is clear to Hegel that the relationship between the One and the multiple is an (analogical) foundation for a theory of social organization, an ontological basis for politics. To attack the dialectical unity of the One and the multiple, then, is to attack the primacy of the state in the formation of society, to insist on the real plurality of society.
>
> (HARDT, 1993, p.13)

As a professor teaching research methods in a university setting, I find myself engaged with the question of what "true" decolonization of research would look like, notwithstanding previous studies on the topic (e.g., Fraser, 2004;

Gegeo & Watson-Gegeo, 2001; Hollway & Jefferson, 2000; Lawler, 2002; Reviere, 2001; Reyes Cruz, 2008; Smith, 2012). Among the main features in such studies is the involvement of community in terms of how we come to know what we know; yet, the dominant process of knowledge production continues to relegate community knowledge as emotional and uncivilized (Reviere, 2001; Smith, 2012). Based on this argument, decolonization in research is a call for the acknowledgment that research has been used (and continues to be used) as a colonial tool to demarcate and systematize knowledge in ways that expunge some knowledges as emotional while affirming others as true and rational (Gegeo & Watson-Gegeo, 2001; Reyes Cruz, 2008; Smith, 2012; Wehbi, 2017). To that end, research is gendered, raced, and classed (Reviere, 2001; Reyes Cruz; (2008) Smith, 2012), meaning that its process has material and symbolic consequences (Harrington, 2005; Smith, 2012; Wehbi, 2017). In short, the research process defines how we construct and visualize the world in terms of being developed and underdeveloped (Wehbi, 2017).

Foucault (1980) says that knowledge is intractably connected to power. This interlocked essence of power and knowledge means that those who produce knowledge control its consumers' reality, value, and ways of being (Reyes Cruz, 2001). This means that knowledge production is an industrial process of truth making and determines whether one is human or subhuman (Wehbi, 2017). Those who engage with the meta/physical sense of knowing (read irrational/ broken/subhuman) are consigned to animal instinct while those who engage at a mental state are exulted as human and rational citizens. This means that knowledge producers are regarded as citizens while those who consume that knowledge are viewed as alien and easily deportable.

The essence of deportability is a confirmation of the fact that the emotional state has no place in knowledge production, thus creating a sense of homelessness. This means that emotions reside at the intersection of citizenship and non-citizenship—at the borderline, a space of exception where law can cease to exist and where violence is normalized and regulated (Razack, 2015). For a while, those who have citizenship to produce knowledge have been heterosexual, White abled men, which has simultaneously relegated the rest of humanity into border spaces, defined here collectively as a space of violence, brutality, nature, and incivility. This claim posits knowledge as being gendered, raced, classed, and dis/abled.

Claiming "true" decolonization as a process of humanizing research is a methodology that may return us to the "original" method of colonizing knowledge. To identify a particular decolonial strategy as a cannon of truth is problematic and in itself colonial. A case in point is the profusion of qualitative knowledge that seemed White and alienated other ways of knowledge (e.g.,

Afrocentric, Indigenous) as not being rational enough while simultaneously engaging White middle-class women as having outgrown their emotionality, which is discussed later in the chapter (Reinharz, 1992; Wahab et al., 2015). Social work as a profession has played a big role in the confirmation of women's rights, which encompasses labour rights, voting rights, and other social justice issues. Social work researchers and practitioners have used qualitative research approaches as a standpoint of affirming their place to citizenship and yet the same research methods have returned a science of quantitative truth. While returning may be employed as a reflexive move to measure our success, I argue that settling to quantitative as the measure of such a success is problematic.

This feminist qualitative historical juncture situates "true decolonization" as an evasive term and praxis that always slip out of our hands just as we "arrive' to claim 'true decolonization. All too often we speak of numbers (i.e., quantitative research) as colonization through the reduction of human stories (Faulkner & Faulkner; 2014). As social science researchers, our take has always been that qualitative research methods are an alternative to the coloniality of quantitative scientific methods. While that may be "true" in a way, it is also untrue—more so when we engage reflexively to these qualitative methods which seemingly seek recognition from without (read: the science of quantification). This chapter offers a critically reflexive process of untying the hidden truth about these qualitative methods to bring forth new decolonizing orientations to research, which are not by themselves the end or final definition of a true decolonial research method. In this chapter, I look at critical reflexivity as a necessary "tool" for unwrapping colonial narratives hidden bellow and above qualitative research methods and approaches, so that researchers can acknowledge their place of interlocked and intersected privilege and oppression in ways that displace their comfort of how they do research.

This chapter looks beyond the process of "digging deep" as a critically reflective process to research and begins a wider conversation of how critically decolonial research can also be a process of displacement and therefore a critically community-based research process. To engage in this process, I first underline quantitative positivist research as a colonial process (Smith, 2012). In this chapter, positivism borrows from the philosophical orientations of French philosopher Auguste Comte. This philosophy believes in the order of things: systematization, logic science, and empiricism (Aliyu et al., 2014). To Comte, society was divided into theological, metaphysical, and scientific stages, and he was a proponent of the latter stage. This chapter looks at decolonizing the research process in knowledge production and truth making from multifaceted dimensions. After that, I engage with the saviour syndrome of a White qualitative research process and discuss how it is implicated in the coloniality of marginalized groups. I look at different approaches to research in ways that open colonial quantitative research hegemony that still exists within the qualitative process of producing knowledge. I will end with a "conclusive" word of opening research futurities lead by social work. My role in this chapter is to open new conversation on how coloniality continues to be manifested in the ways of how we produce and consume knowledge quantitatively and qualitatively.

2   Quantitative Knowledge Production

It is supposed that between all the events of a well-defined spatio-temporal area, between all the phenomena of which traces have been found, it must be possible to establish a system of homogeneous relations: a network of causality that makes it possible to derive each of them, relations of analogy that show how they symbolize one another, or how they all express one and the same central core; it is also supposed that one and the same form of historicity operates upon economic structures, social institutions and customs, the inertia of mental attitudes, technological practice, political behaviour, and subjects them all to the same type of transformation; lastly, it is supposed that history itself may be articulated into great units – stages or phases – which contain within themselves their own principle of cohesion.

(FOUCAULT, 2002, pp. 9–10)

Research as a process of producing knowledge continues to be framed within a colonial framework (Harrington, 2005; Smith, 2012; Wehbi, 2017). Quantitative positivist research as a colonial practice employs numbers as a necessary determining factor of what is true. The belief in positivist research is that there is a truth out there and the role of the research is to retrieve/uncover it from its hidden state of nature (Aliyu et al., 2014). Such hidden spaces are identified as emotional and irrational and as such for any truth to appear the researcher must engage with emotional elements in their state of nature in ways that reduce them to one truth. Positivist research is therefore a process of compressing emotions to force out the truth. The process of compression is also the process of reductionism whereby emotional aspects of being are discarded in the process of truth making. When discussing reductionism, I speak of the process through which the whole is made to disappear for the sake of its subset which then comes to define the lost and forgotten whole. The process of disappearance is metaphoric in the sense that the death of the whole is a necessary evil of producing the single truth. This whole is the emotional part of what constitutes the being and as such it's an ethical and a fundamental element of any process of knowledge creation, yet it is through its death that truth is made real.

To speak of compressing the emotional whole as an ethical process is to impress the loss of life for the existence of truth. Knowledge production and truth making therefore become a process that is biopolitical and an administration of life in ways that determine who is to live and who is to die (Foucault, 1997), hence exemplifying the materiality of knowledge and power. To put this in the human perspective, one must look at how human life is reducible to its minimum life for it to exist. To speak of minimum is to speak of bare life—a life that is displaceable, replaceable, and discardable. By this I mean that human life ceases to be an ethical prerogative in research and can easily be dislocated and evacuated for the sake of seeking this one scientific truth. Such is also the process through which people's storied lives are replaced with a number that is assumed to tell the truth about the human. That means that the production of the human through research is simultaneously the loss of life. We are human beings because we live a storied life. Stories gives us the reason to exist. The simplification of such stories into a numerical sense is to claim the death of humans and as such an administration of whose life matters and whose is grievable when lost (Butler, 2009). That some lives can be grieved while others remain lost speaks of the extent to which research as an accounting of lives for some also discounts others as non-existent even in death. To speak of research as evacuation and as an account of life is to look back at the history of colonization and the role science plays in the displacement of communities.

Bromley's (2003) work on spatiality and surveying creates a vivid picture of displacement and production of space/s through numbers and the role of law in the process of such production and dislocation. The use of surveys, which is a commonly used research tool and which Bromley speaks of in his work, is a testament of how research is implicated in colonialism. Research continues to be a process of producing and administrating spaces and bodies in ways that mark some bodies as citizens and others as aliens. The use of numbers allows the production of spaces through freezing of bodies in ways that regulate and police and thus rend such bodies as homeless and placeless. To speak of freezing such bodies is to scrap out their emotions, spiritualities, and histories from their psyche, allowing them instead to be replaced with a colonial number meant to conserve them in Western rationalities and realities, which enhances their perpetual surveillance and displacement.

Allow me to push Bromley's spatial grid making and engage with Foucault's disciplining and punishment of bodies to bring the implication of how we produce knowledge through imprinting pain and suffering to the marginalized population. As discussed earlier, human being is storied life. To remove a story from the being is to kill its very existence as being. What Foucault's work looks at is the process of cutting through the flesh of people in order to retrieve a truth that can be packaged and sold in the market. The key to this element of production of the other through pain is market rationality. This brings the material purpose of number in the current market economy. Numbers are a necessary evil in grid making and determine whose life and story will be grieved and whose life will be lost (Butler, 2009).

On the other hand, positivist research also looks at the order of things. There is a hierarchy involving who does the research, how the research is done, what can be determined as knowledge, and whose values and realities will count in knowledge (Gegeo & Gegeo, 2001). Key to any positivist research is the role of rationality and the place of the rational self. In this perspective, there is always a truth that can be found in emotional spaces and only rational beings are capable of finding that truth. To be a rational being is to occupy the space of the mind and intention and break away from the emotions and nature. To engage with emotions is to displace the self from the community of humans. To that end, any being who is emotional is subsequently subhuman and in conflict with the law. This has both material and symbolic perspectives in terms of who is allowed to create knowledge and who will consume it. Those who produce knowledge come to be identified as human and rational while those who consume it occupy the place of the disposable emotional others who must be saved from themselves through research. Research become a process of saving humanity from their emotions and their state of nature, which is nasty, brutish, and short (Renz, 2018). On the other hand, the demarcation between the mind and the body as a quintessential element of scientific research is a gendered process where men are seen as the producers of knowledge and women as consumers. It is also a racialized process where Whiteness is the quintessential definition of rationality and research and other racialized bodies as just templates of knowledge.

Positivist researchers believe that society orients the individual and believe in the quantification of human experiences. They believe that there are facts out there that control social realities of individuals. Those realities can be identified through quantification methods that help understand human beings. In positivist research, there is an organized, orderly, and systematic process of creating knowledge right from the point of identifying the problem, reviewing the literature, design, data collection, and analysis. The positivist system of knowledge production looks at the production and measurement of truth as a process that can be done in a controlled environment, which makes it easy to generalize its aftermath to the whole population. Knowledge from a sample population is operated in a laboratory-like environment, one in which researchers are expected to be objective and distant from what they are investigating. The process of objectivity also means objectification of the participant to their simplest atom that can be easily investigated. The sample, which is a subset of the population, is then taken as a representation of the population (Faulkner & Faulkner; 2014). The process of objectification is a process of compression through expulsion of emotion which allows for the squeezing out of a singular truth. Speaking of erasure of emotions, Foucault (2002) says:

> For history in its classical form, the discontinuous was both the given and the unthinkable: the raw material of history, which presented itself in the form of dispersed events—decisions, accidents, initiatives, discoveries; the material, which, through analysis, had to be rearranged, reduced, effaced in order to reveal the continuity of events. (p. 8)

This method pays attention to reliability and validity as the fundamental place of objectivity. Reliability looks at the consistency of a measure while validity pays attention to the accuracy of a measure (Faulkner & Faulkner, 2014). Some of the measures used (like surveys) are believed to be objective and rational and that they can help to eliminate any subject position of the researcher. The majority of positivist studies are large scale in scope and pay attention to patterns. In positivist research, there is a greater look at relationships between two or more variables (Faulkner & Faulkner, 2014). A variable is any feature that changes in a study. There are many kinds of variables, but the two primary variable are independent and dependent. The independent variable helps change the characteristics of the dependent variable (Faulkner & Faulkner, 2014). For example, income as an independent variable influences the divorce rate. While that may be construed as the truth, there are other aspects beyond income that need to be controlled to produce this one truth that supports the above premise.

3   Mapping Qualitative Research Geographies

Qualitative methods are intractably connected to feminist and other rights movements. Qualitative research has focused mostly on issues pertaining to social justice and transformation. Women and other subjugated populations continue to question the centrality of quantitative research as the only means of producing knowledge. The power of knowledge to orient the public and private spheres of life is in itself a manifestation of a gendered, racialized, and classed society and the implication of a knowledge production. Looking at knowledge production through a spatial scheme helps to understand why knowledge is power (Foucault, 1980) and how White heterosexual men can organize the public sphere to exploit, dehumanize, and remove (i.e., colonize) any emotional sense from rational order of knowledge. This speaks of the role of knowledge in the production and extermination of societies based on their skin colour, gender, and other social aspects.

To speak of such a colonial and violent removal illuminates the role of research in policy making and implementation and subsequent erasure of bodies marked as broken because of their emotions (read: objectification). Such bodies are earmarked as subhuman and social excesses that must be eliminated if they are not civilizable. The art of marking deplorable others is raced, gendered, classed, and authorized through the science of quantification. In this sense, knowledge production as a process remains a pure process of producing knowledge and subsequent production of the other through race, gender, and class. Those who produce this knowledge are therefore expected to be pure in thought and intention and devoid of their emotional embodiment. The assumption of purity (i.e., objectivity) marks out women, children, the disabled, and Blacks from the process of knowledge production while earmarking them as only knowledge templates (Foucault, 1979). This split between the knower and the template helps define the role of the mind as the place of knowledge production (i.e., the researcher) and subsequent references of men as the space of knowledge and rationality versus others (i.e., women, racialized, and Black populations) as spaces of degeneracy, brokenness, and emotionality. Black and racialized men are not rational based on their race and as such cannot be allowed to be at the so-called dinner table of making knowledge. Race becomes a technology of defining who constructs knowledge, whose is to be produced, and whose truth matters. This aspect of truth making marks the era of social demarcation as explained in the archeology of knowledge (Foucault, 1980, 2002).

It is worthy to recognize how qualitative methods come to define how knowledge is emotional rather than entirely confined within the scope of rationality (Smith, 2012). Qualitative methods were predominantly led by White middle-class women, such as Margaret Mead who conducted anthropological research among the American Samoa. In social work, we have Mary Richmond who developed a social diagnosis methodology that was steeped on person in environment. This became a time when White middle-class women sought to have recognition within the social construction of knowledge. This growth of qualitative research methods coincides with urban centres and demarcation of the rural from the city (Richmond, 2017). These are the times of immeasurable socio-economic and cultural upheavals as more people move from the country into the urban centres. Industrialization brings a new form of imagining our society more so in terms of social and economic aspects. The role of rational knowledge is limited in terms of understanding the social aspect of a growing urban centres.

The overflow of populations from the country into the city is an issue of concern for the city and urban developers (who are predominantly men). What a great time to involve women in the qualifying and cleaning. Women like Mary Richmond take the role of social work and are expected to lead the way in the controlling the entry of the country into the city while also controlling the country already in the city. To speak of the overflow of population is to make a connection of how the city becomes raced, classed, gendered, and impure by the country. The home (read country) breaks the very sanctity of the public space and so the rational man must find ways of constraining this overflow through the woman. To say that such containment was violent is an understatement. This is because qualitative methods controlled this overflow in terms of where they went and who they met in the city. It is not farfetched if I say that qualitative methods were a psychic boundary within the city that no one saw or would think of its operation. It had the art of panoptic technology and helped to control social movement of city immigrants in the name of helping them or permitting friendly visits (Richmond, 2017). It controlled the flow of the country into the city unverifiably, consistently. Sometimes this control seemed charitable to the country in the city and yet it would be used as a social control mechanism of the degenerate. Qualitative methods was equated to the panoptic system where the White women would be in the watchtower overlooking who crosses the physical boundary between the country (read also home/private space) to enter the city (public space) while simultaneously controlling the movement of the country in the city. Women like Mary Richmond and Jane Addams in social work and Margaret Mead in anthropology took this role of the prison warden.

To that extent, qualitative methodology is implicated in the control of emotions from flooding the city. The role of a panoptic system and research in this argument paints a picture of a system that used White women as border patrols and prison wardens while simultaneously rendering them unnecessary. There is a sense in which the system could operate with or without the White women. To claim this is to say that even by bringing emotions into the operation of the city, women would also be erased simultaneously. For example, women were always expected to rationalize their emotions as depicted by the work of Mary Richmond who had to qualify her methodology of working with clients. To claim the self-operation of the tower to control the overflow of the country into the city would also mean that only rational women would be allowed into the city and be "trusted" to operate the panoptic system. To speak of a panoptic social system in the city is also to say that women were used as border control agents. This means White women were used to control and mark racial purity of the city and that their Whiteness provided a rational edge to their work. To have this rational edge, qualitative methods sought the guidance of quantitative methods in rationalizing the city, through the use of different qualitative research approaches. These approaches are narrative, phenomenology, case study, ethnography, and grounded theory.

4   Qualitative Approaches

The narrative approach believes in the power of the stories as a tool of decolonization. It draws its disciplinary background from anthropology, literature, history, sociology, and psychology (Creswell, 2007). The approach looks at how we construct ourselves using narratives and claims we live a storied life (Bell, 2017; Friedman, 2017). In this approach, stories or narratives help construct people's realities, values, and ways of being. This qualitative method looks at the question of representation as complicated and unending. This approach also speaks of collaboration in social construction of realities (Padgett, 2017). The approach can be used as an exploratory process of understanding individual experience (Creswell, 2007). As a research method, the narrative approach employs interviews and documents to document people's experiences. In terms of data analysis, the approach employs "restorying" (Creswell, 2007). This means providing a chronological order in the form of theme of how a story was made and experienced. It is in restorying that issue of representation supposedly takes a rationalized tangent and needs a political discussion to understand rationalization of emotions. Questions of who does restorying and from which context one may rationalize another person's experience epistemologically essential. For instance, how would you bring together another person's experience without collapsing (since we are stories, read collapsing as the death of the person) it? To apply the term collapsing into themes is to figuratively claim that as researchers we may be implicated in the death of the other. To collapse the story of the other is to claim that they are broken and emotional and as such a researcher holds the privileged position of a high priest who can ethically appraise the broken other from their stories. This is an implication that narrative researchers must live with even as they decolonize the rationality of the qualitative research. This is colonial and has been used to mark societies as underdeveloped and in need of the other to write their stories (Mbembe, 2001, 2016; Wehbi, 2017).

The phenomenological approach to qualitative methods owes its place to the works of Edmund Husserl and Martin Heidegger. It comes from disciplines such as psychology, education, and nursing (Creswell & Poth, 2018; Padgett, 2017). The approach believes that reality is connected to one's consciousness. This approach looks at experiences of people to a phenomenon. A researcher must bracket out to understand experiences of a people who experience a phenomenon. Bracketing involves withdrawing the researcher's past experience from the analysis of participants' experiences (Creswell & Poth, 2018; Padgett, 2017). This is called phenomenological reductionism. This is assumed to enhance objectivity and allow clear understanding of participants' experiences with a phenomenon outside the researcher's past experiences. This to me makes every connection to the quantitative process of mind and body split, where the researcher remains the objective and rational thinker while the phenomenon occupies the emotional space. The second step in phenomenology is horizontalization whereby the researcher identifies specific participants' statements that help them answer their research question. The third part of phenomenology is clustering of meaning where the researcher brings together participants' statements into themes leading to an organized structural description of "how" the phenomenon was experienced by the participant. The researcher also provides the "what" of the phenomenon through a textual description of the data (Creswell & Poth, 2018). This process of writing and reduction of participants' experiences to a phenomenon into "what" and "how" is problematic in the sense that people's lived experiences cannot be simplified and assumed to be universal to everybody else who has experienced a phenomenon (Creswell & Poth, 2018).

Phenomena are experienced differently based on gender, race, and other aspects of social construction. As a Black man, my experience of unemployment may be different from another Black man's. A great example is my doctoral work on experiences of Kenyan men in Toronto in terms of unemployment. It was clear that Kenyan men could be unemployed not just because of their skin colour but also because of their Kenyan accent (Nyaga, 2019). To assume this phenomenon can be collapsed into one experienced universal essence is flawed and implicates the researcher in epistemological violence and imperialism (Butler, 2009).

Grounded theory borrows from sociology and come from the works of Barney Glaser and Anselm Strauss (Creswell & Poth, 2018). This approach looks at a process, and action or interaction as a definitive approach to theory (Creswell & Poth, 2018). This approach to qualitative studies seeks to generate a theory built on raw data from participants. The researcher goes to the field and collects data from participants and looks for patterns from data collected from participants. It is a back and forth journey from a research office and into the field up to the point where data is saturated. In this approach, memoing is an important aspect of generating theory in that the researcher jots down ideas as he collects and analyzes the data. This provides an architectural framework of the process under investigation. In this approach, the data is organized into themes, patterns are identified to bring forth open categories, and a single category is selected to be the focus of theory, followed by axial coding that helps generate a theoretical model (Creswell & Poth, 2018). The intersection of those categories forms the selective coding which forms the theory. A critically reflexive question to ask is how our focus to theory may be precluding the very lived realities of people. As expressed in this chapter, this qualitative approach may seek to create a wealth of academic theoretical frameworks on the backs of people who live a particular social issue like racism and sexism. If such theories are not meant to transform people's social realities, then the approach is a futile activity. The second flaw is based on who makes the decision that data is saturated. This ethical and epistemological question needs to be discussed and contested.

Ethnography is connected to the study of values, behaviours, and cultures of a group of people who have lived together in a location for a while. It is about studying a cultural sharing group and involves extended time in the field. The key is to identify and come up with one singular way of their lives (Creswell & Poth, 2018). One of the major ethical issues in this research is going native. This means that when a researcher stays long in the field, chances of the research emotionally connecting with the participants increases, which blurs professionalism and rationality. A critically reflexive question that needs to be asked is how the researcher can stay in the field with participants and yet remain outside that community: Why would "going native" be ethically problematic and why erect rational borders? Is it all about rationality or is it being with the community? Could this affirm the fact that data collection is a tourist enterprise to feed the self while remaining distant to the participant? This emotional (body) and rational (mind) split methodology of data collection that affirms the rational place of the academic tower is unethical and inhuman, and for any research to be transformative, ethics need to be at the forefront of knowledge production. Levinas says that to come close to the face of the other is to lose one's world (as cited in Thomas, 2004). Research should be about losing one's self rather than placing credence to understanding the other. People are both rational and emotional beings and to mark "going native" as rationally offensive is ethically and humanly violent.

Case study borrows from psychology, political science, medicine, and law. Case studies seek to develop an in-depth examination of a single case within a setting (Creswell & Poth, 2018). A case which may be a community is identified and bounded. Case study is defined by the boundaries you create to a specific case. It applies multiple sources of information from observation, interviews, and many others to report case description and themes (Creswell, 2007). My take for this approach is the reduction of people's experiences into cases, which can be managed through bounding them or creating a boundary (read walling). This is ethically problematic in the sense that it reduces or rounds-up people's experiences into a single universal case.

5   Critical Analysis of Qualitative Methods

This chapter argues that these qualitative approaches are disciplinary in latent and manifest ways. I also argue that the approaches operate as a boundary of determining who is rational and emotional and as such curtails the overflow of the city by the country. Through these approaches, disciplines like anthropology came to be ratified as the only emotional entities that could operate in the city so long as they operated rationally. Through this approach, academic and subsequent social and cultural control of the degenerate other was affirmed and made to look normal. No wonder women like Margaret Mead would be able to enter Indigenous communities of Papua New Guinea. We need to read this act of studying the other as the process of the city writ large into the country to control the degenerate other at the point of entry. We also need to look at this process of entering the country as a process of rationalizing the emotional other so that by the time they come out of the country and return to the city, they can claim their masculinity. Research is thus a process and a technology of constructing gender through the elimination of the racial other. By joining the Indigenous peoples of Papua Guinea as a researcher and coming out of it unscathed, Mead was confirmed as a masculine rational being. From this perspective, we come to a point where qualitative research and its approaches continue to be implicated in the erasure of communities.

Horizontalization (check phenomenology) should be seen within the perspective of enjoining decolonization with community praxis. Horizontalization should also be seen within the perspective of humility in that we as researchers "lay down" our expertise and acknowledge the role of other knowledges. I look at laying down as a process of breaking away (read displacement) researcher knowledge in ways that accommodate others. To "return" and allow the self to be "displaced" is a critically reflexive process of finding self among others and being ready to be summoned and addressed to our limitation. Such a process of "return" and "displacement" should be necessary process of re-orienting how to create knowledge to fit within community needs. In a nutshell, the process of knowledge creation is equally important in the opening colonial wounds to remind us of our implication in the decimation of communities.

To engage with the process of "return" is to be reminded of your place of maternity. I argue that we occupy emotional spaces that are a necessary place of defining how we come to know. To speak of maternity is to claim our human place in knowledge production. My wager is that the process of "return" as a critical reflexive praxis in research is to recognize our past as necessary place of becoming. I argue that return to the past is not archaeological but genealogical (Foucault, 1980), in that research should not just be a recovery but a scrutiny of what is recovered. That process of scrutiny should be ready to displace the known into unknown in a process that is unending. To return is to engage with the psychic self in ways that we "recover and uncover ourselves" from colonial construction and demarcation. I argue that the process of "true decolonization" is a process of bringing to life our suppressed selves into the process of knowledge creation. The process of decolonization is equally a process of dislocation in recovering ourselves.

To dislocate is to move from the ivory tower and recognize the role of community in knowledge production. Dislocation enables researchers to recognize their nomadic presence in searching knowledge. It is a recognition of the state of homelessness research. As a researcher, there is no place to lie down and have comfort. Rather, the researcher is always in a state of flux and "domiciled" in the street. To speak of the street in research is to recognize research as a humbling process. To be humbled is to lose what you know and yet remain comfortable in that discomfort. To speak of research as a street-based praxis is to recognize the agency of research as a transformative process.

I also argue that disciplinary walling in qualitative research denies the growth of robust qualitative studies. To be placed in such disciplinary cubicles is not any different from the panoptic process of celling prisoners. My wager is that qualitative studies need to break away from this epistemological mode of disciplinary demarcation and open new possibilities that allow a connection to lived experiences of study participants. I argue that social work is at a very opportune moment of leading a breakaway from this panoptic disciplinary control. For a while, social work has always sought the guidance of this approach in its search to be scientific. My wager is that for social work to be in this disciplinary otherness or homelessness is a strength. To be in the street is transformational and allows voices of participants to be heard. The problem we currently have as researchers who employ White and hegemonic qualitative approaches is that they do not speak to our lived realities. They seem to collapse our values and realities as explained previously. As a Black social work researcher, I would rather be on the side of the street instead of being in a cubicle and losing my human side. I would rather connect with my emotional Black self than wear a White mask (Fanon, 1967).

6   Concluding Remarks

I started this chapter by imagining true decolonization. What is in "trueness" that needs to be found to claim decolonization: Should decolonization be a term tied to "lost" and now "found" and what would that mean for such a term epistemologically, ontologically, axiologically, and methodologically? If decolonization of research is something sitting somewhere and needs to be saved, what would happen to those other forms of knowledges that are left out in the saving of this one decolonized "truth"? Maybe my quest for this "truth" could be a "return" to the original sin of what we run away from. My wager is that to "return" is necessary for our awakening. To "return" is a reminder of our blindness to truth and a necessary point of digging deep to our colonial implication. To "return" is to come to terms that knowledge is not final but a circular process of producing knowledge. I would argue that to "return" is not just a process of "digging deep" but a displacement of the soil that make our realities and values. In a sense, knowledge production should not just be vertical process of excavation but also the art of widening or horizontalization of the same.

References

Aliyu, A. A., Bello, M. U., Kasim, R., & Martin, D. (2014). Positivist and non-positivist paradigm in social science research: Conflicting paradigms or perfect partners? *Journal of Management and Sustainability* 4 (3): 79–95. https://doi.org/10.5539/jms.v4n3p79.

Bell, E. E. (2017). A narrative inquiry: A Black male looking to teach. *The Qualitative Report* 22 (4): 1137–1150. https://nsuworks.nova.edu/tqr/vol22/iss4/12/.

Bromley, N. (2003). Law, property and the spaces of violence: The frontier, the survey and the grid. *Annals of the Association of American Geographers* 93 (1): 121–141 https://doi.org/10.1111/1467–8306.93109.

Butler, J. (2009). *Frames of war: When is life grievable?* London: Verso.

Creswell, J., & Poth, C. (2018). *Qualitative inquiry and research design: Choosing among five approaches* (4th ed). Thousand Oaks, CA: Sage.

Fanon, F. (1967). *Black skin, white masks.* New York: Grove Press.

Faulkner, S., & Faulkner, C. (2014). *Research methods for social workers: A practice-based approach* (2nd ed.). Chicago: Lyceum Books.

Foucault, M. (1979). *Discipline and punish: The birth of the prison* (A. Sheridan, Trans.). New York: Vintage Books.

Foucault, M. (1980). *Power/knowledge: Selected interviews and other writings, 1972–1977* (C. Gordon, Ed. & Trans.). New York: Pantheon.

Foucault, M. (1997). *Society must be defended* (D. Macey, Trans.). London: Penguin.

Foucault, M. (2002). *Archaeology of knowledge* (A. M. Sheridan Smith, Trans.). Milton Park, Abingdon, UK: Routledge.

Fraser, H. (2004). Doing narrative research: Analysing personal stories line by line. *Qualitative Social Work* 3 (2): 179–201. https://doi.org/10.1177%2F1473325004043383.

Friedman, M. (2017). Unpacking liminal identity: Lessons learned from a life on the margins. In H. Parada & S. Wehbi (Eds.), *Reimagining anti-oppression social work research* (pp. 99–111). Toronto: Canadian Scholars' Press.

Gegeo, D., & Watson-Gegeo, K. (2001). "How we know": Kwara'ae rural villagers doing Indigenous epistemology. *The Contemporary Pacific* 13 (1): 55–88. https://doi.org/10.1353/cp.2001.0004.

Hardt, M. (1993). Conclusion: An apprenticeship in philosophy. (N – New ed., pp. 112) Minneapolis: University of Minnesota Press. doi:10.5749/j.ctttspkt.9.

Harrington, C. (2005). "Liberating" critical ethnography: Reflections from Fiji garment industry research. *Anthropology Forum* 15 (3): 287–296. https://doi.org/10.1080/00664670500280901.

Hollway, W., & Jefferson, T. (2000). *Doing qualitative research differently: Free association, narrative and the interview method.* Thousand Oaks, CA: Sage.

Lawler, S. (2002). Narrative in social research. In T. May (Ed.), *Qualitative research in action* (pp. 242–258). Thousand Oaks, CA: Sage.

Mbembe, A. (2001). *On the postcolony.* Berkeley, CA: University of California Press.

Mbembe, A. (2016). Africa in the new century. *The Massachusetts Review* 57 (1): 91–104. https://muse.jhu.edu/article/612965.

Nyaga, D. (2019). *Re-imagining Black masculinity: Praxis of Kenyan men in Toronto* (Doctoral dissertation, University of Toronto). TSpace. https://tspace.library.utoronto.ca/handle/1807/97580.

Padgett, D. K. (2017). Choosing the right qualitative approach(es). In *Qualitative methods in social work research* (3rd ed., pp. 31–56). Thousand Oaks, CA: Sage.

Razack, S. (2015). *Dying from improvement: Inquests and inquiries into indigenous deaths in custody.* Toronto: University of Toronto Press.

Reinharz, S. (1992). *Feminist methods in social research*. Oxford: Oxford University Press.

Renz, U. (2018). Self-knowledge and knowledge of mankind in Hobbes' *Leviathan*. *European Journal of Philosophy* 26 (1): 4–29. https://doi.org/10.1111/ejop.12227.

Reviere, R. (2001). Toward an Afrocentric research methodology. *Journal of Black Studies* 31 (6): 709–728. https://doi.org/10.1177%2F002193470103100601.

Reyes Cruz, M. (2008). What if I just cite Grasiela: Working toward decolonizing knowledge through a critical ethnography. *Qualitative Inquiry* 14 (4): 651–658. https://doi.org/10.1177%2F1077800408314346.

Richmond, M. E. (2017). *Social diagnosis*. Russell Sage Foundation. (Original work published 1917).

Smith, L. T. (2012). Colonizing knowledges. In *Decolonizing methodologies: Research and indigenous peoples* (2nd ed., pp. 61–80). London: Zed Books.

Thomas, L. (2004). *Levinas: Ethics, justice, and the human beyond being*. Milton Park, Abingdon, UK: Routledge.

Wahab, S., Anderson-Nathe, B., & Gringeri, C. E. (Eds.). (2015). *Feminisms in social work research: Promise and possibilities for justice-based knowledge*. Milton Park, Abingdon, UK: Routledge.

Wehbi, S. (2017). The use of photography in anti-oppressive research. In H. Parada & S. Wehbi (Eds.), *Reimagining anti-oppression social work research* (pp. 39–46). Toronto: Canadian Scholars' Press.

CHAPTER 2

Research Methodologies
Histories, Issues, Tensions

Rose Ann Torres

1   Introduction

Research is a process of looking for information to help us develop an idea one that we can use to address an issue. As such, I sought out references in the literature corresponding to the history of research methodology, but interestingly I could not discover any written materials on this matter. What I have been seeing in the literature is the history of universities that were built by the colonizer, and from here research began. Because this chapter focuses on the critical perspective of research, I will show how research has been used since time immemorial and include a discussion on Indigenous research methodology. Although my chapter focuses on critical research methodology, there first is a need to understand its histories, its original objectives, and how it has been used to dehumanize individuals, groups, and communities. When we talk about history, we must ask ourselves: which history/ies? What is history? Is history about time? These are some of the questions that I grapple with as I write this chapter.

2   Histories

Without romanticizing the histories of Indigenous communities before colonization, I envision these histories as something communal, without forgetting that conflicts also exist among the members of the community. These conflicts could be in relation to any disagreement amongst the members of the community. The difference of this community conflict to colonial conflict is the method that had been used to resolve such conflict (e.g., if the conflict is about who should be the leader in the community). They have used methods that are rooted in their own culture, traditions, and practices that were passed on to them by their ancestors. The members of the community did not rely on any information from the outsider. This was at a time when there were no invaders from other countries, a time when there was no other race dictating to them on how to resolve their own issues. In other words, there was no colonization yet. The question then is, did research methodologies exist during this pre-colonization period?

Based on the histories of healing in the Philippines, research has been used in the Indigenous communities even before colonization. The practices of Aeta, Isneg, and Igorots peoples in healing prove that research had been key in the success of their healing (Torres, 2015). For example, one of the methods of their healing is to use *in-ina* (the healer) in finding the reason why the person is sick (Torres, 2012). The *in-ina* methodology explores why a person is sick. One methodology that an *in-ina* uses is to ask the *ispirito* (spirit). The *in-ina* seeks to question why the person is sick and the reasons why he/she is sick. The *in-ina* also ask the *ispirito* to explain to her what she needs to do so that she can perform healing to the sick person. Through the information that the *ispirito* gives to the *in-ina*, the *in-ina* uses this information to heal the person. The *in-ina* has the responsibility to collect the data from the *ispirito* and ana-lyze the data so that she knows how to apply the process of healing to the sick person. Through this healing practice, the healer can help the sick person in their community. This practice of knowing and understanding the nature of an illness which has been used since the beginning of time in the Indigenous communities in the Philippines is a form of research.

If we define research from a colonial perspective, then research methodol-ogies started when colonization started. However, if we define research from a critical perspective, we cannot define history as time, date, or year. If we define history as time, date, and year then we end up excluding other histories that are not based on these categories. We have to re-imagine the meaning of his-tories in a way that will include everyone's history. Research has many histo-ries, and I say histories because different Indigenous communities have been using research from different times, spaces, cultures, practices, and traditions. Wilson (2001) explains Indigenous methodology as follows:

> To me an Indigenous methodology then becomes talking about rela-tional accountability. As a researcher you are answering to all your rela-tions when doing research. You are not answering questions of validity or reliability or making judgments of better or worse. Instead you should be fulfilling your relationships with the world around you. So your meth-odology has to ask different questions: rather than asking about validity or reliability, you are asking, Am I fulfilling my role in this relationship? What are my obligations in this relationship? The axiology or morals need to be an integral part of the methodology so that when I am gaining knowledge, I am not just gaining in some abstract pursuit; I am gaining

> knowledge in order to fulfill my end of the research relationship. This
> becomes my methodology, an Indigenous methodology, by looking at
> relational accountability or being accountable to all my relations. (p. 177)

Including a discussion of Indigenous research methodology in this section of
my chapter is to show that research has been existed in the Indigenous communities. Through the Indigenous research definitions and nature, we can
realize that Indigenous research stems from their way of life. It is rooted from
their culture, traditions, beliefs, values, relationship with natures and others.
It is based on community practices, a practice that have been passed on to
generation after generation. It is always about the others, because through the
others they can see themselves. Histories of research is not about "time", it is
about understanding that research is not a set of rules, regulations, and protocols, rather it is about acknowledging that we all learn from each other. And we
need the other to understand ourselves and our communities.

3   Issues and Tensions in Research: Power and Privilege

We cannot limit our understanding of research from one history and one reality alone (Torres, 2010). We have to look at research beyond one history. We
have to extend our understanding of research so that we do not eliminate any
histories that have been part of the creation of research methodologies. The
project of colonization was about collecting gold, silver, and spices, among
other goods, from different countries. It was also about stealing the knowledge of the Indigenous people. "They take their seeds and their knowledge to
their home country, usually without their permission, and they then patent
drugs from these plants" (Tauli-Corpuz, 2006, p. 18). In the process of colonization, elimination of Indigenous people was the main activity (Smith,
1999). Indigenous members of the communities subjected by colonization
were killed, raped, and used as slaves. To extend these conquering activities of
the colonizer they established schools, hospitals, welfare benefits, insurance,
churches, charities, and other institutions that continued to propagate their
idea of power, control, and privilege. These institutions also meant to discipline the individual (Foucault,1997). These institutions were the ones to give
researchers approval to conduct research. The rules and regulations that were
used for any research project were coming from Western criteria. These criteria
have been used as the model to be followed whether the research project is
focused on Indigenous communities or other cultures. These rules and regulations have been the only way to be followed.

These rules and regulations before colonization had not been imposed by the Indigenous people. They followed their own way of life, which was for community well-being. For example, in Canada before colonization, it was all about community well-being, but when colonization came to Canada there was no research without colonization. What I mean by this is that we have been using research as a way to explore the lives of the Indigenous people. Institutional Review Board (IRB) is one of the mechanism to legalize research agenda and at the same time the IRB uses colonial rules to approve research study as long as we showed commitment to the mission and vision of the IRB. This IRB is from a colonial institution that imposes all the rules in terms of research rules that have been defined and expressed to protect the researcher and participant. This is a way institutionalizing research and forgetting the voices of others. Even when we claim that our research is about Indigenous people, ironically the rules and regulations used to assess such research study are under colonial rules. The question is, who has the power in the research process? Before we answer this question, there is a need to define power. I will use Foucault's (1997) definition of power. I will define power and then I will demonstrate how it becomes an issue in the research process. First, that power is exercised and not possessed. Second, power is both productive and repressive. Third, power comes from the bottom. In the research process, let's look at how power plays in every part of the process. First, the researcher plans for a research project. While planning the research project, the research always takes into consideration the rules and regulations of how to conduct a research project using a research approach. The foundation of qualitative and quantitative approaches are colonial in nature except for Indigenous research methodologies that are based on the culture and their way of life. When the researcher begins the research project, the only power that a researcher has in this process is the research topic. But even in choosing a research topic there are times that we choose them because of an outside force. This outside force could be a funding agency that is interested into a topic. As much as the researcher is exercising the power that a researcher possesses, the research needs to comply with rules and regulations from the university. So, the degree of researcher power in the research process is contested based on the regulatory ethics board.

When it comes to power as both productive and repressive, in the research process the researcher can argue that this definition of power is both present. A researcher may experience oppressive feelings based on the colonial rules that a researcher needs to follow. For example, when I conducted my research, I was the one who chose the topic, but for the process, I had to keep referring to the rules on how to conduct a research. Research is a term that has been used by Western universities to collect data about an individual, groups of people, and communities. To embark on research means that you have an approval from the IRB committee from an institution, a university, or an agency most especially when the methodology is to interview an individual or group of people. An IRB is an institution that determines if a researcher complies with all that is required from the ethics board. In these rules, some were relevant to my topic, but some were not relevant at all. This feeling of ambiguity was confusing and conflicting in ways that took away the power that I believes I had for my research project. When I do not follow the rules that it has nothing to do with my research project, then I feel that I have the power; however, as soon as I realize that I have to always be in line with the research university guidelines, then the repressive definition of power exists. So, this definition of power as both repressive and productive in the research process does manifest in the researcher experience.

Productive and repressive definitions of power exist in the research process, however their existence are not in equal levels. As a researcher, I felt more repression rather than production in my research journey. What I mean by this is that in the activity of research, a researcher is more in a state of repression than production because of the surveillance and the regulatory guidelines that a researcher has to follow until the very end of a research project.

In terms of power that is coming from the bottom, Foucault talks about how even the subjugated have power. Again, in the research process, this definition of power is contested. In the research the subjugated subject is both the researcher and the participant. The researcher has the power to choose the participant and at the same time the participant has the power to agree or not agree to participate. The power becomes contested when the researcher must comply with the IRB guidelines on how to conduct interviews, what questions need to be asked, et cetera. The power of the participant is contested when the researcher gives all the rules that need to be followed. We cannot forget that these rules are not coming from the researcher, but these rules are from universities. The researcher here becomes the agent of the university. Both the participants and the researcher are bound to follow the requirements that have been imposed by the regulatory board of ethics. They must be eligible to be a researcher and a participant. Power here is a research issue, because when it comes to the roles of both researcher and participant, they are both confined by the regulatory mechanisms that have imposed by university. The question is where does power belong? This is an issue that cannot be resolved. It seems that power in a research process is an imaginary concept. There are times that researchers may think that they exercise the power while conducting a research study, but there are times that this power does not exist at all.

We are confounded with the disciplinary and regulatory technologies that are present in every step of a research processes.

Privilege is another issue that I would like to include in this section. What is privilege? Where does privilege come from? What are the requirements to be a privileged individual? Is privilege a fluid term? In this chapter let me adapt another term: freedom and honor. If privilege is freedom and honor, is research then a privilege? Some of us will say it's a privilege but to some it is not. To analyze these two contested notions of privileges, I will use again the position of a researcher and a participant. As a researcher, I can say it is a privilege if you are the principal investigator. You have somehow power to choose the topic that you want to research on, however, this power becomes meaningless when we begin to follow rules and regulations on how to conduct research, how to deal with the participants, how to disseminate the information, and all things that come with regulations. For example, the regulation of confidentiality is not bad, but the question is for whom? The straight answer here is to protect the participant. Was the participant part in this creation of confidentiality? Did they ask the participant's opinion when the regulatory board created the confidentiality rules? I believe that participants need to be protected, but the issue here is the creation of protection without the knowledge of the participant on how the participant wants to be protected. So,the question of privilege is about who gets to set the rules and regulations that will be used to regulate the participants.

4   Ownership

In research, the issue of ownership is inevitable. When participants share their stories, would it be automatic that they own the research? According to the research protocol, they do not own the research. Who then owns the data? Some would argue that it's the researcher, but even the researcher does not own the data. After being used for a dissertation or for report purposes, the collected data will be discarded. The data can also be used for publication and in this publication, the publisher retains the copyright. When you look at this kind of research activity, we can easily find out that in the process the participant was completely erased. The participant has been disremembered in the process. When we disremember the participant who gave all the information, this research becomes not transformative but rather violent in nature. The disremembering of participants is violent in nature because of how the disposability happens in ways that are hidden in the process. This may be hidden but we must remember that everything the participants share for the research is a story about their lives. A story about their pains and suffering that no one else can understand except the participants themselves. A pain because of the existing inequalities of the society that was created by and for the privileged few. When we erase the value of pain, we also erase the value of the human being. When the value of human being is erased, then nothing else matters. The only thing that matters in this process is the question of values.

What is our axiological assumption when it comes to the question of which life matters? In research, an axiological assumption is important to consider because it will bring us back to what is important to us. As we conduct research, we carry with us the values that we believe. So, if our values are focused on transforming the society that we live in because we are aware of the racial, gender, and class injustices, then we are also cautious on how to treat the participant. We have to follow the ethical responsibility of respecting the participants' experiences. According to Madison (2012),

> By "ethical responsibility," I mean a compelling sense of duty and commitment based on principles of human freedom and well-being and, hence, a compassion for the suffering of living beings. The conditions for existence within a particular context are not as they could be for specific subjects; as a result, the researcher feels an ethical obligation to make a contribution toward changing those conditions toward greater freedom and equity. (p. 5)

Madison explains how an ethical responsibility guides us in the steps of conducting research and also how we consider the other human being with respect and understanding that their life is important. Our sense of duty is not only about following the rules and regulations on how to conduct research but also about empathy for others. Our empathy for others will give us a greater understanding that research is not only about knowing someone else's life but also that research is about understanding the life of others in addressing the inequalities and inequities of this society. The question of how we understand the life of others is important to pay attention to. Before we can understand the word life, we have to ask ourselves the question of what life means to us. If life is about service to others, then we can relate this to research. We conduct research because we want to serve others through the information that we collect through our research. As we use a participant's life to do service for other lives, we have to begin this service to the life of the participant. How do we do this? The ability to include the participant in every process of research is very important. However, the question of who knows best is always the barrier of why participants do not have equal power in the development of research. The participant can only be included when it is time to answer the question. This always happens in most of the research that we do; we only have time to consider their voice when they are asked questions. Are we doing the service for life?

We go back again to the question of how do we balance our ethical responsibility to our responsibility to the university and to the participant? Ethical responsibility is not all about a question of how do we do things because it is our moral obligation? We need to also think about the consequences of the things we do. For example, the purpose of life is to serve others, however, as we serve others, we are doing disservices to others. We gather information because we want to address the racial injustices of racialized people. While we do this, we forget that the other who is giving ways to address this issue also experience the same thing. One of the possibilities to resolve this is to think about where we all link. Where does the researcher, participant, and the society link? We link in a word called purpose. In this purpose where we link means we do things to serve others. The importance of doing this is that it places value on others. When I say value, I do not mean "price"; I define value as something of higher importance regardless of race, class, gender, sexuality, and other socially constructed differences.

5   Conclusion

In this chapter, I discussed the history, issues, and tensions of research. I explored the issues in relation to power, privilege, and ownership when it comes to research. These are the things that we go through when we conduct research. I believe there are more depending on the race, gender, class, sexuality, and ability of a researcher.

References

Foucault, M. (1997). *"Society must be defended": Lectures at the Collège de France, 1975–1976*. London: Picador.

Madison, D. S. (2012). Introduction to critical ethnography: Theory and method. In *Critical ethnography: Methods, ethics and performance* (2nd ed., pp. 1–18). Thousand Oaks, CA: Sage.

Martin, K. (2002). Ways of knowing, being and doing: A theoretical framework and methods for Indigenous and indigenist re-search. *Journal of Australian Studies* 76: 203–214. https://doi.org/10.1080/14443050309387838.

Smith, L. (1999). Decolonizing methodologies: Research and Indigenous Peoples. London, UK: Zed Books Ltd.

Steinhauer, E. (2002). Thoughts on an Indigenous research methodology. *Canadian Journal of Native Education* 26 (2): 69–81.

Tauli-Corpuz, V. (2006). Our rights remain separate and sistinct. In Tauli-Corpuz, V. & Mander J. (Eds.), Paradigm wars, (pp. 13–21). San Francisco, CA: Sierra Club Books.

Torres, R. A. (2010). Fanon's pedagogical implications for women's studies in the Philippines. In G. J. S. Dei (Ed.), *Fanon and the counterinsurgency of education* (pp. 133–155). Rotterdam: Sense.

Torres, R. (2012). *Aeta Indigenous women healers in the Philippines: Lessons and implications* [Doctoral dissertation, University of Toronto]. TSpace. https://tinyurl.com/y4lnahlo.

Torres, R. & Nyaga, D. (2015). The politics of cultural representation. *Sociology Study Journal* 5 (9): doi: 10.17265/2159-5526/2015.09.

Weber-Pillwax, C. (1999). Indigenous research methodology: Exploratory discussion of an elusive subject. *Journal of Educational Thought* 33 (1): 31–45. https://doi.org/10.11575/jet.v33i1.52552.

Wilson, S. (2001). What is an Indigenous research methodology? *Canadian Journal of Native Education* 25 (2): 175–179. https://tinyurl.com/yca4ksoe.

CHAPTER 3

Torn Apart

Racialized Feelings and the Ethics of Doing Research with One's Own Community

Fritz Pino

So you are a Ph.D. student at the University of Toronto?" "Yes", I replied. "But you speak Filipino very fluently! Where did you learn it?" I answered, "In the Philippines!" "Oh, so you were born in the Philippines?" "Yes, I was, and I grew up there too", I said. "Oh, I thought you were born here!" "Why so?" I asked. "Because you said you are a researcher and a Ph.D. student at the University of Toronto, so I thought you finished your education here [Canada]! Did they recognize your degree from the Philippines?" I said, "No. They didn't. I had a master's degree in the Philippines completed that's why they were able to accept me in another master's program here [Canada]. So I took a master's of Social Work program here in Toronto before I applied for the Ph.D". "Oh, You're lucky! Your case is exceptional. They were able to accept you. I really thought that you were born here because you are there [University of Toronto].

1   Introduction

The above epigraph was based on one of my encounters in my early years of doing a community research project as part of my training in the doctoral program. The research was situated within my own community – the Filipino community in Canada. As a first-generation Filipino immigrant myself, born and raised in the Philippines, and identify as transgender woman, I critically reflect on this encounter, especially on the ways in which my own folk wondered about the place where I was really born – Canada or in the Philippines – since I was affiliated with a Canadian university and was performing one of their typical roles: doing research and knowledge production. Hence, in this encounter, my engagement with academic research plays a significant role in the production of the assumption of being a 'Canadian-born'.

I argue that this encounter tells something about the colonial practices of research and how it reinforces essentialist notions of identity among racially marginalized communities. In this context, the discourse of 'Canadian-born

Filipino' by my own folk has an underlying story. It emerged from the very experience of discrimination, marginalization, and displacement of many Filipino immigrants from the Philippines whose academic degrees were not honoured and not considered as a full professional degree in most academic institutions in Canada (Kelly, 2009). Here, the concept of deprofessionalization and de-skilling as forms of racialization are important to name in this context (Coloma et al., 2012). Solely being 'Filipino' without the 'Canadian' seems inadequate and unimaginable to be seen as the typical researcher within dominant academic spaces. My community folk used the discourse of 'Canadian born' so he can make sense of my embodied Filipino identity who was engaging with university academic research activities in the community.

However, the use of 'Canadian-born Filipino' by my own community folk as a way to make sense of my identity as a Filipino researcher has reinforced the essentialist notion of identities. Here, I was no longer considered as an 'authentic Filipino', one who was born and raised in the Philippines, because I was able to perform research activities with a Canadian university. By doing so, I deviated from the normative construct of being a Filipino within the Canadian nation-state. Meanwhile, the discourse of Canadian-born also reinforces the stereotypical notion that being a 'Canadian-born Filipino' has greater mobility and chances of success in academia compared to a non-Canadian-born Filipino. Such is a stereotypical assumption because it conceals the very lived experiences of racial barriers, struggles, and trauma of Canadian-born Filipinos as they navigate Canadian academic spaces, which often dismiss their very presence and that lead them to stop their education and leave academic spaces (Mendoza, 2012). Ultimately, however, the discourse of 'Canadian-born', reinforces the social position hold by a 'Canadian' subject, which usually refers to a 'White, hetero-cis male', as the authentic and legitimate figure for an academic researcher (Dei & Johal, 2005).

In this critical analysis of the link between birthplace and the practice of research where discourse of 'Canadian-born' has emerged, in this chapter, I seek to also focus on critically deconstructing my own feelings and emotions that I have felt or have evoked during the encounter, especially when the label 'Canadian-born' was imposed on me. I felt as though I was being cut-off, distanced, or separated from the community that I claim to belong due to my engagement with academic research. That is to say, my academic research persona renders me as a mere 'outsider' and a mere 'witness' to the struggles of my very own community. The persona created a seemingly invisible boundary that separates me from my own community's issues of deskilling, deprofessionalization, and racial discrimination so that I would appear objective, distant, and a neutral observer of their experiences.

What does it mean for racialized researchers to highlight their emotions and feelings upon wielding Western academic research for their own community? How would these feelings and emotions, which I describe as 'racialized feelings', be taken up by the Canadian nation-state? How do such emotions and feelings reveal the limits and possibilities of research?

By foregrounding feelings and emotions in my analysis of this encounter, I aim to reiterate the generative critique of critical race and feminist thinkers and writers who highlighted the importance of affect and emotions as legitimate sources of knowledge and worthy of analytic empirical theorization as they promote critical and emancipatory forms of knowledge (Cheng, 2001; McElhinny, 2010). This is important to consider given that research has been historically based on hetero-patriarchal and masculine sensibilities of the Enlightenment scholars that demanded researchers to disengage with one's feelings and emotions because they do not produce objectivity, neutrality, and I would say, a de-politicized form of knowledge that can be applied universally (Dei & Johal, 2005).

This chapter then is a critique of such hetero-patriarchal and masculinist forms of knowledge that do not consider emotions and feelings as ways that can also reveal the limits and possibilities of particular socio-cultural objects, situations, and structures such as the practice of academic research. I argue that by focusing and unpacking my feelings and emotions opens up conversations and insights on the ways in which academic research, which historically is a colonial tool (Dei & Johal, 2005), reinforces what Foucault (1982) termed as 'dividing practice' of hegemonic institutions of power. In other words, paying attention to my feelings and emotions as a racialized researcher reveals the divisive impact of particular objects and practices such as Western academic research invented by dominant Eurocentric institutions of power. By doing such deconstructions, I hope to offer insights around the ethics of doing research within one's own community as a racialized researcher.

To discuss my points further, I lay out three subsequent sections. First, *Wearing A Researcher's Hat* where I critically interrogate my identification with research itself, and how such research persona impacts my sense of belonging and relationships in my own community. Second, *Becoming a Feeling Subject* offers a psychoanalytic deconstruction of my feelings and emotions when being implicated by the hegemonic practice of academic research. Finally, *Taking Action* foregrounds the impact of emotions in research endeavors to fuel affirmative actions as an ethical response among racialized researchers.

2   Wearing the Researcher Hat: Engaging with One's Own Community
for Research

Reading Foucault and other critical race scholars (Dei & Johal, 2005; Tamboukou & Ball 2003; Villenas, 1996), I have come to realize that research in itself is a technique of control since it has the purpose of seeking knowledge about the population in order to properly manage and govern them. Research endeavours are practices that sustain academic disciplines' regimes of truth and such regimes of truth also shaped research practices (Peters, 2004). By participating in research, researchers are implicated and constituted in such a truth making game (Peters, 2004). By mastering and wielding such a tool of research, researchers can then properly manage their (own) population.

During my initial encounter with academic research, I had refused to identify with the term 'entry into the community' because it does not capture what I know of my own subject position and personal experiences. As a first-generation immigrant in Canada, I have always been visible in the Filipino community such as in the church, in various Filipino organizations, groups, and associations, including home parties, and religious celebrations, and funerals. Claiming to have entered into the community signifies that I do not belong as though I am a Western scholar who performs research with strange cultures in order to render such research as objective (Ahmed, 2000; Kanuha, 2000; Villenas, 1996).

However, while claiming as not a stranger in my community, I was pushed to be one upon wearing the research hat[1]. Here, I would say that I am not 'entering' the community for the first time, but, rather 're-entering' given the role that was associated with the research position, thus the term 'outsider' (Creswell & Poth, 2018). Consequently, while wearing the research hat, I felt as though I am away or distant from my own community. The hat indeed carried dominant frameworks that rendered me as a thinking subject because it seemed to be upholding only my intellect or cognition to enable a posture of objectivity. Indeed, the researcher persona was countered by a different reaction as I was being seen and treated as a 'Canadian-born Filipino'. The discourse of 'Canadian-born' then produces a position of privilege as I was labelled 'exceptional' – one that has not been fully impacted by racial and class marginalization that many first-generation Filipino immigrants experienced simply because they saw me being in academia and pursuing higher education.

---

1   Research hat is a metaphorical term to symbolize my role as a researcher, including the kinds of dominant framework that I have been exposed to in school.

The context through which the discourse of 'Canadian-born Filipino' as a privileged subject can be rooted from the ways in which Filipinos have been taught via colonialism and imperialism about the West or Canada. This is related to the idea of Edward Said (1979) who revealed the racialized and orientialized constructions embedded in the socio-cultural and historical relationships between East and West. The Western nation Canada has indeed been imagined as more modern, culturally advanced, and technologically progressive as compared to an Eastern nation, the Philippines. The circulation of these notions about Western and Eastern nation-state spaces conceals the very unequal cultural and economic relationships that have historically been existing and impacting the East, including those spaces being constructed as the 'Third World' such as the Philippines. The racialized construction of the Philippines maintains Western superiority and domination (Coloma, 2009; 2012a).

The discourse of 'Canadian-born' that circulated in the community is then an effect of colonialism that has impacted the mindset of marginalized subjects, allowing them to continue to sanctify the West, including the practice of 'research', which is its cultural object. Consequently, the problem of this discourse then is that it also impacts intergenerational relationships among Filipinos in diaspora. The discourse of 'Canadian-born' indeed produces two kinds of Filipino subjects in Canada: 1) one born in Canada, and (2) one born in the Philippines. While Filipinos born in Canada has been imagined as more privileged given their cultural capital (e.g. English language skills and adaptation to Western cultural norms and practices) that allowed them to easily access Canadian academic spaces, including the ability to engage in research compared to non-Canadian born Filipino, the discourse also constructed them as objective, hence, devoid of feelings and affect deemed 'Filipino'. This assumption conceals Canadian-born Filipinos' very experiences of marginalization and discrimination as racialized bodies, and at the same time reinforces their colonial trauma reflected in their experiences of alienation from parental and familial culture.

Meanwhile, 'Filipino-born in the Philippines' also produces an image of marginality and victimhood, a less privileged positionality because of the ways in which their cultural resources do not seem to serve the Canadian mainstream; hence, they won't be able to enter and engage academic spaces. This discourse then continues to exhibit racialization and disempowerment, thereby emerging as a normative script that Filipinos born in the Philippines themselves continue to believe in.

This aspect of the discourse of 'Canadian-born' rooted in the colonial discourse about 'Canada' becomes what Foucault (1982) considers as a 'dividing practice'. As Foucault (1982) writes, 'Dividing practices are an objectivizing process in which the subject is either divided inside himself or divided from others (*away from others, as in differentiating from others*[2]; p. 126)'. This discourse of 'Canadian-born' Filipino as a 'dividing practice works to mark, classify, and categorize' (Foucault, 1995; p. 272) Filipinos so that they can be properly managed, controlled, and regulated within Canada, that is, to identify *who or which Filipino* can be part of such privileged academic spaces in Canada. In other words, the discourse of 'Canadian-born' serves to identify and determine who can be accepted or rejected within a particular Canadian institution or even within the Canadian nation-state in general.

The ultimate purpose of marking and classifying Filipino bodies (either as Canadian-born or not) is to economize[3] the resources of the space so that not all Filipinos can access or can be allocated with the resources of the space. According to Foucault (1978), "To economize is part of the practices of managing the space so as to maintain control and domination of the space including those who inhabit the space" (p.234). Consequently, the economizing practice is the normalization[4] of the discourse of 'Canadian-born' as the only group who can enter or deserve to be in academia. The normalized discourse suppresses the desire and imagination of non-Canadian born Filipinos in accessing Canadian nation-states' resources, such as in participating and venturing into Canadian academic institutions.

As the discourse is consumed as 'true', individuals (e.g., racialized subjects) may then participate in such dividing practices. Indeed, this was reflected in my encounter with my community folk. I was automatically classified as Canadian-born because I was able to access academia. This reveals that the economizing practice of the dominant discourse is not something that is necessarily imposed or enacted from the mainstream or colonial institutions but moved towards historically marginalized communities so they can be 'policing' and 'scrutinizing' each other: determining who can be part of or not part of the privileged academic space. The notion of 'birthplace' becomes a site of contestation, serving as an automatic marker of one's identity that can determine possible success or failure. This division disrupts possible solidarity work among diverse Filipinos to combat colonialism and interrogate the dominant powers that impact their own community and relationships.

---

2   Emphasis added: refers to my feeling of being distant from my own community.

3   See Foucault (1995 edition), *Discipline and Punish*, p. 272.

4   Here, normalization of the discourse of Canadian-born is attained by treating it as a *natural* phenomenon since the division is based on "country of birth", a particular inevitable circumstance based on common sense.

Indeed, wearing the research hat seemed to iron my racialized and queer identity as it becomes associated with being a 'Canadian-born'. It seemed to elevate my marginalized position just because of my affiliation with Western academic institution. This elevation, however, marked me as different from my community, let alone, has distanced me from the community that I am intimately connected with.

3   Becoming a Feeling Subject: Coming to Terms with the Rewards of the Privileged

What have I gained in being perceived as 'privileged'? What is/are the return/s of such complicity and participation to hegemonic practices? In this context, wearing the research hat has erased my immigrant persona that it distanced me from the community that I intimately identified with. By assuming the role of an 'outsider' researcher, it separated me from the people, including the research participants, who seemed to be unable to be in the academic space where I am in. I argue that this is the affective and emotional effect of the dividing practice of the discourse of 'Canadian-born': it has a splitting effect between my own self and my own community.

Wearing my research hat has indeed produced feelings of melancholia. The melancholia was a result of a failed expectation from the idea that if I do research within my own community, such a research engagement could also somehow compensate my feelings of nostalgia and longing as an immigrant and diasporic subject who has been separated from my homeland. This indicates then that academia seemed to always already disconnect and separate racialized subjects from their own community, especially when dominant knowledge being taught and introduced sends an underlying tone that de-historicize racialized communities' experiences of marginalization. I thought engaging research in my own community would be the remedy of such longing, separation, and nostalgia.

Furthermore, the feelings of melancholia continues as my expectation of Western academic research to somehow rekindle my sense of belonging in my own community has failed. Indeed, in the encounter, I was no longer considered as an authentic member or part of the Filipino community due to my affiliation with academia. Being marked as not fully belong, unsettled feelings of loss occupy my entire being. Indeed, I named such feelings as melancholia (Cheng, 2001).

Following Freud, Cheng (2001) describes melancholia as a feeling of loss whereby the subject refuses replacement of a loss object. Such a refusal to replace the loss object is necessary in order to maintain the structure of loss-but-not-loss (Cheng, 2001). This means that the subject is stuck with feelings of loss itself that is made possible by active denial and exclusion of the loss object. Wearing the research hat provides the condition for such a melancholic feeling to exist: The research hat allow me to feel the loss from being separated and no longer fully part of my community – their everyday conversations, their ways of understanding and interpreting particular situations and phenomenon. These cultural practices now appear as somewhat contradictory or opposite to the kinds of dominant conversations and interactions that I have within academic spaces.

However, within such a situation of loss is also a feeling of liking the transformation that I have within myself or even liking the loss itself that I do not want to move out or away from it. This 'liking' was due to the privileges associated with such transformation, and therefore, the feelings of 'loss' itself becomes associated with privilege. Melancholia then carries ambivalent feelings: the like and the not like of the loss that is similar to Filipinos' relationship with academia as both an experience of marginalization and privilege.

Realizing and acknowledging such feelings of ambivalence, however, ultimately resulted in feelings of guilt and shame of embracing colonial embodiments and legacies, as well as in participating in the governing function of research. As this shame and guilt for both liking and disliking the loss continue to envelope my body, my very venture into the social and political issues that my own community face came another set of feelings and those are of anger and pain. Such pain and anger devoured my feelings of guilt and shame. This condition, according to Cheng (2001) is a cannibalistic self-interpellation and self-infliction as though I am whipped, tortured, and slapped for taking and wearing the research hat. The marginalized lived condition that I have witnessed in my own community is nonetheless part of my own reality that I cannot escape from, though was only temporarily concealed upon wearing the academic research hat. The feelings of pain and anger upon re-witnessing my community's struggle in Canada during my research engagement with them taint my position of privilege upon wearing the research hat; upon liking the situation of loss.

Given the existence of these ambivalent feelings in doing research with my own community, I have come to realize that as a racialized researcher, my work is not only about using and engaging the intellectual or rational dimension of myself, but also, the emotional/affective dimensions. I began to see that research is not only an intellectual labour but also an emotional one. The emotional labour in research should then be counted as work. The consideration of emotion as labour in research disrupts the idea of an intellectual – a subject of the Enlightenment who can best himself/herself by using one's rationality only. Meanwhile, those who are engaging or highlighting their emotions along with their cognitive thoughts such as women, trans, queers, and racialized subjects – are being questioned of their validity and legitimacy and hence are prevented to be part of the production of knowledge.

However, it is indeed important to recognize how race plays into this process of emotional labour in research. What does it mean then for me, as a racialized (Filipino) researcher, who engages with the emotional aspects and labour of research, carying emotions of ambivalence, melancholia, shame and guilt, and ultimately anger and pain? What does it mean then to be seen as someone who can negotiate and even write or make sense of such feelings and emotions?

I contend that such feelings and emotions produced from or enacted by a racialized subject or body is also read as racialized feelings. In her analysis of the ways in which Asian American bodies are read, Ross (n.d., as cited in Da Silva, 2007) writes: "the white man can best the yellow man in turning off work. But under bad conditions, the yellow man can best the white man, because he can *better endure* spoiled food, poor clothing, foul air, noise, heat, dirt, discomfort, and microbes" (p. 216).

Ambivalence, melancholia, shame and guilt, and anger and pain are feelings of discomfort, something displeasing, and not pleasurable at all as they are produced from being torn apart between spaces of marginality and spaces of privilege. These feelings are racialized feelings as they become discursively normalized as being *naturally* produced by a racialized body. Such a discourse works to justify the production of racialized thoughts towards the body of a person of colour. Hence, a racialized researcher engaging unpleasant emotions in research would then be seen as just a 'natural' experience for them and as they can *better endure* the unpleasant feelings and emotions.

4   Taking Action

The production of such racialized feelings then should not be treated as an individual response but rather as a result of the hegemonic structural processes, discourses, and practices that continue to split communities of colour. Here, wearing the academic research hat, the symbol of my complicity and participation in academia's practices of knowledge production, did not only shaped me as an intellectual, rational subject but also someone who felt particular feelings and emotions. Experiencing and embodying such emotions and feelings are difficult and painful as it characterizes feelings of being torn apart and hence being relegated in the in-between position (Coloma, 2008;

Villenas, 1996). I contend that the difficult and painful feelings and emotions are disciplinary practices towards racialized subjects as reflected in the notion that they can 'endure' such pain and difficulty since they are a resilient subject.

Emotions are productive (McElhinny, 2010; Razack, 2007). Such feelings of pain and difficulty indeed were a call for affirmative action. Indeed, the research is geared towards developing programs and services as well as for advocating for policy changes. Experiencing and witnessing the very difficulties in our very own community demands concrete actions towards change. The results of our study served to impact policy to improve the lives of people in our community. The research also made possible for the establishment of certain support programs in our community.

Here, we witnessed that research is a peculiar site and exists in a paradoxical position. On one hand, it has been a technique of controlling and colonizing the population including governing one's affect – and that needs to be continually critiqued and reflected on . On the other hand, research also has become the site of self-knowledge where we can come to know ourselves as being implicated by its hegemony. In practice, we can treat this as an instrument that can mobilize social justice efforts; thus an instrument for subversion. Perhaps, paying attention as to how we are formed into various subjects of research – emotional, rational, or combination, being mindful and attentive to the socio-historical locations of people, bodies, and communities who are wielding such an academic Western instrument, thereby debunking the idea that all researchers are the 'same', and becoming intensely vigilant to the circulation of nation-state discourses around race and other markers of difference that maintain certain forms of dominance and power of particular normative bodies and subjects – can be an initial move towards a more ethical response of thinking about the idea of research being carried out by a racialized researcher.

References

Ahmed, S. (2000). *Strange encounters. Embodied others in post-coloniality.* London and New York: Routledge.

Cheng, A.A. (2001). *The melancholy of race. Psychoanalysis, assimilation, and hidden grief.* Oxford: Oxford University Press.

Coloma, R.S. (2008). Border crossing subjectivities and research: Through the prism of feminists of color. *Race Ethnicity and Education* 11 (1): 11–27.

Coloma, R.S. (2009). Destiny has thrown the Negro and the Filipino under the tutelage of America: Race and curriculum in the age of empire. *Curriculum Inquiry* 39 (4): 495–519.

Coloma, R.S. (2012a). White gazes, brown breasts: Imperial feminism and disciplining desires and bodies in colonial encounters. *Paedagogica Historica* 48 (2): 243–261.

Coloma, R.S., McElhinny, B., Tungohan, E., Catungal, J.P.C., & Davidson, L.M. (Eds.). (2012). *Filipinos in Canada: Disturbing invisibility.* Toronto: University of Toronto Press.

Creswell, J.W., & Poth, C.N. (2018). *Qualitative inquiry and research design: Choosing among five approaches.* (4th Ed.). London: Sage Publications.

Da Silva, D. F. (2007). *Toward a global idea of race.* Minneapolis: University of Minnesota Press.

Dehli, K. (2008). Coming to terms: Methodological and other dilemmas in research. In K. Gallagher (Ed.), *The methodological dilemma. Creative, critical, and collaborative approaches to qualitative research* (pp. 46–66). Toronto: University of Toronto Press.

Dei, G.S., & Johal, G.S. (2005). *Critical issues in anti-racist methodologies.* New York: Peter Lang Publishing Inc.

Foucault, M. (1978). Governmentality. In P. Rabinow & N. Rose (Eds.), *Selections from the essential works of Foucault 1954–1984.* (pp. 229–245). New York: New Press.

Foucault, M. (1982). The subject and power. In P. Rabinow & N. Rose (Eds.), *Selections from the essential works of Foucault 1954–1984.* (pp. 126–144). New York: New Press.

Foucault, M. (1995). *Discipline and punish.* (2nd ed). New York: Vintage Books.

Kanuha, V. K. (2000). "Being" native versus "going native": Conducting social work research as an insider. *Social Work* 45 (5): 439–447.

Kelly, P.F., Astorga-Garcia, M., Esguerra, E.F., & the Community Alliance for Social Justice, Toronto. (2009). *Explaining the deprofessionalized Filipino: Why Filipino immigrants get low-paying jobs in Toronto.* Toronto: CERIS – The Ontario Metropolis Centre.

McElhinny, B. (2010). The audacity of affect: Gender, race, and history in linguistic accounts of legitimacy and belonging. *The Annual Review of Anthropology* 29: 309–328.

Mendoza, G. M. (2012). Educated minorities: The experiences of Filipino Canadian university students. In Coloma, B. McElhinny, E. Tungohan, J.P.C. Catungal, & L.M. Davidson (Eds.), *Filipinos in Canada: Disturbing invisibility* (pp. 360–381). Toronto: University of Toronto Press.

Peters, M. A. (2004). Educational research: games of truth and the ethics of subjectivity. *Journal of Educational Enquiry* 5 (2): 50–63.

Razack, S. H. (2007). Stealing the pain of others: Reflections on Canadian humanitarian responses. *The Review of Education, Pedagogy, and Cultural Studies* 29: 375–394.

Said, Edward. (1979). *Orientalism.* New York: Vintage.

Tamboukou, M., & Ball, S. (2003). *Dangerous encounters: Genealogy and ethnography.* New York: Peter Lang Publishing Inc.

Villenas, S. (1996). The colonizer/colonized Chicana ethnographer: Identity, marginalization, and co-optation in the field. *Harvard Education Review* 66 (4): 711–730.

PART 2

Types of Critical Research Methodologies

∵

CHAPTER 4

Critical Ethnography
Discussions of Ethics and Principles

Rose Ann Torres

This chapter explores critical ethnography in relation to ethics and principles. I expand on Creswell's (2007) work on critical ethnography discussed in his book *Qualitative Inquiry and Research Design*. Creswell (2007) states clearly in his definition of critical ethnography that this "approach is in response to current society, in which the systems of power, prestige, privilege, and authority serve to marginalize individuals who are from different classes, races, and genders" (p. 70). This definition of critical ethnography speaks about a clear purpose of research—one that calls for emancipation for oppressed individuals. My only concern about Creswell's way of defining critical ethnography is that it is not clear to which race, gender, and class he is referring. There is a need to name these specific categories of life experience in order to avoid essentialism. And when examining Creswell's procedures for conducting an ethnographical study, it is also not well explained based on race, class, and gender. Although I acknowledge that Creswell's ideas are important, they need to be expanded upon from a critical perspective. As Soyini Madison (2014) asks,

> What does it mean for the critical ethnographer to "resist domestication"? It means that she will use the resources, skills, and privileges available to her to make accessible—to penetrate the borders and break through the confines in defense of—the voices and experiences of subjects whose stories are otherwise restrained and out of reach. This means the critical ethnographer contributes to emancipatory knowledge and discourses of social justice. (p. 6)

Soyini Madison gives us a clear explanation of what constitutes critical ethnography: We need to use whatever resources we have to challenge the structural systems, institutions, and individuals regarding the injustices perpetuated in our society. This means also that even our intentions underpinning our research need to be challenged and questioned.

Critical ethnography as a public health qualitative research methodology is important to understand because whenever we talk about public health, it means knowing and understanding the health of the population. But in knowing and understanding the health of the population, one requires data or evidence to derive a certain conclusion about such health. There is a need to understand how information is being collected because the process of doing so is as important as the outcome. Public health does not only mean the health of the population; we also need to understand fully the population on which we are focus.

My objective in this chapter is to expand upon Creswell's (2007) ideas posited in is definition of critical ethnography and procedures for conducting an ethnography. I first will discuss why critical research becomes a public health qualitative research methodology. I will explain how I decided to focus on critical ethnography as public health research methodology, and discuss the transnational framework in which I locate myself. I then discuss a procedure for critical ethnography as a public health qualitative research methodology, including principles and ethics, and offer some concluding remarks.

1   Public Health

My doctoral research focused on the public health of Indigenous women in the Philippines, particularly the Aeta women (Torres, 2012). In this research, I looked into how Indigenous women dealt with issues corresponding to diseases in their community. I have known this community since I was young and have seen first-hand how they address issues of public health in their community. The Indigenous women collectively define public health not just as the health of the whole community but also the health of particular individuals who suffer any illnesses. In short, they look at health from an individual, institutional, and whole society perspective. They focus on the health of individuals and the whole community as part of their own contribution as healers.

My decision to focus on public health and how Indigenous women address diseases is because I believe that critical ethnography is an interesting methodology to use. In writing this chapter, I try tried to address my research question on how Indigenous women address public health in their community; however, a pattern emerged. This pattern of experiences centers on how they have been discriminated and marginalized as healers in their own country. This pattern did not only happen during the time I conducted my research but rather stems from the time colonization began in the Philippines. The Philippines was under the Spanish colonial rule for 500 years and since then other colonial powers started to invade the Philippines. Every now and then, Indigenous people have been the target of abuse that has dehumanized their existence as the original inhabitants of the Philippines. The history repeated itself so often that Filipinos themselves have internalized colonization. Through this internalized colonization, they are implicated in the ongoing struggles of the Indigenous peoples in the Philippines, including the Aeta women. This kind of treatment did not only happen to Indigenous populations in the Philippines but also to the Aboriginal peoples in Canada, where I now reside. Such oppression became a pattern for Indigenous peoples globally, through the appropriation of land and the creation of colonial policies that strip away their rights to exist in their own countries.

My research in the Philippines adopted a critical ethnographical approach and I used talking circles as a methodology to collect data. In my dissertation, I did not explain that my study was a critical ethnography because I have a negative view about such the theoretical approach called "ethnography." In my academic experience, I have read ethnographic studies and through these studies I have seen how Indigenous peoples have been dehumanized (Torres, 2012). However, when I became a Professor of Research Methodologies in a university setting, I encountered literature on critical ethnography. And as I reflected on my research journey, including the research I conducted among the community of Aeta women, I realized that what I used was a critical ethnography.

It was a critical ethnography because for a long period of time before I embarked on my research, I had lived among the Aeta community. My parents used to own a farm along the Sierra Madre mountain range. I had the opportunity to learn and understand the Aeta people's way of life. They were very gracious to me in showing and explaining their culture and traditions. For example, my mother used to sell dried fish; instead of selling it to earn money, she used to exchange it with other goods so that my family had the opportunity to taste other kinds of food (Torres, 2012). As part of their culture, Aeta people used to practice such bartering with my mother. My mother had given them dried fish, which they exchanged for wild deer meat. Because of this practice, I have tasted delicious wild deer meat.

I had also seen how the military used forced to evict people from their own ancestral land. As I noted in my doctoral research,

> Furthermore, while the colonizer's main goal was to acquire wealth, yet they understood that social integrating forces would make the communities resist. Laws were set up to deny property and religion and to control the spiritual domain. They understood too that healers in Indigenous communities bore organizational and leadership qualities much like the banking, legal and religious sector elites of their own cultures. Undermining them was therefore tactically important. Brute military

force was necessary, particularly if control was to be sustained over long periods.

(TORRES, 2012, p. 40)

These kinds of atrocities were real among the community of Aeta people. I have seen how they suffered. These are some of the reasons why I decided to focus my study on them. My study focused not only on the injustices they experienced but also on how they have been addressing these social, economic, political, and spiritual injustices. I explored how Aeta women used their healing practices in resisting neo-colonization. I showcased their resiliency in the midst of the different struggles that they face on basis of their ethnicity, race, class, and gender.

I was also interested in understanding the way that Indigenous Aeta women address public health. I went to their community not just to ask questions about their healing practices, but also to understand the patterns of how they address public health and how they have been treated as members of a larger society. It is interesting to note that they were treated as a knowledgeable member of their own community; however, as they joined other individuals outside their community, patterns of discrimination and marginalization began to manifest. For example, one of the participants in my study, Rang-ay, stated:

> My experience with the Filipinos is bad. One day, I went to the market in town to sell fruits and vegetable. A man and a woman approached me and asked the price of saging or banana. I told them the price, instead of buying, they took two pieces and peeled them right in front of me and ate them. I was happy to see that they enjoyed my banana and hoped in my heart that they would pay me. Instead, after eating, they left without paying me. They did not even thank me. I was sad because it was very apparent that they did not respect me. This is one example of my experience from these Filipinos, there were more and they were even worse.
>
> (TORRES, 2012, p. 12)

In understanding the public health of this community, it is important to use critical ethnography because as research, it is not enough to know that a community suffers certain diseases; we also should understand the history, culture, beliefs, language, and behaviors of that community.

Public health is not about looking at the general experience of a population merely in terms of their health but also the history of a population. Critical ethnography is an important methodology in public health because we want to make structural, institutional, and individual changes. Health is not just about making the physical healthy but also making the environment, government, beliefs, and other systems healthy. Public health is about the web of life—the interrelationship of everything that encompasses what life is all about. The moment we disconnect the smallest part of the web of life, the precarity of public health is revealed. This web of life that exists in each member of the public can only be understood through critical ethnography. Critical ethnography is about immersing oneself to the other self in order to fully understand the life of the other.

2   Transnational Feminist Framework

Transnational feminism is a framework that focuses on the intersectionality of experience, both local and international. It posits that while we travel across borders, we face different spaces, such as culture, beliefs, languages, and health. As we encounter these things, we also carry our own and others will also have the chance to understand our culture, beliefs, language, and our notion of health through us. These cultures, beliefs, languages, and experiences with health help us make sense of our new experiences in the new space that we are in. However, as much as we travel with our own culture, beliefs, and language, they are fluid and amalgamate to the other cultures, beliefs, and languages that we encounter in the new spaces. This does not mean that we forget our original practices; rather, when we are in this new space our knowledge expands and we look at things in a different way while we simultaneously go back to our original culture, beliefs, and language. There is something in this original culture, beliefs, and language that we cannot forget while we learn new things. Especially when we encounter oppression in the West; we go back to our culture, beliefs, and language to get knowledge on how to respond.

Such oppression derives from race, class, and gender. For example, as a Filipina in the West, I have been treated as somebody who does not belong. In one of my classes, I introduced myself as Dr. Torres. Then, one student addressed me as *Ate*, which in the Filipino language means older sister. I wondered why the student called me Ate, even though I introduced myself as a Doctor. From a critical perspective, the student wanted to bring me back to where he thought I belonged. This student is not innocent at all. He was being both racist and sexist to me at the same time. The student did not want me to settle in the West; he wanted to remind me that Canada is a country where I am not supposed to belong that I don't count as a "real professor" even if I have the qualifications. At that moment, what mattered to the student is that the message he was sending to me was clear. I got it! At that moment I felt that

I was being evicted. So, how did I respond? I smiled, but my heart was in pain. I smiled because I remembered that this student belongs to a system with a history of racism, sexist, and classism against racialized individuals like me. That racism is systemic, however, by saying this I am not forgetting the fact that the student belongs to this system and the system will not work without the student's participation. We are all part of this structure. Some decide to work against the structure while others choose to obey the structure. The student opted to follow the racist and sexist structure. The way this student treated me comes from deeper systemic issues. However, this does not mean that I am sanitizing this particularly experience; as much as the student played a big role in my sense of eviction, we cannot forget that there is a stronger force behind him, and that is the structural system to which he belongs.

This question of "who belongs" and "who does not belong" implicates racism, classism, and sexism because a particular race, class, and gender belongs to a particular place (Torres, 2010). The people who do not belong are racialized, and I do not belong because I am Filipina who supposedly belongs in a so-called Third World country. I belong when I am considered as a participant or subject of a study, or when I work in an area where dominant race are not supposed to work. This system allows me to work in a caring and service-oriented workplace. However, this does not come easily because before an immigrant becomes an immigrant, health is the first thing to be checked. Even when all other requirements are met, when one's health does meet the requirements of Canada's Ministry of Health, one cannot cross the Canadian border. Health means everything; there is no economy without health, there is no environment without health, there is no government without health. For this reason, it is important to learn about one of the ways of doing research in the area of public health.

3   Critical Ethnography as a Public Health Qualitative Research
       Methodology

The major components of critical ethnography according to Creswell (2007) "include a value-laden orientation, empowering people by giving them more authority, challenging the status quo, and addressing concerns about power and control. A critical ethnographer will study issues of power, empowerment, inequality, inequity, dominance, repression, hegemony, and victimization" (p. 70). This value-laden orientation is not about passing judgment when it comes to people's culture, beliefs, and other practices. It is about allowing individuals to express their own concerns and ideas about issues. It is not meaning making on behalf on the individual. It is not making assumptions as to what individuals say about the issues. It is about letting individuals make the meaning of what they say. When we as researchers make meaning on behalf of participants in a study, then we are infusing our own biased assumptions, and this does not make ethnography critical.

Critical ethnography is about empowering people by giving them authority (Creswell 2007) to share their own ideas or opinion on the issues. Before I expand upon Creswell's idea, I must first problematize the word "giving": When we talk about giving empowerment, there is a notion that we own and have the authority to give that power. The question is, "how do you see the other"? Are you seeing the other as powerless? Who are we to give authority to others? When we talk about empowering people by giving them authority, it suggests to me that researchers are the only individuals who have the power and the authority to give power. This in itself is a manifestation of how we undermine the participant's existence. Critical ethnographers need to think beyond themselves and the notion that only they have the power and authority. We have to rethink critical ethnography by seeing power in the ethnographer and the participant alike. We use critical ethnography because we believe that some members of the population in today's society are experiencing inequality and inequity, and that public health issues exist because our society is racist, sexist, homophobic, anti-Black, and anti-Native among other issues that contribute to the degradation of public health. Critical ethnography allows ethnographers and participants to understand each other by immersing themselves into each other's lives so that they can work collaboratively in liberating each other from the injustices perpetrated by society, institutions, and individuals.

I totally agree with Creswell (2007) when he describes that critical ethnography has the capacity to challenge the status quo and represents a way to address concerns about power and control. We use critical ethnography in understanding public health because we have manifested inequalities in society. For example, a Filipina gives birth through caesarean and during the operation medical staff accidentally cut another organ, and she must then use catheter for a month afterwards. The question is, is this a form of negligence on the part of medical staff who assisted her in her operation? Why did it happen to a Filipina? In Canada, she has been marked as a nanny or caregiver (Torres & Nyaga, 2017). Where is the respect of life? In this kind of research, critical ethnography is appropriate because it challenges the state that is racist and sexist. Critical ethnography will not only look at the experience of a racialized individual but also explore the other experiences in the community. A critical ethnographer looks at the pattern of how racialized groups have been treated in the health care system and how the health care system discriminates against

such groups in terms of care. Critical ethnography as a public health research
methodology will expose the discriminatory practices facing immigrants in
the health care system. The health care system in Canada only cares about the
desirable population while the undesirable population (i.e., immigrants) are
not considered important. Before racialized individuals become immigrants,
their health is the most important qualification; however, the moment they
become immigrants, their health becomes the least important. This seems so
contradictory, but when a society was built on the mechanisms of injustices,
this society continues to practice exactly the same mechanisms as it pretends
to be the most benevolent place to live in.

Creswell's (2007) description of critical ethnography as an approach that
questions power and control is on point. This is an important aspect of critical
ethnography because as we delve into the lives of the participants and want
to know more about their health, then our focus should be to challenge the
power and control that exist in their everyday lives. So too should the power
of a researcher over the participant be challenged. In Canada, power and control belong to the state through policies and regulations that are rooted in the
country's colonial history. Canada describes itself as a country that believes
in inclusivity and respects multiculturalism but based on the experiences of
immigrants it is clear that cultural hegemony exists. This cultural hegemony
is about the existence of White culture as the norm in Canadians society. All
practices are based on White culture, and the culture of the immigrants does
not exist. Public health is based on a White policy definition of health. A critical ethnographer will question this notion of health. The misconception of
immigrants as an undesirable population is key in using critical ethnography
as a public health research methodology because it exposes the insidious practices of the state, institutions, and individuals.

4   Procedures in Conducting Critical Ethnography as a Public Health
        Qualitative Research Methodology: Ethics and Principles

In this section, I use Creswell's (2007) procedure for conducting ethnography
from his book *Qualitative Inquiry and Research Design: Choosing Among Five
Approaches*. I will expand each procedure in relation to public health. The
main question that is central in each procedure is identifying how they apply
to conducting critical ethnography as a public health qualitative research
methodology. The first procedure is to determine if ethnography is the most
appropriate approach to use to study the research problem. Ethnography is
appropriate if the needs are to describe how a cultural group works and to

explore the beliefs, language, behaviors, and issues such as power, resistance, and dominance" (Creswell, 2007, p. 70). The first procedure focuses on understanding the nature of the research question. What does the research question focus on? What does it entail to address the research question? For example, the research can seek to identify the public health issues facing Filipinos in Toronto's Regent Park neighborhood. This research question focuses on the public health issues of Filipinos in Regent Park.

When we talk about public health, we want to comprehend the health issues of Filipino families in Regent Park. The research question wants to shed light on the health issues of a particular community, not just an individual. In this research question we can know that its concentration is the health of the Filipino population in Regent Park. To identify the health issue, there is a need to know the pattern of their daily lives (e.g., What kind of diet do they usually follow? What time do they eat?). We also want to apprehend their culture, behaviors, and beliefs in terms of health so that we can recognize the pattern of their way of life. Some of these questions are important to consider in order to know which qualitative research approach we need to use. While we consider this aspect of their lives and look at patterns, we also have to remember that their way of life is fluid. We cannot take patterns as practices that are stagnant and never change. Through a transnational framework, we can perceive that the connection between their practices in terms of health care from their country of origins to Canada play an important role. As they practice their way of life from their country of origin, they simultaneously incorporate the practices that they are learning in their new spaces that they occupy. Though Creswell is not discussing it in relation to public health, we can still use this first procedure when we look at public health because it helps us identify the appropriate approach to address the research question. Because critical ethnography seeks to change the status quo through addressing issues, we can us this approach as our methodology.

The second procedure is to "identify and locate a culture-sharing group or study. Typically, this group is one that has been together for an extended period of time, so that their shared language, patterns of behavior, and attitudes have emerged into a discernable pattern" (Creswell, 2007, p. 71). I have to carry on the research question that we use in the first procedure: What are the public health issues facing Filipinos in Toronto's Regent Park neighborhood? In this research question, we can perceive that it focuses on a group of individuals because it is asking about the public health issues facing Filipinos in Toronto's Regent Park neighborhood. We can observe that the research question would like to recognize the public health issues that Filipinos are confronting in this research question. We can also notice that this research question's emphasis is on the public health issues of a certain group. Its attention is the experience of a certain group who show patterns of behaviors and practices. While the research question focuses on patterns, its motivation is to address public health inequalities and inequities in the community of Filipinos. As it looks at the culture-sharing that Filipinos practice, critical ethnography also centers on the implications of policies that govern Filipinos. These policies could be health, labor, immigration, and criminal justice. All these policies are interconnected in governing the Filipino community, so the policies have implications for the Filipinos' health. While we are looking at the culture-sharing practices of the Filipino community, critical ethnography has to take into account other influences on their health. In this research question, procedure two is applicable.

The third procedure according to Creswell (2007) is to

> select cultural themes or issues to study about the group. This involves the analysis of the culture-sharing group. The themes may include such topics as enculturation, socialization, learning, cognition, domination, inequality. ... The ethnographer begins the study by examining people in interaction in ordinary settings and by attempting to discern pervasive patterns such as life cycles, events, and cultural themes. (p. 71)

Having the research question in mind, procedure in conducting ethnography is critical. What I want to pay attention to in this procedure is when we use critical ethnography and it involves a culture-sharing group, it is important to make an analysis focused not only on what the culture tells us but also on how the culture evolves from a transnational body and how the culture has been influenced by external factors. The factors that I am referring to in this chapter are the marginalization and discrimination that Filipinos are facing. When we talk about marginalization, the question is: in what way? For example, in terms of job opportunities, most of these Filipinos obtained university degrees before they immigrated to Canada; however, the moment they landed in Canada, they faced the problem of de-professionalization (Torres & Nyaga, 2017). They cannot get jobs based on the degrees they obtained from universities in the Philippines. They are forced to work as caregivers, servers, factory workers, and other service workers. This contributes (negatively) to their health. For example, an individual is forced to work as a janitor in spite of being a credentialed engineer. The effect of this kind of experience results in depression and disorientation. If this individual has a family and is experiencing such health issues, the question is: how will it affect their family relationship? In this third procedure, as much as we look into the pattern of the culture-sharing group, we have to also rethink the individual experiences in order to draw conclusions from the generalization. I like Padgett's (2017) notion that in details we see the devils, without totally evading the common experiences of the group we are studying.

The fourth procedure is to "study cultural concepts, determine which types of ethnography to use. Perhaps how the group work needs to be described, or the critical ethnography may need to expose issues such as power, hegemony, and to advocate for certain groups" (Creswell, 2007, p. 71). This fourth procedure speaks about concentrating on the concepts in a culture, but this concept we already know from our research question. What I want to emphasize in this procedure is how to expose power and hegemony. First of all, we can only expose the power and hegemony based on the research question that we want to address. Like our research question that we use in this chapter, we are looking into the public health issues that Filipinos are facing in Toronto's Regent Park neighborhood. This research question alone talks about exposing public health issues. When you want to know the public health issues that minority groups are facing, it is about concentrating on the powerlessness of this group, while uncovering the power of the state and the institution. The reason why we describe the powerlessness of the Filipino group is because Canada has a colonial history of marginalizing minority groups. For example, the live-in caregiving policy for Filipino women is racist and sexist (Torres & Nyaga, 2017). One reason why this is racist and sexist is the policy only gives caregivers permanent resident status when they finish their 24-month contract from an employer, where they live in and perform their duties as nannies. This in itself shows how Canadian policies are racist and sexist. Through this procedure, we need to use analysis that is not only centred on the individual and group but also on the different institutions that govern them, and the structural system that dictates how people live in Canada—the structural system that maintains power and control over everything that we do. The analysis should look into how each sector is implicated in the public health issues.

The fifth procedure is to "gather information where the group works and lives. ... Gathering the types of information typically needed in an ethnography involves going to the research site, respecting the daily lives of individuals at the site, and collecting a wide variety of materials" (Creswell, 2007, pp. 71–72). Ethnography concentrates on data collection where the group lives and going to the research site, but critical ethnography is not only interested in gathering information; it also pays attention on how this gathering of information takes place. Are we considering and respecting the wants, needs, desires, and spaces of the participant? Are we giving participants time to think about what they want to say and to not say? Where does our motivation lie? These are just some of the questions we need to ask ourselves as we use critical ethnography in researching public health issues. Health is a private matter to some of the groups. How do we then deal with this privacy when we know very well that this research is a public matter? How do we reconcile the desire of the participant to make it private and at the same time public in order to change the status quo? Is using anonymity enough in addressing this? What can we add so that we can respect the desire of the participants as we advocate for the issues that they are facing? Also, in this part of the procedure, it is important to build a relationship within the members of the community, which takes time and effort. However, establishing a relationship is necessary so that there is respect and care for one another. It is easy to gather information, but we have to ask ourselves about the kind of information that will be given to us when there is no trust and respect. As critical ethnographers, we must think and rethink about how we develop trust and respect within the members of the community.

The sixth and final procedure "is a holistic cultural portrait of the group that incorporates the views of the participants (emic) as well as the views of the research (etic). It might also advocate for the needs of the group or suggest changes in society to address needs of the group" (Creswell, 2007, p. 72). This procedure is critical, and I want to adapt it in critical ethnography as a public health qualitative research methodology. What I want to add here is the participants' voices in conversation with the voice of the ethnographer. Participants should not only be given the role of storytellers but also given a role in analyzing those stories. This analysis should be used not only for the purpose of adding quotations from the participant; the final product should also include participants' analyses. A critical ethnographer must remember that the author of the story knows better that anyone else. Some may argue that in academic writing, theory must guide the analysis. But who created the theory? Theory was created based on a study that has been conducted from an individual or a community who experience injustices. Therefore, theory already exists from the story of a participant.

5   Conclusion

The chapter explored critical ethnography as a public health qualitative research methodology through a transnational framework. It discussed how a transnational framework guides in looking at critical ethnography and how a research question can be developed that focuses on public health. It explored the meaning of public and addressed the question of how critical ethnography can be a useful approach in public health.

It also examined the procedures of conducting ethnography discussed by Creswell (2007) and used it as a reference for the procedure that can be used by critical ethnographers in conducting research on public health issues. In order for me to do this, I included a research question as a point of reference in all my discussion of the procedures. I decided to do this because without a research question, I cannot possibly discuss how a procedure can be critical in nature. Since my research is located among the Filipino communities, I then used this group as my participant. Also, using a transnational framework, it is wise to use this community for I know, as a part of the community, we always connected to our country of origin while simultaneously adapting to our new country. The intersectionality of our local and international experiences has a strong influence in how we see the world around us. It has a strong connection to how this community resists different forms of oppression and how they navigate their everyday lives. This local and international connection is also important in how the community looks at the public health issues that they are facing.

References

Creswell, J. (2007). *Qualitative inquiry and research design: Choosing among five approaches* (2nd ed.). Thousand Oaks, CA: Sage.

Padgett, D. K. (2017). *Qualitative methods in social work research* (3rd ed.). Thousand Oaks, CA: Sage.

Soyini Madison, D. (2014). *Critical ethnography: Methods, ethics and performance.* Thousand Oaks, CA: Sage.

Torres, R. A. & Nyaga, D. (2017). Gendered citizenship: A case study of paid Filipino male live-in caregivers in Toronto. *International Journal of Asia Pacific Studies* 13 (1): 51–71. https://doi.org/10.21315/ijaps2017.13.1.3.

Torres, R. A. (2012). *Aeta women Indigenous healers in the Philippines: Lessons and implications* (Doctoral dissertation, University of Toronto). TSpace. http://hdl.handle.net/1807/32830.

Torres, R. (2012). Exploring indigenous spirituality, activism and feminism in the life of my mother. *Canadian Women Studies Journal* 29 (1–2): 135–140.

Torres, R. (2010). The role of indigenous knowledge in the promotion of anti-racism education in schools. In *Our schools/our selves: Anti-racism in education: Missing in action. Canadian Centre for Policy Alternatives Journal* 19 (3): 239–254.

CHAPTER 5

My Blackness Is African

Looking at Kenyan Man through Black/Afrocentric Methodologies

Dionisio Nyaga

1   Introduction

> Though theory may guide and inspire us in composing a lay summary, designing interview questions, or coding data, it is not theory but a methodological process that directs the completion of the task. The relationship between theory and method has a long and provocative history reflected in disciplinary boundaries and research traditions privileging one over the other, as well as defining them as exclusively separate spheres.
>
> (MADISON, 2005, p. 12)

> The Negro ... exhibits the natural man in his completely wild and untamed state. We must lay aside all thought of reverence and morality—all that we call feeling—if we would rightly comprehend him. There is nothing harmonious with humanity to be found in this type of character. Hegel then promises himself not to ever mention Africa again, for "it is no historical part of the World; it has no movement or development to exhibit." What we properly understand by Africa, he concludes, "is the Unhistorical, Undeveloped Spirit, still involved in the conditions of mere nature."
>
> (MBEMBE, 2016, p. 91)

Historically, research has been used to define communities as backward and uncivilized (Smith, 2012). This colonial representation of the other is an issue with which the African continent continues to struggle (Mbembe, 2001). This chapter argues that Africa can represent itself in ways that are valid and responsible. This chapter is an outcome of a study that was undertaken among 10 Kenyan men in Toronto to identify ways in which they faced anti-Blackness in terms of employment, education, and immigration. This narrative Afrocentric qualitative study attempted to understand the role of accent in racial elimination of Kenyan men in Toronto. The study also attempts to understand the representational limitations of Black masculinity in terms of experiences of Kenyan in education, labour, and immigration. With those limitations, the study reconceptualizes Black masculinity by including Indigenous masculinities as another way of representing Kenyan men in Toronto. The following were the major research questions:

1. How does accent affect Kenyan men in Toronto in terms of labour, immigration, and education?
2. What are the limitations of Black masculinity in the representation of Kenyan men in Toronto?
3. What is the role of Indigenous masculinities in representing Kenyan men's issues in Toronto?

Using accent as the foundation of re-imagining Black masculinity and Blackness, the study found racial erasure of Kenyan men in educational, labour, and immigration policies. The study found Black masculinity and Blackness to be complicated and complex and as such research as a process needs to rise to this complexity of Africaness and Blackness. This chapter will showcase one among the many ways to undertake African-oriented research. It will present some of the nuances of African ways of knowing as central spaces of undertaking an African-based research. Drawing from scientific positivist studies, this chapter re-imagines the objectivist aspect of research as presented in the West. It is important to underline that this is not a cultural competence course of the "how" of doing research but rather a roadmap that has multiple known and unknown orientations.

2 On Representation of Africa

Positivist research borrows from the work of Auguste Comte, who believed that truth can be produced in orderly and systematic means, and that such truth can be valid and a true representation of the object so researched. Colonial and imperial systems of knowing continue to utilize a positivist paradigm to measure and gender knowledge production as either rational or emotional (Faulkner & Faulkner, 2014). This colonial representation is replete with colonial dualism of knowers and objects of study and provides the rationale to subjugate and colonize communities through the civilizational process of Western rational knowledge. Such measures erase the voices of participants through their reductionist process. Such processes do not consider communities' agency and resiliencies as forms of resistance. Some Black scholarship (also read Black masculinity) is embedded in colonial national metadata that erases the emotional role of inquiry. Such records do not represent fully sub-liminal voices of marginalized communities, and hence misrepresent the experiences of Black community. Much of the data does not speak to, account for, or represent the "hidden transcripts coded defiance" communities (Chavez et al., 2008) but rather presumes to understand the experience of Black com-munity as though Blackness was one straight and neat jacket. Certainly, such data cannot explain or even attempt to understand the experiences of Kenyan men, let alone Black communities.

The way studies on Black/African communities has been undertaken in the past is hegemonically colonial and gendered (Mbembe, 2001; Reviere, 2001; Wehbi, 2017). Mbembe (2001) has underlined the representation of Africa as a child, and whose story must be told by the West. This is tied to the belief that Africa cannot tell its story and requires the West for it to be known. Wehbi (2017) paints a picture of the Global South (read Africa) as broken and needy child who needs the West for its survival. Both Mbembe and Wehbi have pro-vided a framework through which research can be used to stamp or mark spaces as degenerate and in need of the White saviour. This racial representa-tion of Africa as broken and immoral continue to be supported through posi-tivist research from the West as valid and believable. Mbembe (2001) says that Africa is identified as a needy child whose story must be told by the rational other (Wehbi, 2017). Colonial researchers have constructed African communi-ties as intellectually broken, therefore rationalizing the need to write stories on behalf of Africa/ns (Mbembe, 2001, 2004). This patronizing and devaluing rep-resentation of the Black other is under scrutiny from Black scholars who call for research based on cultural humility and humanness (Chavez et al., 2008). With this colonial past, Black scholars are now calling for African-centred research that pays attention to African/Black context, histories, and experi-ences (Asante, 1998, 2007; Dei, 2011; Jones, 1991; Kubrin & Wadsworth, 2009; Kukushkin & Watt, 2009).

3   Decolonizing as a Methodology

Madison (2005) says that theory and research require a change in paradigm when doing research among communities (Chavez et al., 2008). If theory is tailored in ways that speak to the experiences of participants, then the fabric of social justice in knowledge production is realized. A social justice researcher needs to provoke and blur the neat division created between the researcher (read the West) and the participant (read Africa) in ways that reflect both as knowers and creators of knowledge (Gegeo & Gegeo,

2001). This is a process of decolonizing knowledge production in ways that acknowledge that power between the researcher and participant are critically reflective and reflexive and allow other ways of knowledge to be respected as authentic and truthful.

To decolonize the process of knowledge production means blurring power (Foucault, 1980), positions (Wehbi, 2017), language, and discourse hegemonically used in research (Arribas-Ayllon & Walkerdine, 2017; Gegeo & Gegeo, 2001). According to Tomic (2013), speaking on the gendered research,

> Unless feminists dared to think independently from the dominant ideas in sociology, a sociology highly dominated by patriarchy, it was not possible to contribute meaningfully to the discipline. I am a feminist academic with an immigrant background writing at the beginning of the 21st century. English is my second language (ESL). My life and work are inseparable from the dichotomy of Standard English/ESL. While through Lemert's influence I integrate my life experience into my teaching and research, through Acker's metaphor of "getting the man out of [one's] head," I have been encouraged to get the power of Standard English and whiteness out of my head to be able to reflect and write on the connections between Standard English, colonialism, whiteness, and the ESL immigrant experience. (p. 2)

This perspective of getting the "man out of the head" is a decolonial process of dispositioning rational knowledge production as the only way of truth-making. This form of decolonizing knowledge production troubles the researcher to identify how they are implicated in colonial, patriarchy, and Whiteness. The process of decolonial research means analyzing the researcher's implicit and unconscious epistemological, visceral, and lateral violence and imperialism toward the marginalized (Butler, 1990). A well-meaning researcher may well suppress their community in ways that espouse colonialism and capital accumulation.

To undertake a decolonial research, a researcher reflects on their biases in ways that are critical and reflexive (Creswell & Poth, 2018; George, 2017; Wehbi, 2017). The researcher acknowledges participants are knowers and experts of their experiences (Gegeo & Gegeo, 2001; George, 2017). The researcher is made aware that they are facilitators of knowledge production (George, 2017). Decolonial research is participant-led, and it benefits communities in meeting their daily needs. Research becomes a process that is organic and grounded on the needs of the community (George, 2017).

4   Afrocentric Indigenous Research

This study sought to deconstruct the methodologies and methods used to "study" Black men in America. Based on the distinct experiences of Kenyan men in Toronto, this study applied a Transnational Afrocentric Indigenous (TAI) qualitative narrative methodology. According to Penner and Saperstein (2013), "qualitative research methods are the most appropriate means of studying the intersectional complexity of social difference, in part because they tend to be better suited to identifying mechanisms and process rather than broad patterns" (p. 321).

Qualitative methods look at the complexities of communities based on their experiential stories and narratives steeped in their context and histories (Baumeister & Newman, 1994; Berg, 1998; Cohler, 1994). The qualitative narrative study decolonizes through feminization of the research process as a dance (Chavez et al., 2008) and recognizing subjugated bodies of knowledge like songs, cultural beliefs, values, and poetic knowledges (Butler, 1993; Elliott, 2005; Hickson & Hickson, 2016; Reinharz, 1992; Stanley & Wise, 1991) as fundamental to the research process. A qualitative study questions, disturbs, and decolonizes the taken-for-granted ivory tower position of the knower as the essence of knowledge (Hollway & Jefferson, 2000) by invoking local narrative as a powerful point of knowledge production (George, 2017). Madison (2005) says

> Critical social theory evolves from a tradition of "intellectual rebellion" that includes radical ideas challenging regimes of power that changed the world. As ethnographers, we employ theory at several levels in our analysis: to articulate and identify hidden forces and ambiguities that operate beneath appearances; to guide judgments and evaluations emanating from our discontent; to direct our attention to the critical expressions within different interpretive communities relative to their unique symbol systems, customs, and codes; to demystify the ubiquity and magnitude of power; to provide insight and inspire acts of justice; and to name and analyze what is intuitively felt. (p. 13)

A qualitative narrative methodology validates experiential knowledge of both researchers and the participants (read Africa/n) in ways that allow multicentric bodies of knowledge production to appear (Cajete, 2000; Chilisa, 2012; Craig, 2009; Dei, 2000, 2011; Fraser, 2004; Gardner, 2003; Gegeo & Gegeo, 2001; Gergen, 1999; Graham, 1999, 2005; Reyes Cruz, 2008). Such knowledges are holistic and meet the well-being of the participant by centralizing and authenticating their self-esteem and determination (Smith & Sparkes, 2009). A qualitative narrative study is participant-led and galvanizes local powers as necessary in decolonizing normalized knowledge and firming local needs (Creswell & Poth, 2018; Gegeo & Gegeo, 2001; Labov, 2006; Lawler, 2002; Nelson, 1998).

Narrative research approach troubles the dominant discourses on research (Fraser, 2004; Mazama, 2003; Reviere, 2001). Bhabha (1994) says

> In keeping with the spirit of the "right to narrate" as a means to achiev-
> ing our own national or communal identity in a global world, demands
> that we revise our sense of symbolic citizenship, our myths of belonging,
> by identifying ourselves with the "starting point" of the other national
> and international histories and geographies. It is by placing herself at the
> intersections (and in the interstices) of these narratives that Rich empha-
> sizes the importance of historical and cultural re-visioning: the process of
> being subjected to, or the subject of, a particular history "of one own"—a
> local history—leaves the poet "unsatisfied" and anxious about who she is,
> or what her community can be, in the larger flow of transnational history.
> (p. xx)

Storying, which is central to Afrocentricity, is the research process of knowl-edge production that recognizes that social justice, "truth," and harmony are necessary points of looking back to self and others (Asante, 1988; Fraser, 2004; Mazama, 2003; Reviere, 2001). A social justice researcher who employs a nar-rative approach recognizes, acknowledges, and disturbs power, discourse, and language use in knowledge production (Creswell & Poth, 2018). This decolonial process breaks down the prevailing power dynamics between the researcher and participants in ways that centralize, recognize, and acknowledge histor-ical injuries and collective trauma meted on participants (read Africa/ns). To that end, the participants and the researcher work together in mutual respect and make relationships built on those histories. Consequently, the participants have a sense of ownership in the research process and its outcome, and the researcher takes the responsibility of facilitating the processes of knowledge repatriation.

Through the Afrocentric narrative research process, the participants stand apart from their stories, sentences, and words in ways that allow a rethinking of what they say. This provides a space for both the researcher and the partici-pants to question what has been presented by the participants while allowing the participants to be critical of their presentation. Such a process is back and forth and never seeking to arrive. Each participant adds their contributions into the fabric of narratives in ways that enrich the understanding of social life while transforming research into an artistry.

An Afrocentric research methodology ties to the principles (canons) of Afrocentricity, which are Umoja (unity), Kujichagulia (self-determination), Ujima (collective responsibility), Ujamaa (cooperation), Nia (aim), Kuumba (creativity), and Imani (faith) (Asante, 1988, 2007; Reviere, 2001). These principles examined, guided, and facilitated the processes of this study. Afrocentric research unites people in producing knowledge, hence making the process relational rather than individualistic. This makes research an organically oriented knowledge production process that affirms participant experiences as truthful and believable (Faulkner & Faulkner, 2014). Such aspect is steeped on the needs of the participants and the role the research plays in social justice.

This ties to Asante's (1980, 1988, 2007) calls for Ma'at and Nommo in community processes. According to Reviere (2001),

> Ma'at is "the quest for justice, truth, and harmony," and in the context of this article it refers to the research exercise itself, in harmony with the researcher, being used as a tool in the pursuit of truth and justice. The ultimate goal of Ma'at is that of helping to create a more fair and just society. Nommo means "the productive word," and here it describes the creation of knowledge as a vehicle for improvement in human relations. (p. 711)

Afrocentric studies focus on issues faced by Black communities in the West (Asante, 1988, 2003). As such, Afrocentric research methodology provided a relevant way of understanding injustice meted on one form of Blackness (Kenyan men) at the behest of the other. Afrocentric methodology includes the participant as a stakeholder (collective responsibility) in the research process (Asante, 1988, 2003, 2007). Afrocentric methodology works with and celebrates the Indigenous process of knowledge production guided by relationship building, love, respect, and reciprocity. The seven principles of Afrocentricity work under the guidance of the Indigenous framework.

Afrocentric Indigenous research brings people together to share themselves to each other (Reviere, 2001). Research is a community-based project (Ujamaa) rather than an individual endeavour (Gegeo & Gegeo, 2001). This methodology looks at the research process as collaborative work where knowledge production is *in situ*. It politicizes how knowledge is produced and disseminated. These principles orient research as a transformative praxis meant to bring change in communities (Asante, 2006; Borum, 2007; Graham, 1999, 2005; Reviere, 2001). For example, participants were engaged in deeper analysis of their narrative in ways that transformed their thinking but also allowed collective imagination between the researcher and the participants. This made the interview process communal and acknowledged the participant as knowers based on their own experience. The role of the researcher was to facilitate their new formations of knowledges to appear and disturb taken-for-granted metanarratives (Gegeo & Gegeo, 2001). An Indigenous perspective to Afrocentric research helps to mitigate the very danger of canonization of research. Afrocentric research cannot be without Indigenous knowing of African people both at home and in the diaspora.

Indigenous qualitative methodology validates the power of storytelling in transforming the socio-cultural needs of communities (Creswell & Poth, 2018). Stories come to be modes or avenues of sharing the experience of research participants to trouble the colonial representation of the African other as broken (Mbembe, 2001). Such sharing is based on a concerted effort on the part of the researcher to actively listen and affirm participants' experiences as expressed in their stories. Active listening is key in building respectful relationships with participants. Indigenous methodology asserts respect, reciprocity, relationship-building, and love as the framework of storying and knowledge production between the participant and the researcher. It troubles the language, power, and discourses that control the research process (Cajete, 2000; Dei, 2000, 2011; Gegeo & Gegeo, 2001; Reyes Cruz, 2008) by introducing subjugated voices as truthful and powerful sites of decolonization. Through active and respectful listening, researchers and participants form alliances that trouble the taken-for-granted research processes.

Reviere (2001), quoting Alice Walker on Afrocentric research methodology, starts by saying

> I believe that the truth about any subject comes when all sides of the story are put together, and all their different meanings make one new one. Each writer writes the missing parts to the other writer's story. And the whole story is what I am after. (p. 709)

This connects to Bhabha's (1994) role of iterative process of narration. Knowledge production comes to be oriented as a process of connected relationship between knowers, which disorients the dominant knowledge production processes. The role of an Afrocentric Indigenous researcher is to actively listen, validate, facilitate, and acknowledge localized bodies of knowledge as expressed through the stories given by the participant. In this sense, knowledge comes to be a gift to the community by participants.

An Afrocentric Indigenous narrative methodology looks at narration as transformative, subversive, and a counter discourse to colonial metanarrative (Asante, 1998; Dei, 2000; Gegeo & Gegeo, 2001; Reviere, 2001). It seeks to deconstruct totalizing discourse and language (Foucault, 1980) that look at participants as broken and damaged by identifying them as co-producers of knowledge (Gegeo & Gegeo, 2001). It seeks to actively involve the participant in the process of knowledge production (Reyes Cruz, 2008). An Afrocentric Indigenous narrative methodology identifies the participant as the expert and the researcher as the learner. It seeks to inconvenience the colonial rational order of producing of knowledge by complicating the dual relation between the researcher and the participant (Chavez et al., 2008; Dei, 2011; Gegeo & Gegeo, 2001; Smith, 2012). This methodology is guided by a decolonial process of research as representational politics (Baskin, 2005; Bhabha, 1994; Dei, 2000; Smith, 2012). The Afrocentric research paradigm troubles the taken-for-granted ideals, thoughts, and feelings.

This methodology is grounded on Black and African experiences and the racial and gender ordering of knowledges and knowledge production. It is a philosophical understanding of material and symbolic racial and gender expulsion of Kenyan men in knowledge production. It celebrates the diversity of cultures and knowledge as sites of strength rather than weakness. It seeks to centralize the desire of Kenyan men in the diaspora as an important point of emergence and counter discourse.

The researcher in this study paid attention to what the participants were saying as well as their gestures and body language to make sense of participants' stories. He did not interrupt the participant and would seek clarity to understand the participant. The researcher was patient with the participant and would not interrupt. In his study, the researcher applied paraphrasing and questions as reflective and analytical pieces of bringing attention to the importance of participants' comments. Such points allowed the speaker (participant) to analyze and bring forth a new dimension to their story (analysis) while learning new information (epiphanies) from their story (Creswell & Poth, 2018).

Through this approach, Kenyan men living in Toronto provided this study with rich data that explains their experiences and those of others in ways meant to bring social justice in labour, education, and immigrations process in Canada. This approach created a relationship of purpose between the researcher and participant (Asante, 1988; Chavez et al., 2008). According to Madison (2005),

> Conquergood frames dialogue as performance and contends that the aim of "dialogical performance" is to bring self and Other together so

they may question, debate, and challenge one another. Dialogue is framed as performance to emphasize the living communion of a felt-sensing, embodied interplay and engagement between human beings. For Conquergood, dialogue resists conclusions. It is intensely committed to keeping the meanings between and the conversations with the researcher and the Other open and ongoing. It is a reciprocal giving and receiving rather than a timeless resolve. The dialogical stance is situated in multiple expressions that transgress, collide, and embellish realms of meaning. Dialogue is both difference and unity, both agreement and disagreement, both a separation and a coming together. For Conquergood, ethnographic, performative dialogue is more like a hyphen than a period. Dialogue is therefore the quintessential encounter with the Other. (p. 9)

The process of dialogic interviewing democratizes research in ways that include and affirm subjugated voices, while recognizing the complexities and violent encounters between the researcher and the participant. This research process allows the researcher to enter the participants' spaces with an open mind, validate their voices, and acknowledge them as experts. Knowledge production is not an end but a means of creating relationship through respect and love. The researcher guides or facilitates production of knowledge (Reyes Cruz, 2008) while the community takes the lead and ownership of knowledge production. A researcher works with the participants in ways that effect social change and justice (Harrington, 2005). Narrative study decolonizes Eurocentric determination of the participant as damaged by celebrating interstitial points of emergence as important points of strength (Tuck, 2010). Research comes to be seen as a celebration of community (Smith, 2012).

This study critically reflexed and reflected on the colonial politics of knowledge production. The study looked at the relations of power between colonial state institutions and their interaction with Kenyan men. The study looked at the effect of accent and how the Kenyan men are racially profiled in education, labour, and immigration. The study applied an Afrocentric Indigenous perspective to decolonize policies using participants' stories. Their voices (read accents), once defined as emotional, became the central pillar of decolonizing a masculine rational form of knowledge production. Their stories feminized the research process by celebrating emotions as a form of decolonizing rational process of knowledge production. The powers of migrant Kenyan men as expressed in their stories came to trouble the totalizing and normalizing processes of knowledge and production of truth in ways that affirmed alternative ways of visualizing the migrant Black other as capable of writing their stories. This disturbed the settled sites of gendered knowledge production in ways that validated migrant accents, histories, and ways of life as relevant in knowledge production while effecting policy change.

5   Ethical Principles

The researcher explained in simple and accessible language the purpose of the study and the role of participants. Due to the ethical consideration, the study used pseudonyms in order to keep participants anonymous. The study also removed all identifying information like demographics to keep information provided confidential and maintain anonymity. The researcher made sure that the written consent form was signed and dated.

The researcher informed all participants that they could decide not to answer part or all the questions and that such a decision would not interfere with the relationship they had with the University of Toronto. They were also told that they could withdraw from the study at any time, that they could withdraw their comments at any time, and that such a move would not interfere with the relationship they had with the University of Toronto. The researcher also explained to the participants the benefits and risks of the study. This study had minimal risk and was passed by the University of Toronto Ethics Board. The researcher provided the participants with the consent form and allowed them to go through it and ask questions or seek clarification. It is after the participant signed the consent form that the researcher commenced the interviews.

6   Infusing Indigenous Afrocentricity in the Methods

This study identified participants as experts of their own life and therefore considered them co-producers of knowledge (Gegeo & Gegeo, 2001). The researcher acknowledged their position and power as researcher in ways that allowed them to be vulnerable and humble to learn from the participants' lived experience. The interviews became more of a conversation between the researcher and the participant. This was a way to break the historical ice brought about by determination of the researcher as the expert and the participant as a template of knowledge production (Foucault, 1975). The role of the researcher was to actively listen to the participant without interrupting them. Interview questions were based on the conversation but tailored in ways that would help answer the interview question while maintaining the conversation between the researcher and participant. This means that the interviewer had to understand the interview questions and find a way to balance what the participant said and how that answered the interview question. The key is to break the horizontal power between the colonial role the interview schedule plays in directing researcher interviews. The role of the interview question was to learn from the experiences of the participant.

While the interviews were ongoing, the researcher found time to critically analyze some of the comments of the participants with them. Participants had time to reflect on their comments and their implication to Kenyan communities both in Canada and the world. This played the role of subverting the colonial depiction of African bodies as incapable of making sense and writing their own stories (Mbembe, 2001). This aspect also helped break the colonial order and system of research process. According to Faulkner and Faulkner (2014), the research process can take multiple forms that allow the subaltern subjects to speak (Spivak, 1988, 2003). In this sense, research becomes a process of representational politics and uncoupling the colonial gendered metanarrative that the participant is irrational and incapable of writing their own story. From this perspective, the researcher takes the role of facilitating the process of researcher while the participant directs the process. This study was participant-led and accommodated participants' views in deconstructing and subverting the design, tools, and process of study (Harrington, 2005). This way of looking at data collection as also analysis (conversational interviews) was decolonial, efficient, and effective while also allowing the participants to open up to their hidden and coded experiences (Chavez et al., 2008).

The interview process took the form of a dance where the researcher kept reflecting on when to get in and when to withdraw, when to ask questions, and when to allow conversations to continue. Dances are a major aspect of African values and culture. This reflexive back and forth process of critical reflection is necessary in terms of affirming and validating participants' points of view. This process allowed the feminization of the research process in ways that also allowed emotions to take central role. Emotions are key means of knowledge production among the African communities. Emotions helps connect the being to the spiritual place where knowledge is believed to emanate. The interview was more of a coffee-house discussion between the researcher and the participant, allowing democratization of representations and knowledge production (Habermas, 1984, 1987, 1989). This is core in the Afrocentric research perspective which looks at knowledge production as being steeped in communities' needs and experiences (Asante, 1998).

It is important to bring on board the voices from the margin by integrating and validating their complexities and iterative incompleteness through the narrative qualitative form of data collection (Creswell, 2013). This study looked at the experiential stories of Kenyan men as an essential form of reimagining their needs and aspirations. The researcher decided to focus more on the voices of participants and how they inform the interview schedule. Rather than the interview questions leading the conversation, the participants spoke to the question in ways that deconstructed and reinvented new forms of understanding Black communities and Kenyan men. Narrative is an important component that connects the researcher and the participant in producing knowledge (Clough, 2002; Czarniawski, 2004; Fenstermacher, 1994; Harrington, 2005). It accommodates and validates participants' emotions in decolonizing the research process (Borland, 1991; Fontana & James, 1998; Franzosi, 1998). This process of data collection and analysis is pegged on validation, respect, and creating long-lasting relationships with communities, which is a core aspect of Indigenous and Afrocentric knowledge production.

7   Interview Process

Most interviews were done at the University of Toronto, Ontario Institute for Studies in Education (OISE) library. The interview schedule contained 11 questions. The interview time was between 45 minutes to 1 hour. Before the interview, the researcher introduced himself and the study and had the participants sign the consent form. After that, participants introduced themselves. This provided time to build rapport and relationship with each participant (Faulkner & Faulkner, 2014). Relationship building is a key component in African cultures and a fundamental part of the process of knowledge production. The interview focused on creating initial relationships with the participants; thus, the researcher would spend the first few minutes discussing something that was not connected to the study, but which interested both the researcher and the participant. Topics would range from family issues to Kenyan politics, which would help break the ice and create familiarity between the co-creators (i.e., participant and researcher). In Indigenous and Afrocentric research paradigms, relationship building is key in interviewing (Reviere, 2001; Smith, 2012). It denotes respect through interest in participants' ideas and thoughts and humanizes the interview processes.

The researcher actively "read" the participants' body language to determine their comfort levels. Then, discussion would slowly orient to the focus of this study. It is at this point that the researcher would remind the participant about audio recording. Such an interruption was made when the researcher realized that the discussion was delving into the research focus. The interruption was respectfully and ethically done in ways that maintained the relationship. Respect and relationship are a key component of African values. This speaks of why we need to pay attention to humanness rather than fronting knowledge as prior or ethics. For example, the researcher allowed the participant to finish what they were saying and then show interest in what they had said by paraphrasing it and informing them that what they had said was part of the study. It is also at this point that the researcher would discuss the study, its purpose, and the content of the consent form.

Since the study was audio recorded, the interviewer would then gently remind the participant that they would record the conversation and explain why it is necessary. Most of the time, the researcher informed the participants that he needed to concentrate on the conversation they were having and as such recording would help document the conversation in ways that would retain its authenticity. All the participants agreed to be audio recorded. From then on, the researcher also told the participants that this was more of a discussion-based interview, which provided the participants the space to be open and analyze some of their comments. In Indigenous knowledge production, participants are producers of knowledge rather than consumers; as such, the interview process was designed to allow co-production of knowledge. When participants analyzed their comments, it allowed them to create knowledge that humanized their experiences, which is a key decolonial and African-based interview praxis. Sometimes the researcher asked candid and critically reflective questions and the participant would look removed and lost in their thought. The role of an Afrocentric researcher in such moments was to remain silent, present, and comfortable. The presence of the researcher provided assurance and support to the participant that they "get lost." This speaks of an African researcher as companion to others in their journey of searching for themselves. This was not just respectful to the participant but also allowed authentic relationships to flourish. Such a process of losing the self is necessary in reliving participants' experiences in ways that allowed them to introspect on what was hidden in their unconscious through colonization. A good Afrocentric researcher waits for participants to own the journey and when the participants come back, they find familiarity and support from the researcher.

This moment is crucial in analysis processes of knowledge production. Such moments elicit discomfort in researchers in that they are losing the participant or that they are losing their expertise since they cannot control the emotional participant. A decolonial Afrocentric interview praxis allows an Afrocentric researcher to remain comfortable in such discomfort. It is at this point that silence becomes a tool of decolonization. To an Afrocentric researcher, this is an important point at which the participant reaches out to their suppressed self and present it as authentic knowledge. This instant allowed them to reflect on their comments, and the interlocking power engrained in them, to overcome and create knowledges that speak to them. To get lost is a privilege in that those who take the journey come to be defined as human, while those who cannot come to be determined as broken. This means that the interruption of such a process of self-searching is not only disrespectful but also goes against ethical practices of human right. Most researchers, scared of losing their role as rational thinkers, ask irrelevant questions rather than allow the participants to introspect themselves.

The researcher had a hard copy of the interview schedule but instead memorized it. The interview schedule provided questions to be asked but did not orient the interview process. All questions were guided by what the participant was saying. The questions were asked in ways that reflected the discussion but also would answer interview question. These transitional modes of interviewing allowed deconstruction of interviews in ways that the interview schedule and the researcher came to occupy the role of a listener. That meant that the interviewer did not follow the order of questions in the interview schedule. This allowed the researcher to create a comfortable environment for a discussion that was not regulated by the document. This also allowed a reflexive discussion that questioned colonial tools of introspection like the interview schedule and its implications for colonial research and representation.

This form of epistemological disruption is necessary in any research process. The interview schedule is built on subjective lived experience that may not speak to the participant. To suspend its appearance from the discussion means decolonization of interviewing process. It is also ethically allowed in that it reduces pressure on the part of the participant because most people are scared of questions and questioning more so when somebody is using chapter material as a point of interviewing. It also allowed the researcher to ask questions that were relevant to the discussion and that would help answer the research question. Such a decolonial interviewing allows the complication of the research process in ways that embed and connect data collection with its analysis.

8   Data Analysis

Analysis of the data is a political process of meaning-making and representation of what the participant has said (Fraser, 2004; Gegeo & Gegeo, 2001). In this study, the process of data collection was also a time when the researcher engaged with the participant in deeper conversation and analysis of their statement and content. This is fundamental in decolonization of research because it engages the participant in unsealing the neat research process. It also provides a space for participants to engage in knowledge production. Such a break from traditional knowledge production counters the dominant belief that the participant is an object of introspection and cannot perform rational work. As discussed earlier in the interview section, data analyses started in the data collection section. The researcher provided a comfortable environment that made participants introspect their comments.

In any interview, questions are political. How you pose a question determines the trajectory of the study. For this study, questions invited the participant to take part in enriching their comments. For example, the researcher would apply questions to challenge participants standing on social issues. The researcher applied paraphrasing as a tool of making the participants reflect on their statement. Paraphrasing is key in terms of opening new perspectives on the part of the participants. The researcher mirrors back participants' comments so that they can start making sense of what they say. The researcher is expected to open discussion on where the sentiments are coming from and the effect they bring to the lives of other people. The interview process should not be all about validating the participant but also about challenging held-for-granted thoughts and notions as expressed by the participant and researcher.

9   Conclusion

This chapter paid attention to the different ways through which critical reflexivity can help unravel the ways in which we may give life to the very structures we may be looking forward to decolonizing. The chapter identified key areas of decolonization in a research undertaken among 10 Kenyan men living in Toronto. This chapter lays bare the necessity of decolonization and Blackening of research in ways that are transformational in terms of the processes undertaken in any research. Key to this chapter is the recognition that ethics must precede knowledge so that research become an act of being human.

References

Arribas-Ayllon, M., & Walkerdine, V. (2017). Foucauldian discourse analysis. In C. Willig & W. Stainton-Rogers (Eds.), *The Sage handbook of qualitative research in psychology* (2nd ed., pp. 110–123). London, UK: Sage.

Asante, M. K. (1980). *Afrocentricity: The theory of social change*. Buffalo, NY: Amulefi.

Asante, M. K. (1988). *Afrocentricity* (Rev. ed.). Trenton, NJ: Africa World Press.

Asante, M. K. (1998). *The Afrocentric idea* (Rev. and expanded ed.). Philadelphia, PA: Temple University Press.

Asante, M. K. (2003a). *Afrocentricity: The theory of social change*. Chicago, IL: African American Images.

Asante, M. K. (2003b). Locating a text: Implications of Afrocentric theory. In A. Mazama (Ed.), *The Afrocentric paradigm* (pp. 235–244). Trenton, NJ: Africa World Press.

Asante, M. K. (2006). A discourse on Black studies: Liberating the study of African people in the Western academy. *Journal of Black Studies* 36 (5): 646–662.

Asante, M. K. (2007). *An Afrocentric manifesto*. Cambridge, UK: Polity Press.

Baskin, C. (2005). Storytelling circles: Reflections of Aboriginal protocols in research. *Canadian Social Work Review* 22 (2): 171–187.

Baumeister, R. F., & Newman, L. S. (1994). How stories make sense of personal experiences: Motives that shape autobiographical narratives. *Personal and Social Psychology Bulletin* 20 (6): 676–690.

Berg, B. (1998). *Qualitative research methods for the social sciences*. Boston, MA: Allyn & Bacon.

Bhabha, H. K. (1994). *Location of culture*. New York, NY: Routledge.

Borland, K. (1991). "That's not what I said": Interpretive conflict in oral narrative research. In S. Berger Gluck & D. Patai (Eds.), *Women's words: The feminist practice of oral history* (pp. 63–76). New York, NY: Routledge.

Borum, V. (2007). Why we can't wait! *Journal of Human Behavior in the Social Environment* 15 (2–3): 117–135.

Butler, J. (1990). *Gender trouble: Feminism and subversion of identity*. New York, NY: Routledge.

Butler, J. (1993). *Bodies that matter: On the discursive limits of "sex"*. London, UK: Routledge.

Cajete, G (2000). Indigenous knowledge: The Pueblo metaphor of Indigenous education. In M. Battiste (Ed.), *Reclaiming Indigenous voices and vision* (pp.181–191). Vancouver, BC: UBC Press.

Chavez, V., Duran, B., Baker, Q.E., Avila, M. M., & Wallerstein, N. (2008). The dance of race and privilege in community based participatory research. In M. Minkler & N. Wallerstein (Eds.), *Community based participatory research for health: From process to outcomes* (2nd ed., pp. 91–106). San Francisco, CA: Jossey-Bass.

Chilisa, B. (2012). *Indigenous research methodologies*. Thousand Oaks, CA: Sage.

Clough, P. (2002). *Narratives and fictions in educational research*. Buckingham, UK: Open University Press.

Cohler, B. J. (1994). The human sciences, the life story, and clinical research. In E. Sherman & W. J. Reid (Eds.), *Qualitative research in social work* (pp. 163–174). New York, NY: Columbia University Press.

Craig, C. (2009) Learning about reflection through exploring narrative inquiry. *Reflective Practice* 10: 105–116.

Creswell, J. (2013). *Qualitative inquiry and research design* (3rd ed.). Thousand Oaks, CA: Sage.

Creswell, J., & Poth, C. (2018). *Qualitative inquiry and research design: Choosing among five approaches* (4th ed). Thousand Oaks, CA: Sage.

Czarniawski, B. (2004). *Narratives in social science research*. London, UK: Sage.

Dei, G. J. S (2000). Rethinking the role of indigenous knowledges in the academy. *International Journal of Inclusive Education* 4 (2): 111–132.

Dei, G. J. S. (2011). *Studying, researching and teaching African Indigenous knowledge: Challenges, possibilities and methodological cautions*. Pretoria, South Africa: University of South Africa.

Elliott, J. (2005). *Using narrative in social research: Qualitative and quantitative approaches*. London, UK: Sage.

Faulkner, S., & Faulkner, C. (2014). *Research methods for social workers: A practice-based approach* (2nd ed.). Chicago, IL: Lyceum Books.

Fenstermacher, G. (1994) The knower and the known: The nature of knowledge in research on teaching. *Review of Research in Education* 20: 3–56.

Fontana, J., & James, J. H. (1998). Interviewing: The art of science. In N. K. Denzin & Y. S. Lincoln (Eds.), *Collecting and interpreting qualitative materials* (pp. 47–78). Thousand Oaks, CA: Sage.

Foucault, M. (1975). *Discipline and punish: The birth of the prison* (A. M. Sheridan-Smith, Trans.). Harmondsworth, UK: Penguin.

Foucault, M. (1980). *Power/knowledge: Selected interviews and other writings, 1972–1977*. New York, NY: Pantheon.

Franzosi, R. (1998). Narrative analysis: Or why (and how) sociologists should be interested in narrative. *Annual Review of Sociology* 24 (1): 517–555.

Fraser, H. (2004). Doing narrative research: Analysing personal stories line by line. *Qualitative Social Work* 3 (2): 179–201.

Gardner, F. (2003). Critical reflection in community-based evaluation. *Qualitative Social Work* 2 (2): 197–212. doi:10.1177%2F1473325003002002005.

Gegeo, D., & Watson-Gegeo, K. (2001). "How we know": Kwara'ae rural villagers doing Indigenous epistemology. *The Contemporary Pacific* 13 (1): 55–88.

George, P. (2017). Critical arts-based research: An effective strategy for knowledge mobilization and community activism. In H. Parada & S. Wehbi (Eds.), *Reimagining anti-oppression social work research* (pp. 29–38). Toronto, ON: Canadian Scholars' Press.

Gergen, K. (1999). *An invitation to social construction*. London, UK: Sage.

Graham, M. (1999). The African-centered worldview: Developing a paradigm for social work. *British Association of Social Work* 29 (2): 252–267.

Graham, M. (2005). Maat: An African-centered paradigm for psychological and spiritual healing. In R. Moodley & W. West (Eds.), *Integrating traditional healing practices into counseling and psychotherapy* (pp. 210–220). Thousand Oaks, CA: Sage.

Habermas, J. (1984). *The theory of communicative action. Volume 1: Reason and the rationalisation of society* (T. McCarthy, Trans.). London, UK: Heinemann.

Habermas, J. (1987). *The theory of communicative action. Volume 2: Lifeworld and system: A functionalist critique* (T. McCarthy, Trans.). Cambridge, UK: Polity Press.

Habermas, J. (1989). *The structural transformation of the public sphere: An inquiry into a category of bourgeois society* (T. Burger, Trans.). Cambridge, UK: Polity Press.

Harrington, C. (2005). "Liberating" critical ethnography: Reflections from Fiji garment industry research. *Anthropology Forum* 15 (3): 287–296.

Hickson, H., & Hickson, H. (2016). Becoming a critical narrativist: Using critical reflection and narrative inquiry as research methodology. *Qualitative Social Work* 15 (3): 380–391.

Hollway, W., & Jefferson, T. (2000). *Doing qualitative research differently: Free association, narrative and the interview method*. London, UK: Sage.

Jones, L. (1991). Unemployed fathers and their children: Implications for policy and practice. *Child & Adolescent Social Work Journal* 8 (2): 101–116.

Kubrin, C. E., & Wadsworth, T. (2009). Explaining suicide among Blacks and Whites: How socioeconomic factors and gun availability affect race-specific suicide rates. *Social Science Quarterly* 90 (5): 1203–1227.

Kukushkin, V., & Watt, D. (2009). *Immigrant-friendly businesses: Effective practices for attracting, integrating, and retaining immigrants in Canadian workplaces*. Ottawa, ON: Conference Board of Canada.

Labov, W. (2006). Narrative pre-construction. *Narrative Inquiry* 16 (1): 37–45.

Lawler, S. (2002). Narrative in social research. In T. May (Ed.), *Qualitative research in action* (pp. 242–258). London, UK: Sage.

Madison, D. S. (2005). *Critical ethnography: Method, ethics and performance*. Thousand Oaks, CA: Sage.

Mazama, A. (2003). *The Afrocentric paradigm*. Trenton, NJ: Africa World Press.

Mbembé, J.-A. (2001). *On the postcolony*. Berkeley, CA: University of California Press.

Mbembe, A. (2004). Aesthetics of superfluity. *Public Culture* 16 (3): 373–406.

Mbembe, A. (2016). Africa in the new century. *The Massachusetts Review* 57 (1): 91–104.

Nelson, K. (1998). Meaning in memory. *Narrative Inquiry* 8 (2): 409–418.

Penner, A., & Saperstein, A. (2013). Engendering racial perceptions: An intersectional analysis of how social status shapes race. *Gender & Society* 27 (3): 319–344.

Reinharz, S. (1992). *Feminist methods in social research*. Oxford, UK: Oxford University Press.

Reviere, R. (2001). Toward an Afrocentric research methodology. *Journal of Black Studies* 31 (6): 709–728.

Reyes Cruz, M. (2008). What if I just cite Grasiela: Working toward decolonizing knowledge through a critical ethnography. *Qualitative Inquiry* 14 (4): 651–658.

Smith, L. T. (2012). Colonizing knowledges. In *Decolonizing methodologies: Research and indigenous peoples* (2nd ed., pp. 61–80). London, UK: Zed Books.

Smith, B., & Sparkes, A. C. (2009). Narrative inquiry in sport and exercise psychology: What can it mean, and why might we do it? *Psychology of Sport & Exercise* 10 (1): 1–11.

Spivak, G. S. (1988). Can the subaltern speak? In C. Nelson & L. Grossberg (Eds.), *Marxism and the interpretation of culture* (pp. 271–315). Urbana, IL: University of Illinois Press.

Spivak, G. C. (2003). Can the subaltern speak? *Die Philosophin* 14 (27): 42–58.

Stanley, L., & Wise, S. (1991). Feminist research, feminist consciousness, and experiences of sexism. In M. Fonow & J. Cook (Eds.), *Beyond methodology: Feminist scholarship as lived research*. Bloomington, IN: Indiana University Press.

Tomic, P. (2013). The colour of language: Accent, devaluation and resistance in Latin American immigrant lives in Canada. *Canadian Ethnic Studies* 45 (1): 1–21.

Tuck, E. (2010). Breaking up with deleuze: Desire and valuing the irreconcilable. International *Journal of Qualitative Studies in Education* 23 (5): 635–650.

Wehbi, S. (2017). The use of photography in anti-oppressive research. In H. Parada & S. Wehbi (Eds.), *Reimagining anti-oppression social work research* (pp. 39–46). Toronto, ON: Canadian Scholars' Press.

CHAPTER 6

Storytelling

A Critical Narrative Approach

Rose Ann Torres

1   Introduction

Adopting a narrative approach in research is about understanding the life of an individual, or as Creswell (2007) puts it, to "explore" the life of an individual. However, I argue that the narrative approach is more than exploring the life of an individual. What I want to focus on when I use the narrative approach is to understand and imagine the life of an individual. Understanding the life of an individual is about getting permission from that individual to allow me to understand their life. My interest and desire to understand the life of an individual should also be the interest and desire of the individual for me to understand their life. Narrative gives us the venue in knowing this story because the participant's role is to tell us a story. The question is, what part of a story does a participant needs to tell? Where does the story begin and end? When do we know that story is the right story to share? Who should make the call on when to end the storytelling? These are some critical questions.

The question of what story a participant needs to tell is a question of power. This is about power because it centers on who has the right to determine what story needs to be told. I would answer this question through my objective of writing this chapter. As I focus on narrative research methodology, one of the qualitative research methodologies I am coming from a decolonial transnational feminist perspective. A decolonial transnational feminist perspective is about centering the intersectionality of my experiences as a scholar who lived in the Philippines and now lives in Canada. These experiences from my communities, friends, schools, the borders, immigrations, and from my mother, father, brothers, and sister when I grew up with them in the mountain lives with me as I continue to live in Canada with my husband and my children. These memories that I have here and abroad are tools that I use simultaneously as I write storytelling as a critical narrative approach. I characterize this perspective from a decolonial transnational perspective because it is rooted in my own lived experience a being that was amalgamated through the process of colonization that continues to exist in my journey of belonging here and abroad. However, I am fully aware of this amalgamation and I continue to ask critical questions on how I live my everyday lives.

To answer the question of who has the right to determine what story needs to be told is all about the participant's wishes and desire to share whatever story. A researcher using a narrative approach recognizes the power and privilege that a researcher possesses, and also recognizes the power and privilege of the participant. As much as the researcher has the power to know a certain part of the story of the participant, the participant also has the power to tell the part(s) of the story he or she wants to share. This part of the narrative approach is about balancing the power of both the participant and the researcher. The question of how to balance the power will only happen when the researcher and the participant are willing to have a dialogue about this issue. This requires openness, honesty, and humility between the researcher and the participant. A dialogue is meaningless when the dialogue between the researcher and the participant is not honest, open, and humble. It does not carry any meaningful intentions, beliefs, and values. This results to unequal power.

The next section of my chapter is a discussion of what constitutes a narrative approach as one of the qualitative research methodologies. This section explains why there is need to discuss storytelling as a critical narrative approach.

2   Narrative Approach: A Research Methodology

The narrative approach "... begins with experiences as expressed in lived and told stories of individuals ... a specific type of qualitative design in which narrative is understood as a spoken or written text giving an account of an event/ action or series chronologically connected" (Padgett 2017). The question of which experiences are to be considered researchable is based on contextual information. If this experience has the answer to the research question, then this experience becomes an important part of the study. However, we must be mindful that even if this experience has the answer to the research question, it all depends on if the owner of the experience is ready to tell the story.

There are different types of narrative approach. The first is biographical study, in which the researcher writes and records the experiences of another person's life (Creswell, 2007). The second is autoethnography, which is written and recorded by the individual(s) who are the subject of the study (Friedman, 2017). And the last one is oral history, which is about gathering personal reflections of events and their causes and effects from one individual or several individuals (Creswell, 2007). All these types of narrative approach are interested in hearing the stories of the participants. "The unit of analysis of narrative approach is about studying one or more individuals and data collection is achieved primarily through interviews and documents (Creswell, 2007, pp. 78–79)". The narrative approach is interested in studying one or more individuals' lived experiences to best address the research problem of the study. Lived experience is where we can find the answer of what the research is looking for. It is where the everyday experiences of the participants are recorded and this is where we can see how the participants experience the society in which they live.

According to Clandinin and Connelly, there are different procedures for adopting a narrative approach (as cited in Creswell, 2007). This is important to include in this chapter so that we critically transform these procedures in a way that is more inclusive and relevant to both researcher and participants. The first procedure is "to determine if the research problem or question best fits narrative research" (Creswell, 2007, p. 55). The narrative approach is focused on collecting the specific lived experiences of a single or more individuals. Capturing the detailed stories of an individual or groups is a necessary part of the narrative approach because this is where the researcher can find out if the story answers the research question. The second procedure is to "select or more individuals who have stories or live experiences to tell, and spend considerable time with them gathering their stories through multiple types of information" (Creswell, 2007 p. 55). The key in narrative approach is the time to spend in understanding the story of an individual. If a researcher has limited time, then the narrative approach may not be the right approach, because there is no way you can understand the life of an individual without having ample time for listening to, reading, and understanding their stories. It is also important to have time to get to know the individuals because without knowing the participants, listening or reading their stories may not be enough to understand their lived experiences. This lived experience is a process, therefore understanding involves another process. The third procedure is to "collect an information about the context of these stories" (Creswell, 2007, p. 56). This is an important procedure of a narrative approach because without knowing the context of the story it is impossible for the researcher to thematize and analyze the story. The fourth procedure is to "analyze the participants' stories, and then 'restory' them into a framework that makes sense. Restorying is the process of reorganizing the stories into some general type of framework" (Creswell, 2007, p. 56). The last procedure is to "collaborate with participants by actively involving them in the research" (Creswell, 2007, p. 57). This collaboration means different ways of working with the participants as the researcher disseminates the results of the research project. This collaboration can be in the form of publications, workshops, and conferences. It can also be in the form of giving back in the communities where the participant lives. There are different ways of doing this, if there is an agreement between the researcher and the participant on how to work together on the project.

3   Storytelling

This section of the chapter looks at storytelling in the narrative approach. "Storytelling is a compelling strategy used by marginalized groups to understand a person's life. The value of narratives lies in giving the audience an opportunity to understand the experience of the storyteller (Bell, 2017, p. 1137). Storytelling provides an account of people' lived experiences as expressed through their emotions. Storytelling is a popular method used by Indigenous and racialized groups to retell their story of marginalization, inequalities, discrimination, and other issues that concern them. Storytelling is a powerful way of giving meaning to the experiences of people. It is also a powerful way to collect data because through this way you can hear the details of lived experience. This section of the chapter focuses on how storytelling becomes critical. I separate it in two parts: (a) as researchers, how can we use storytelling from a critical perspective; and (b) how can we as participants use storytelling in a critical way in giving our testimonies about our lived experiences. I chose to focus on how to use storytelling critically from both the participant's and the researcher's perspective so that this chapter can be used by either the researcher or the participant.

3.1   *Storytelling as a Critical Narrative Approach: Researcher Perspective*
As researchers, our main objective is to gather data that can possibly address our research questions. Storytelling is one of the ways of collecting data through interviews; we listen to the stories of the individual or a group of individuals. The focus of this section is: as researchers, how can we make sure that storytelling as a narrative approach is critical? We must agree that our role as researchers is to listen to the individual who will give the story. In the previous section, I described the process of narrative approach. In these approaches I do not have any problem. My focus is on how we make sure that storytelling is critical. First, as a researcher "open time" is a key component to follow when we ask the participant to tell a story about their lived experiences. "Open time" means we cannot impose when to begin and when to end a story to be told. We have to understand that our position at this time is to listen. And when we put ourselves in a position to listen, time therefore must be open. We need to

understand that telling a story needs time, energy, memory, and passion. We have to be able to put ourselves in the place of the individual who tells the story. In telling a story, time is important because the process of remembering the stories that we want to tell can take time. These stories might have happened a long time ago or recently. To go back to this event in our lives means we need the time to do it. As we go back to the past and remember the experiences, this can create a sense of joy, sadness, or anger. To have this emotion means you need time to gather your thoughts as you simultaneously deal with the emotions that come along with the story you are sharing.

It also takes a lot of energy to tell a story. This energy is a feeling of strength that you need as you retell your story. This energy is a strong feeling that you need to have in order to express the emotions and give words to the experiences that you had in the past. Telling a story without energy is difficult because you cannot make sense of the event that you are sharing. The energy will help you give meanings to the event that you are sharing now.

The other part that we need to remember when somebody tells their story is that we need to have the memory to go back to the past events of our lives. This memory will help us to understand and make meanings of our experiences. This memory will help us remember the joy, struggles, and achievements that we had in our lives. Most of the time, as researchers, we use storytelling not because we want to know the beautiful experiences of the participants, but we want to know their struggles and sufferings. As researchers we have to be honest with ourselves and the participant that the focus of the story is about the challenges that a participant experiences; for example, a research problem may be to focus on understanding why a Filipina experiences racism in the Canadian society. This research problem tells us what we want to know or what we want to hear from the story of the participant. So, as we listen to the participant's story, we focus on how their story can be aligned to the issue of racism. Telling a story about racism needs time, energy, memory, and passion. The memory comes in to understand how a story can be considered racist. Memory is important to have so that we can pay attention to the different events in our lives. Storytelling is not all about sharing any story but rather is about sharing a story that is relevant to the research question; for this you need memory.

Passion to tell a story is necessary so that we can pay attention to every detail the story. Our experiences in life happen in every moment, whether planned or unplanned. To tell a story in a moment that you do not expect to happen can be very different. Like the example that I use, the research question is focused on racist experience. I believe none of us expect to experience racism, or we do not want to experience it at all, because it gives us pain and suffering. This pain can have a long- and short-term effect on our well-being, therefore you do not want it to happen. However, as researchers this is what we want to focus on. We have to remember that as the participants tell their unexpected racist experience of their lives, you need to have a passion to tell this kind of story so that you can give a detailed chronology of the experience in order to be part of the racist experience. Passion is a necessary component in telling a story so that the participants can make the researcher realize that the story is a racist experience.

I enumerated some of the things that a storyteller needs to have in order to tell a story so that a researcher can understand what it entails to tell a story. As researchers, we disremember how to tell a story when we are in the moment of wanting to know the details of the story. In this way we become selfish because we want to focus on addressing the research question and we forget the position of the participant who is doing the storytelling. As researchers, we become focused on our need to address the research question and forget how hard it is to tell a story. As researchers from a Euro-centric perspective, we focus on the steps of how to conduct the right research based on the procedure that an approach needs to follow, and in the process we disremember the participant's memory, passion, and energy while telling the story. As researchers, we focus on the ethics protocol and forget that the participant is a human being who needs compassion and care.

As researchers there is a need to remember that as we disremember the participants' time, energy, memory, and passion to tell their story we are not only re-creating another pain in the lives of the participants but also contributing to a deeper oppression in their lives. How do we contribute to the deeper oppression when we already include them in our research? I like to remember that research is a colonial project. It is a colonial project to know the lives of others so that we as researchers have something to publish. It is a colonial project because we want to explore the lives of others so that we have something to use as an evidence to prove that our hypothesis is correct. It is a colonial project because it is about collecting data that we call empowering but, in the process, we disempower the participant. This is important to know so that we can reflexively know our implication to the oppression of the individual we are using as our research participant. This is important to acknowledge so that we can implicate ourselves in every process that we do in our research. If research is a colonial project, we have to also acknowledge that the moment we use research in our academic exercise we are already colonial actors and actresses. The question is how do we address this colonial exercise? There is a need to see the position of a participant so that we can understand the participant's positionality. Although I argue that this can be problematic because there is no way we can understand fully the position of a participant when we are the researcher, I am including this part through my experience as a participant. In the next section of this chapter, I shift my positionality as a participant. This is a necessary process for me so that I can engage fully with what I am going to share with you.

3.2 Storytelling as a Critical Narrative Approach: Participant Perspectives

As participants we need to remember that we do have power in the research process. Power can only exist in the process when a participant acknowledges that power belongs to anyone who acknowledges it. When I talk about power, it is power that comes from our own being. This is a power that we have when either we decide to tell or not tell our story. I acknowledge that we have different forms of power. One of them is a juridical power that belongs to the state (Foucault, 1980). When this power is being exercised, some are given privileges, and some are being oppressed. This kind of power chooses to exalt a particular race, gender, class, sexuality, and other forms of differences. And when this kind of individual rules, other races, genders, and sexualities are meant to be ruled out and controlled. The racialized individuals who belong to these categories can be called an undesirable population. As a participant you may belong to this undesirable population; I want to acknowledge the power that you have. It may not be a juridical power, but there is power to tell a story because this story is a story that only you can tell, and you own it. You own the decision to tell or not to tell your story. You can decide on different ways to tell this story. You can decide to begin from a different vantage point. You can decide to end whenever you feel like ending the story. And most of all you can decide to name your story in any way you want.

This for me is a power that a participant for a narrative approach has through storytelling—a power that a participant does not exercise when telling a story, especially when we tell a story of oppression. This does not mean that the participant does not know about it, but sometimes the researcher controls the whole session of telling the story, therefore the participant has no choice but to follow the structure that has been presented. This structured way of conducting research implicates the researcher as to why the participant feels disempowered when telling a story. It also implicates participants of feeling disempowered because of forgetting that whatever position we are in, we can always derive our power from within. As much as I say this, I acknowledge that this is not about blaming one another but rather about looking from the individual, to the institution, and the system for the ways in which each of these contributes to the disempowerment of the participant.

The other thing that a participant should remember is that to tell a story is a privilege. I understand that privilege comes from a dominant race, gender, and class, but I do not want to undermine the privilege that we have as we tell the story. I conducted a research study among an Indigenous community in the Philippines, and as a researcher I felt privileged to listen to the stories they told me. It is a privilege to tell stories because you can direct how the listener thinks about the idea you are sharing. It is a privilege because you can control the stories you want to share. It is a privilege because you are answering a research question and no one else have the same answer as yours. It is a privilege because you have the power to categorize the stories you are telling. As a participant, storytelling becomes critical when you allow yourself to flow with power and privileges regardless of race, class, and gender. This different form of social construct becomes a powerful tool to tell a story that can change the perception of what it takes to have a race, gender, and class like yours.

4 Conclusion

In this chapter I discussed the narrative approach as one of the research methodologies. I explored different procedures in conducting narrative approach. I also explained what constitutes a narrative approach and how storytelling becomes a key feature of the narrative approach. I also explained that I do not have any question in terms of the procedure on how to conduct a narrative approach.

This chapter focused on how storytelling becomes a critical narrative approach. I discussed a researcher's ways of understanding storytelling as a critical feature of narrative approach. I also explained a participant's ways of looking at storytelling from a critical point of view. I explained ways in which a participant can embrace power and privilege in storytelling.

References

Bell, E. E. (2017). A narrative inquiry: A Black male looking to teach. *The Qualitative Report* 22 (4): 1137–1150. https://nsuworks.nova.edu/tqr/vol22/iss4/12/.

Creswell, J. (2007). *Qualitative inquiry and research design: Choosing among five approaches*. Thousand Oaks, CA: Sage.

Foucault, M. (1980). *Power/knowledge: Selected interviews and other writings, 1972–1977*. New York: Pantheon.

Friedman, M. (2017). Unpacking liminal identity: Lessons learned from a life on the margins. In H. Parada & S. Wehbi (Eds.), *Reimagining anti-oppression social work research* (pp. 99–112). Toronto, ON: Canadian Scholars' Press.

Padgett, D. K. (2017). *Qualitative methods in social work research* (3rd ed). Thousand Oaks, CA: Sage.

Smith, L. T. (1998). *Decolonizing methodologies: Research and indigenous peoples* (2nd ed.). London: Zed Books.

CHAPTER 7

Research as an Inconsolable Mourning
Reimagining Pedestrian Research

Rose Ann Torres and Dionisio Nyaga

> Publics are historically conditioned and socially concrete "things";
> that is, they emerge or are dissolved in specific locations, they are
> shaped by the technologies and material culture to which they are
> subject, and they also serve the production of knowledge.
> (EMDEN & MIDGLEY, 2013, p. 3)

∴

We are writing this chapter at a time when police brutality and the apprehension of Black men in America continues to be normalized. Black men must wrestle with the decision of whether to mask themselves (Fanon, 1968) from racial profiling (Tanovich, 2006; Tator & Henry, 2006) or from the COVID-19 pandemic (Mukherjee, 2020), as both situations take away their breath. Research on Black communities shows a population struggling with different terminal diseases like cancer, diabetes, and the human immunodeficiency virus, among others. Pandemics like COVID-19 continue to wreak havoc in Black neighborhoods by compounding existing historical injustices in the Black community (Hutchinson, 2020).

A 46-year-old Black man named George Floyd was killed by four Minneapolis, Minnesota police officers because he had given a shop attendant a fake $20 bill. This is not the only time a Black man has died in the hands of police officers, which in many instances involved a plea to be allowed to breathe (Aymer, 2016). Several police officers pinned Floyd on the ground, while police officer Derek Chauvin pressed his knee on Floyd's neck in what seemed like standard practice. No amount of pleading from Floyd to be allowed to breathe made Chauvin loosen the pressure on Floyd's neck. Several bystanders videotaped the incident, which was later uploaded and went viral. This chapter seeks to engage with videography as a research method and critical Black video reflexivity as a methodology of mourning Black deaths and making Black lives matter.

1   Grievability of Blackness

The history of slavery of Black people provides a stark picture of how labor can be appropriated for capital accumulation. Black and marginalized bodies historically have been placed on the edges or the shadows of the world, waiting to be exploited, discarded, and forgotten. This speaks of the fact that Black citizens cannot be imagined within the current rational economic world order as humans instead of modes of production that can be used and discarded at will (Akuno, 2015). Blacks cannot own but rather continue to be imagined as property. This and the next argument help explain why Floyd, who was driving a Mercedes Benz and accused of providing a fake $20 bill was really a Black aberration that had to be corrected through his death. This has research meanings and consequences, as will be discussed later in the chapter.

The death of George Floyd and other previous incidences of institutionalized Black deaths speaks of the unliveable life of Black bodies in the hands of violent police. A police officer squeezing the life out of a Black man speaks of colonial brutality that continues to demarcate Black bodies as being non-existent. The act of pressing a knee on the neck of Floyd and other Black men by police officers is an expression of colonial power imprinting itself on Black bodies, marking those that will be lost and those that will be allowed to continue to breathe. We argue that while this may seem like a unique case and that the police officers in question are just some so-called bad apples within the police sector, these police officers are an expression of a violent colonial system that continues to brutalize Black bodies and mark them as injurable, broken, and ungrievable (Butler, 2009).

We are living at a time when Black and other marginalized bodies have become disposable, deportable, injurable, and yet ungrievable (Butler, 2009, 2015; Nyaga, 2019). To speak of disposability of Black bodies is to say that such bodies are not human but rather constitute social excesses/refuse/waste that must be cast out of human community, thus imagining Black lives and bodies as "superfluous" populations. The term Black as "superfluous" is applied to mark Black bodies as living in the shadows of economic structures, where their labor is precarious and their bodies disposable (Bauman, 2004), deportable, and injurable (Aymer, 2016). Galabuzi (2001, 2006) remarks that the Canadian labor market is emblematic of racialized migrant labor as being disposable and marks racial bodies as not belonging in the body politic.

The fact that Black is not imaginable/intelligible speaks of the fact that Black is forgettable and non-existent. In fact, Black is not seen as a living being but rather a non-living item or property that can be owned and sold or discarded when it is not needed (McKittrick, 2006). This speaks of the way in

which Black is objectified and always seen as waste to be used up and discarded. This Black spatial methodology has fundamental consequences in
research, more so when Black bodies occupy the place of materiality and are
imagined as templates of knowledge production rather than intelligible bodies. Over time, research has been used as an economic map that determines
who is a citizen and who is and alien and deportable. This chapter argues that
research is implicated in the violent erasure and marking of Black bodies as
ungrievable and injurable. Research has turned Black bodies into templates
of knowledge production reminiscent of the plantation economy. Black bodies have been reduced into mining spaces where they are needed and used to
accumulate wealth and disposed of when it they become unproductive. Such
disposable Black bodies are never imagined as living, which makes it easy for
them to be injured, dispossessed of their lives, and disposed of at will. This is
an ethical question that this chapter attempts to address.

Though this chapter underscores Black life as grievable, it also focuses on
the role of bystanders who took the video of Floyd's death and the role the
video and social media played to document, transmit, and translate anti-Black
racism in ways that brought accountability, transparency, and translatability to
the street. The chapter therefore argues for street-based social justice research
if Black and Blackness is to be grieved and humanized. If there is anything
research learns from the act of anti-Blackness and subsequent anti-Black
demonstration, it is that social justice is beyond the comfort of science.

Documentation as a research tool allows verification, translation, clarification, and transmission of information. To engage with videography as a
research method/ology, this chapter is guided by what Jones and Raymond
(2012) identify as a fundamental question/trick of working with videos as a cultural tool and data, which is to "Ask where the data come from, who gathered
it, what their organizational and conceptual constraints are, and how all that
affected what the [data] I'm looking at displays" (p. 111). Documentation sub-
stantiates the accuracy and completeness of data or information in ways that
are transparent, translatable, and accountable; as such, videography should be
taken as a "cultural record and as data" (Jones & Raymond, 2012, p. 109). While
the video provided a vivid picture of the issue, it took a long time for the police
department to arrest the police officer, which indicates whose truth matters.
It is only after the video went viral that the slain Floyd could be grieved, and
justice could be served.

Technologies of documentation allow the multiplication of witnesses, which
we argue is a necessary ethical ground for social justice and inconsolability
of mourning Black deaths. The riots that followed Floyd's death help affirm
Black research as a necessary tool for mourning the death of Black bodies.

Street-based research enhances the transmission of data from the comfort of science to the discomfort of street demonstration in ways that allow Black bodies to be mourned—and humanized. This scenario should also inform the "how" of knowledge creation that may help change the ways society mis/treat Black bodies in public spaces. This chapter therefore reimagines Black bodies as grievable and intelligible in the research process.

2   Documentation and Videography

Sociologists have been slow to embrace video as an analytical resource. Yet in the same way that photographs can expand our understanding of a setting or a subject beyond what can be recorded by the written word, video can provide a compelling real-time rendering of social life. Indeed, video is already an invaluable "resource for the analysis of human conduct and interactions."

(JONES & RAYMOND, 2012, p. 112)

Video technology or videography is not new in research. It is a process through which videos are made and come to define how we see and engage with our environment (Jones & Raymond, 2012; Wong, 1998). Videography is divided into three categories: opportunistic, ongoing, and institutional (Jones & Raymond, 2012, p. 112). Opportunistic videos are those that are taken when a third party (not a researcher) comes across an incident; they are supposed to report an isolated incident (Jones & Raymond, 2012). Ongoing videos usually record incidents or encounters over a period of time, while institutional videos record surveillance incidents, most often stores, police cars, or in public spaces. All these videos are third party, which means that there is no researcher involved in their production.

This chapter argues that documentation of Black individuals' deaths should not only be an act of preservation and conservation (read archival methodology) of Black cultural information and data but rather a verbing (Walcott, 2003) and vibration of Black and Blackness grounds (McKittrick, 2006) in ways that unsettle the comfort of scientific research. According to Walcott (2003),

This project, then, performs one tiny aspect of black cultural studies. My text acknowledges the possibility of working with difference not as the substance that must be dissolved but as the very thing that needs to be engaged and acted out. It is the engagement that moves this work from naming (nouning), to thinking about the possibility of ushering in much more (verbing). Actors take on roles that are anterior to them. In taking on these roles they are supposed to enact the specific and particular requirements that are either documented by the playwright or commanded by the director. Actors perform the discourses of others as another. Blackness as a discourse, when called up, uttered, and performed, places the question of doing as central to what meanings might be derived from a set of actions. The temporality and spatiality of meaning as applied to blackness requires an acknowledgement of black cross-cultural resonances (creolization/hybridity). (p. 78)

Verbing Black and Blackness is an art or an act of speech that releases Blacks from histories of colonial incarceration brought about by colonial conservation or achieving of Black narratives in ways that devalue Black diversity in terms of gender, sexuality, nationalities, and citizenship. The argument centers on how Black is nouned in ways that silence its resiliency and diversity. This form of conservation generalizes Black histories, values, and ways of being in research, thus returning Black and Blackness to their violent borderlines. To open borderlines of research to diversity, McKittrick's (2006) work on *Demonic Grounds* helps look at Black monster researchers as an ethical necessity that diversify Black cartographies in all their alterity in ways that revise our gaze on Black bodies as research substance. According to Wong (1998),

Meanings of media begin to merge with the meanings of the enacted community, and our questions of audience become issues of acceptance, identification, and use, as well as of readership. Such questions of narrowcast media, nonetheless, raise important issues of audience that reverberate with other pieces in this issue. (p. 91)

Social engagement in production and dissemination of Black video narratives is an important research aspect that advances scientific White research from its colonial purity into demonic grounds that are open to difference.

3   Review of Literature on Videography

Numerous studies look at videography as a source of surveillance (Nilsson, 2008), community health (Wilson et al., 2015), racial inequality (Bowman, 2017; Jones & Raymond, 2012), teaching and learning (Montelongo & Eaton, 2019), and research and critical analysis (Rodriguez, 2017). Li et al. (2017) identified "videography analysis for three types of applications, including content-based video retrieval, video summarization (both visual and textual), and videography-based feature pooling" (p. 2261) as ways in which one can explore video analysis. We argue that video analysis can also be a space for engagement between the eyewitness and the broader social media community (Jones & Raymond, 2012; Wong, 1998). If research is to be reimagined and devolved from its elitist/scientific place of exultation, emotional sentiment of social media users must be reimagined and critically reflected (Jones & Raymond, 2012). The issue to this claim is what happens in the era of social media that is still writ by White narrative and heightened by media surveillance? We argue that critical Black reflexivity will uncouple hidden Whiteness within the social media analysis.

According to Bowman (2015), television continues to provide visual narratives of anti-Blackness. With the growth of social media, there is an exuberance of video production and distribution in ways that have challenged the place of television and allow images to be writ large. According to Habermas (1989), media has taken the role of squeezing the public space into the private space, such that families sit together to witness the pain of the other in the comfort of their homes. This has led to the death of the salon and coffee house, where people would engage more with public policy and politics. This has an important dimension in terms of how we visualize Black research, which has been archived in the shadows and the dark alleys of public space. How do we speak of Black and Blackness in coffee houses that are White and rational? How can public spaces speak the language of Blackness in ways that are conducive to its monstrosity? According to Emden and Midgley (2013),

> If the public sphere continues to carry weight as an explanatory model it needs to be seen, to borrow a phrase from James Tully, as representing a "strange multiplicity" of publics, of interests, of forms of political and social action as well as forms of representation. (p. 3)

This is a fundamental research dimension in terms of democratizing and verbing videos and application of social media in the spread of eyewitness "strange multiplicity" of research analyses.

This chapter argues that the issues of social justice and democratic conversation/analysis of data and cultural visuals should be visible, documentable, translatable, and ingratiated within the concept of social transformation. Videos and the power of social media have pushed documentation of racial disparity in ways that seem to archive (read nouning) and transmit (read verbing) a chronology of Black death, hence allowing accountability and transparency in terms of mourning Black deaths. Recording and subsequent transmission of videos depicting Black encounters with institutional violence allows Black bodies to be grieved. This allows stories of racial inequality to survive time and space in ways that keep Black bodies alert based on a documented racial past. This is an ethical prerogative for Black-based research in that it maintains histories as a necessary ghost that every researcher must engage with. Histories of Black deaths contaminate the very comfort of scientific research in ways that unmap rationality, systemics, and the order of science.

While all the aforementioned studies focus on videos and community development, this chapter seeks to imagine how videos can be applied as a research tool that not only opens multiple discussions of Black and Blackness but also provides a space to mourn Black deaths. This chapter therefore seeks to answer the question: How can videos work as a research tool that engages with Black deaths and grievability?

4   Historicity

For a long time, pictures and videos have played a great research role in documenting issues of race and racism (Jones & Raymond, 2012). As Bowman (2017) notes,

> Bystanders used cell phones to capture the choking of Eric Garner and the shooting of Walter Scott, among other incidents, across the country. Video of these incidents were critical in providing a visual record of confrontations with law enforcement and sparking debate over issues associated with policing and race relations. At the same time, video posted on social media and broadcast on national television has been instrumental in mobilizing efforts to fight for equal protection under the law, holding law enforcement officials accountable for their actions, and raising public awareness about injustice in America. (p. 1)

Video documentation sheds light on anti-Blackness in ways that are transparent, accountable, and prescient, and connects the present to the past. It is important to understand that Black and Blackness is not historically neat and rational but rather has multiple manifestations of racial erasure (Gilroy, 2012; Mercer, 1994; Nyaga, 2019; Walcott, 2003). There are myriads of issues that the Black race faces that are interconnected yet not the same. The problem with video as a documentation of Black history is the universal expression in ways that may be assumed to speak to one form of Blackness. Such an assumption renders Blackness as neat, hence collapsing the term by nouning Black and

Blackness, while it is very clear that Black is amorphous and myriad. The act of collapsing Black and Blackness is ethically problematic in that it freezes the movement (read resistances and resiliencies) of Blackness, to which scientific research is implicated. To collapse Black histories symbolically indicates a form of objectification (slaughtering) or maiming the Black subject into a commodity that can be sold in the market. This is a form of colonial return of the Black subject to the very history of Black as a commodity in the plantation economy. This is a form of reducing and simplifying Black to a commodity that can be sold to the highest bidder, which has been a fundamental role of research more so in a neoliberal society.

To say that research freezes Blackness speaks of the way in which Black and Blackness are demobilized (Walcott, 2003). This is also a form of objectification meant to keep for a longer period a particular historical truth of Black bodies as the true depiction of Blackness and subsequently evicting other Black histories as problematic, pathological, and emotive—hence necessitating the medicalization of the "new Black normal" through neoliberal research methodologies (Nyaga, 2019). This means that one form of historical narrative of Black and Blackness is true and that any other form is subject to interrogation. The material and symbolic consequences to this Black neatness is the pathologization of Black difference in ways that evict other Blacks from citizenship. This is a question of citizenship and subsequent erasure of Blackness for failure to lie within a standard narrative of Blackness. Such a "true story of Blackness" serves a White nation mythology of Blackness, allowing for easy rationalization of original sin that continues to define a White nation state. It simplifies Whiteness in ways that allow easy reparation and assumed reconciliation (read White accountability and transparency) of historical Black pain and suffering.

This chapter argues that such a form of neat Black history has over time been used to soothe the soul of a White nation because it absolves them from any implication to anti-Blackness, hence postponing Black grievability. Demonstration on anti-Blackness becomes a site of White bodies finding ways in which they can purify and forget their nasty and grisly past rather than engaging with that past in ways that do not erase it but rather find discomfort with that Black history. It becomes a site of self-absolution rather than coming to terms with the historical torture of Black bodies. This means that Whites will have to find ways to make peace with that past in ways that allow their allyship to be a process of inconsolable mourning. It allows the White nation not to face their ugly past against Black society.

This chapter argues that for video to sustain Black grievability, an ethical obligation of breaking away from White essentialist narratives that collapse, and freeze Blackness is of the essence. The role of any social researcher is to open multiple forms of narratives that must disrupt the universal story of the Black race. Such a universal story cannot mourn Black and Blackness without critically reflecting on its connection to colonialism and present-day neocolonial systems. Such an essentialist depiction of Blackness only serves as an antidote to White fragility and can never answer to the present maiming of Black men. I argue that for Black and Blackness to be mourned, then the video lens must turn to the multiplicity of Black histories. This will disturb White comfort in ways that will allow new conversations that never arrive but allow the nation to mourn inconsolably the death of Blackness.

This chapter identifies six methodological concepts that attempt to guide the "how" of doing research among Black men. These methodological concepts are:

1.   That Black and Blackness must be a praxis rather than a noun.
2.   That Black is alterable and fluid.
3.   That Black and Blackness is framed in histories of atrocities meted on Black bodies. These histories are complex and myriad and that any attempt to simplify them is colonial.
4.   That illegal operation of power and Black erasure is manifested in the local spaces.
5.   That Black cannot pass and is easily marked.
6.   That to speak of Black power means imagining other forms of struggles as connected to Black struggles.

These are not canonical procedures that are the whole truth of Black and Blackness but rather a guide to how we come to face Blackness.

5   Documentation and Mourning

At the same time, the formation of new social movements and the effects of digital communication technologies, which have combined to generate the widespread phenomenon of cyber protests, are increasingly shaping what is widely perceived as a transnational public space. These developments invite the question of whether there is indeed still a sense in which the public sphere can serve as a counterbalance to the state and whether it can provide an accurate description of the realities of political life.

(EMDEN & MIDGLEY, 2013, p. 4)

With the growth of technology, videotaping has taken a new dimension, in that people have the capacity to produce videos with a touch of button and in their own comfort/discomfort. A while ago, video work and documentation were a career for specific people (Jones & Raymond, 2012). With the new technology of videography, people can videotape an incident using their phone. The growth of social media platforms like Facebook and Twitter has accelerated the circularity of video incidents in ways that are frequent and quick. In fact, one can stream a live video taping what is happening in one area and transmit it instantaneously to other spaces. This form of transmission has led to the shrinking of the home by the public in ways that allow witnessing an incident from a distance while seated in the comfort of one's home. This is both materially, emblematically, and symbolically significant in terms of how we come to see research as social justice work. The home whose comfort has over the time been the comfort of the working class has turned into an active volcano that is spilling its magma into the street in ways that call for social and political justice for Black bodies.

Video research has also allowed for the documentation of Black deaths in ways that not only archive Black deaths but allow inconsolable mourning of the same. Key to the documentation of Blackness is the opening or verbing of Blackness in ways that disturb archival research methodology. To document without necessarily opening multiple conversations of Blackness is colonial and epistemologically imperial. As Walcott (2003) claims, Black cannot be preserved or conserved but rather should be verbed in ways that allow multiple conversations and ways of life to speak. It has been argued that technology has brought to the fore what could have been lost in colonial archival methodology under the tutelage of totalizing knowledge producers (Foucault,).

According to Gilroy (2012),

> As London's errant Metropolitan police have found to their recent embarrassment, those technological innovations have torn through the blanket of secrecy and facilitated the shocking discovery of unacceptable if not criminal behaviour all around. With its high tempo and ease of transmission, digitalia has helped to present routine acts of racist commentary and violence from new angles and in unprecedented ways distinguished by the irrefutable authority of video veracity. There are other consequences too. Anyone who has read through the comments posted underneath a YouTube clip or an article published on The Guardian's Comment Is Free Site can attest that anonymous Internet interaction necessitates a different understanding of tolerance than the variety that is anticipated when contributor identities are verified and trackable. Online, localised racial abuse has been compounded by multinational, white-supremacist crowd-sourcing and is freshly typified in a provocative repudiation of the

fashionable, conservative idea that race-thinking has been overcome and might now be consigned to the past. (p. 381)

Previously, Black deaths were recorded and archived in ways that did not allow Black bodies to be mourned. With technology, Black families have grown exponentially and brought together in ways never seen before, such that the death of a Black man in one territory can be witnessed and grieved in another far away. This has made Black grief and mourning break colonial national borders of grievability in ways that are transformative and political. An online story can be documented and still elicit emotional and political calls for justice for Black deaths.

This chapter also argues that technology has opened traditional spaces that documented Black deaths and made them accessible to the public in ways that are genealogical and political. This complicated retrieval of police brutality on Black bodies allows for a continuous, consistent, and unverifiable grieving of the lost Black souls. This has an ethical obligation of grieving Black deaths in ways that are ceaseless and inconsolable. This allows marginalized Black communities to mourn their lost loved ones in ways that have no closure. This non-closure allows for the opening of past and present Black traumas, which we argue are a necessary antidote for Black social justice. The chapter argues that Black communities need to find a way to negotiate Black trauma in ways that are beyond progressive diversity and connect to other struggles both within and without Blackness.

6   Representation

While we celebrate the very opening of borders in terms of Black grievability, we also need to identify ways in which media technology can be a site of ethical and critical questioning and reflexivity. The question of video research as a form of mis/representation of Black and Blackness is an issue that needs to be addressed to reimagine how data can be a source of social justice and how it can also be used as a tool of racial erasure. As discussed earlier, the video research method has been an important tool that has allowed Blackness to be grieved through maintenance and documentation of data online. It is now clear that while video captures racial incidents, media has allowed continuous flow of data into the public space in ways that have allowed instant analysis and operation of data to arouse social justice movements.

This chapter argues that through videography and social media, information can reach a wide population in ways that allow differentiated analysis of the messages and allow instantaneous justice. This is a key ethical element of opening research to the public space for deeper interrogation leading to social transformation. We argue that videography as a method of data collection and subsequent messaging through social media has changed the social milieu of research in ways that are like a Habermasean coffee house. People can receive the data in the comfort of their house and make "informed" analyses of the data in ways that are transformative and political. While we argue that the home has been invaded by the public through social media and normalized, individualized social movement, we equally argue that it has allowed the organization of such movement. The videos showing police brutality meted on George Floyd provided an online conversation that built up a social movement that went to the street to call for social justice.

This chapter argues that people can now engage with information on social media in multiple ways that can allow social transformation. Days after the death of George Floyd, a group calling for a Black Tuesday requested everyone who supported Black and Blackness to put a Black box in their profile. This was assumed to cause people to pause and reflect on what Black community is facing under the current neoliberal era. A few hours later, there was a call for people to not put a Black square that glorifies one Black representative movement. This was clear a moment of social engagement on Black representation that allowed a critical reflection on Black and Blackness. This chapter argues that such a critically Black reflexive moment is a necessary pointer of reimagining Black and Blackness. For a while, Black bodies have been represented objectified and represented as one entity. This representation has worked to serve White mythology and help sustain the status quo that has consistently served some Black representatives at the behest of the marginalized others. It is now becoming clear that Black and Blackness have been turned into a product for sale in the market. On this claim, everyone including Black representatives are implicated.

7   Critical Black Reflexivity as a Methodology

This chapter argues that for Black justice to prevail, Black critical reflexivity, which is a fundamental research approach/methodology, is a necessary step to social justice. Critical Black reflexivity calls out the self while imagining institutions as sites of anti-Blackness. For a while, issues of Blackness have been looked at as only emanating from colonial structures in ways that absolve any implication of the self. Critical Black reflexivity imagines the self as the political vehicle of the structures and as such implicates everyone. Critical Black

reflexivity is a process of engaging with the self in ways that allow one to identify ways in which they have participated in the erasure of themselves. It is a
process of identifying self-hate perpetrated by colonial systems of oppression,
whereas a Black subject I become a vehicle of eliminating other Black subjects. Critical Black reflexivity allows a Black subject to be vulnerable in ways
that allow reimagination of anti-Blackness allowing for "true" transformation.
Vulnerability is a form of mourning the death of I and the resurrection of me in
ways that can help acknowledge the pain of the other while understanding the
self. In a nutshell, videography and social media allow mourning to be inconsolable in ways that make Blackness to be reimagined beyond a colonial, color-
coated form of social justice. Critical Black reflexivity humbles the self in ways
that help imagine ourselves in the face of the other. Critical Black reflexivity is
an ethical question that helps us understand that while we may be Black, we
are beyond Black based on diversity of histories, values, genders, sexualities,
and cultures, and that no one group of Blackness has the ultimate role of Black
representation

8   Towards Allyship

To argue that critical Black reflexivity is a methodology is to also engage
with the question of whether Black is a closed circuit or an open system.
This chapter argues that while we mourn Blackness, we also need to imagine
ways in which other racialized bodies become templates of social erasure.
We need to imagine how our struggles are connected to other struggles faced
by Indigenous peoples, women, LGBTQ2S+, Asian communities, and other
marginalized groups. Critical Black reflexivity calls for imagining Black and
Blackness beyond colonial measures and markings that deny social solidarity
and connection beyond universalized histories. Marginalized groups continue
to face global erasure in ways that are virulent and yet much like Black racial
experiences. Colonial tools of marking what is Black and what is not can help
fuel sentiment of one struggle being more or less important than the other.
Fellows and Razack (1998) identified ways in which this can lead to toehold on
respectability which is parochial and provincialization of pain which is epistemologically imperial. The ways to bring forth allyship is to imagine the self
in the face of the other. This means losing what we know as formal knowing of
the other (read quantitative research of understanding the other) which helps
unmark social hierarchies of needs and respectability. This means falling prey
to the other in ways that come to reimagine the self as answerable to the other
even before we can think of our obligation to them.

9   Conclusion

This chapter has engaged with videos as a research method and critical Black reflexivity as a methodology of engaging with video research. It is now clear that video and social media have pushed the edges of television in ways that bring out all sides of racial inequality. We can now witness first-hand issues of racial bias and engage and analyze the video in the social media with friends and relatives in quick succession. Technology has spread people's pain and victories in ways that have affirmed and informed Black lives and grievability. While this is true, I am pained to imagine what social justice would look like when social media remains in the hands of a White system. How can Black bodies grieve their loss through a White social media to reimagine Black and Blackness? We also need to engage with the eyewitnesses and the role they play in marking spaces of brutality and the trauma that follows. According to Jones and Raymond (2012),

> The acquisition and analysis of third-party video also raises important ethical concerns regarding informed consent, confidentiality, and anonymity, which leads to a final question that we consider briefly: ... How can social scientists best manage privacy concerns at a time when older notions of personal privacy are quickly eroding? (p. 111)

This is an ethical imperative that future studies need to engage with. There is also a need to begin a discussion on the ethical place of circularity of Black deaths and what that means in terms of social justice. Do we necessarily need videos and pictures of another dead Black man for action and justice to be seen to take place? This ethical question can only be imagined within a framework that is critical, Black, and reflexive, built around inconsolability of mourning Black loss.

References

Akuno, K. (2015, September 4). Until we win: Black labor and liberation in the disposable era. *CounterPunch*. https://www.counterpunch.org/2015/09/04/until-we-win-black-labor-and-liberation-in-the-disposable-era/.

Aymer, S. R. (2016). "I can't breathe": A case study—Helping Black men cope with race-related trauma stemming from police killing and brutality. *Journal of Human Behavior in the Social Environment* 26 (3/4): 367–376. https://doi.org/10.1080/10911359.2015.1132828.

Bauman, Z. (2004). *Wasted lives: Modernity and its outcasts*. Cambridge, UK: Polity Press.

Bowman, M. (2017). TV, cell phones and social justice: A historical analysis of how video creates social change. *Race, Gender & Class* 24 (1/2): 16–26.

Bowman, R. (2015). REVIEW | It's been beautiful: Soul! and black power television. *Iaspm@journal, 5*(2), 82–84. doi:10.5429/2079-3871(2015)v5i2.9en

Butler, J. (2009). *Frames of war: When is life grievable?* New York: Verso.

Butler, J. (2015). *Bodies that matter: On the discursive limits of "sex."* Milton Park, Abingdon, UK: Routledge.

Emden, C. J., & Midgley, D. (Eds.). (2013). *Beyond Habermas: Democracy, knowledge, and the public sphere*. Oxford, NY: Berghahn Books.

Fanon, F. (1968). *Black skin, white masks*. New York: Grove Press.

Fellows, M. L., & Razack, S. (1998). The race to innocence: Confronting hierarchical relations among women. *Journal of Gender, Race & Justice* 1: 335–352.

Foucault, M. (1980). *Power/knowledge: Selected interviews and other writings, 1972–1977*. New York: Pantheon.

Galabuzi, G. (2001, May). *Canada's creeping economic apartheid: The economic segregation and social marginalisation of racialised groups*. Toronto, ON: CSJ Foundation. http://www.socialjustice.org/pdfs/economicapartheid.pdf.

Galabuzi, G. (2006). *Canada's economic apartheid: The social exclusion of racialized groups in the new century*. Toronto, ON: Canadian Scholars' Press.

Gilroy, P. (2012). "My Britain is fuck all": Zombie multiculturalism and the race politics of citizenship. *Identities* 19 (4): 380–397. https://doi.org/10.1080/1070289X.2012.725512.

Habermas, J. (1989). *The structural transformation of the public sphere* (T. Burgen & F. Lawrence, Trans.). Cambridge, UK: Polity Press. (Originally work published 1962).

Hutchinson, E. O. (2020, April 2). Don't leave African Americans out in COVID testing. *The Bay State Banner*. https://www.baystatebanner.com/2020/04/02/dont-leave-african-americans-out-in-covid-testing/.

Jones, N., & Raymond, G. (2012). "The camera rolls": Using third-party video in field research. *The ANNALS of the American Academy of Political and Social Science* 642 (1): 109–123. https://doi.org/10.1177%2F0002716212438205.

Li, K., Li, S., Oh, S., & Fu, Y. (2017). Videography-based unconstrained video analysis. *IEEE Transactions on Image Processing* 26 (5): 2261–2273. https://doi.org/10.1109/TIP.2017.2678800.

McKittrick, K. (2006). *Demonic grounds: Black women and the cartographies of struggle*. Minneapolis, MN: University of Minnesota Press.

Mercer, K. (1994). *Welcome to the jungle: New positions in Black cultural studies*. Milton Park, Abingdon, UK: Routledge.

Montelongo, R., & Eaton, P. W. (2019). Online learning for social justice and inclusion: The role of technological tools in graduate student learning. *International*

Journal of Information and Learning Technology 37 (1/2): 33–45. https://doi.org/
10.1108/IJILT-11-2018-0135.

Mukherjee, D. (2020). Experiencing community in a Covid surge. *The Hastings Center
Report* 50 (3): 10–11. https://doi.org/10.1002/hast.1109.

Nilsson, F. (2008). *Intelligent network video: Understanding modern video surveillance
systems.* Boca Raton, FL: CRC Press.

Nyaga, D. (2019). *Re-imagining Black masculinity: Praxis of Kenyan men in Toronto*
(Doctoral dissertation, University of Toronto). TSpace. https://tspace.library.uto-
ronto.ca/handle/1807/97580.

Rodriguez, A. B. (2017). Teaching guerilla praxis: Making critical digital humanities
research politically relevant. *Transformations* 27 (2): 212–216. https://doi.org/
10.1353/tnf.2017.0019.

Tanovich, D. M. (2006). *The colour of justice: Policing race in Canada.* Toronto, ON:
Irwin Law.

Tator, C., & Henry, F. (2006). *Racial profiling in Canada: Challenging the myth of "a few
bad apples".* Toronto, ON: University of Toronto Press.

Walcott, R. (2003). *Black like who?: Writing Black Canada* (2nd rev. ed.). London, ON:
Insomniac Press.

Wilson, S. M., Murray, R. T., Jiang, C., Dalemarre, L., Burwell-Naney, K., & Fraser-Rahim,
H. (2015). Environmental justice radar: A tool for community-based mapping to
increase environmental awareness and participatory decision making. *Progress in
Community Health Partnerships: Research, Education, and Action* 9 (3): 439–446.
https://doi.org/10.1353/cpr.2015.0066.

Wong, C. H. (1998). Understanding grassroots audiences: Imagination, reception, and
use in community videography. *The Velvet Light Trap* 42: 91–102.

PART 3

Application of Critical Research Methodologies

∴

CHAPTER 8

A Black Woman's Perspective on Leadership and Risk-Taking

Exploring Research Methodologies That Can Transcend the Discourse of Mainstream Leadership Thought

Elizabeth Charles

1 Introduction

Mainstream leadership theories that get positioned as universally applicable to all leaders but are informed primarily by quantitative research methods, tend to center and reify the hegemonic ideas of elite White men. The narrative of objectivity and rationality inherent in these scientific research methods, draws attention away from how a, "… body of specialized knowledge reveals its affinity to the power of the group that created it." (Mannheim, 1936 as featured in Collins, 2009, p. 269). Since spaces of Western leadership researching and theorizing have not been occupied by Black women, our leadership practices have become distorted or largely excluded. When analyzing the experiences of Black women leaders, we can see how these mainstream leadership theories tend to ignore the ontological and epistemological struggles that can inform the strategies of marginalized Black women who have gone on to lead success-fully. What research methodologies can help us understand the ways in which Black women come to be effective in leadership? How can we engage with these methodological paradigms to understand the experiences, knowledges and practices of marginalized Black women who have led successfully? When studies about leadership engage with principles associated with critical inter-sectional epistemology, critical ethnography and personal narrative instead of just with scientific methodologies that tend to centre the positionalities of White patriarchal elitism, they can unveil strategies of successful leadership practices conceptualized by Black women as a result of their ontological and epistemological struggles at the intersection of their race, gender and class status.

2   Method

In this chapter, I will use theories informed by Black Feminist Thought along with principles found in critical intersectional epistemology, critical ethnography and personal narrative to demonstrate how when theories about effective leadership practices evolve primarily from data generated from scientific research methods, they tend to privilege the hegemonic positionalities of White patriarchal elitism and ignore the experiences, knowledges and standpoints of marginalized Black women who have gone on to lead successfully. Analyzing the article, *"If You Want Your People To Be Less Afraid Of Taking Risks, Try Reducing The Cost of Failure"* published in Forbes.com, I will demonstrate how the author's primary reliance on scientific research data to inform his theory about effective leadership and risk-taking, centres and reifies the positionalities and epistemologies of dominant elite White men and ignore those of marginalized Black women. Highlighting the methods of critical intersectional epistemology, critical ethnography and personal narrative, I will demonstrate how when researchers centre the experiences and knowledges of Black women, they can produce studies that uncover different strategies of effective leadership practices informed by a Black woman's standpoint. Sharing my personal experiences with leadership and risk-taking, I will demonstrate how centering the experiences, epistemologies and standpoint of a Black woman can generate theories of leadership that do not generally get conceptualized by a White man's interpretation of the world. While I am acutely aware that relying solely on my experiences in this manner is an approach associated with auto-ethnography and not the type of research methodology one would engage with when trying to capture the experiences of a larger participant group, I use my personal narrative in this chapter to showcase how when you use methods that centre marginalized experiences, epistemologies and standpoints, researchers can unveil practices that tend not to get acknowledged by mainstream leadership theorizing. Engaging with my personal experience in this manner to showcase my knowledge formation, I follow the tradition of other subjugated voices; in particular Black women, who because of our exclusion from White-male controlled spaces of knowledge construction, had to use, "... alternative ways of producing and validating knowledge." (Collins, 2009, p. 270). Doing so, I hope to demonstrate how research about leadership can get to the multiplicity of successful strategies in order to transcend those dominant hegemonic elite White patriarchal discourses that all too often get positioned prominently in mainstream leadership thought.

3   Centering and Reifying Dominant White Male Elitism and Ignoring
         the Experiences and Epistemologies of Black Women: Using
         Science to Theorize about Leadership

In his article, *If You Want Your People To Be Less Afraid Of Taking Risks, Try Reducing The Cost of Failure,* entrepreneur, bestselling author, leadership trainer and Forbes contributor, Mark Murphy engages with data generated from two quantitative online surveys to theorize about how when leaders reduce the cost of failure they can increase risk-taking among employees and contribute to organizational success (Murphy, 2019). One of the studies featured in his article entitled, *"How Do You Personally Feel About Change?"* (Murphy, 2019, para. 6), invites respondents to answer a series of questions. One of these questions asks participants to choose from the following options: "I like taking risks. I would take a risk if it seemed prudent. I avoid risks." (Murphy, 2019, para. 6). According to Murphy, even though 28% of the 10,000 respondents said, "... that they like taking risks, ..." (Murphy, 2019, para. 7), he acknowledges that "... there is a lot of variation depending on the level one occupies in the organizational hierarchy." (Murphy, 2019, para. 7). Analyzing this finding, Murphy highlights that 40% of top executives answered that they like taking risks compared to only 24% of frontline employees who responded feeling the same way (Murphy, 2019, para. 7). The other online survey used in Murphy's article, poses the question, *"What Motivates You"* (Murphy, 2019, para. 9). Out of the 20,000 participants of that study, 26% said they were motivated by security while 16% stated that they were motivated by adventure (Murphy, 2019, para. 9). After presenting these findings, Murphy shares his interpretation of the data that reflects the positionalities, experiences, and knowledges of dominant and privileged elite White men.

According to Murphy, the reason why executives are less risk averse compared to frontline staff is that the cost of failure for these most senior leaders is considerably lower than for the latter group (Murphy, 2019, para. 8). He attributes this difference in cost of failure to a CEO's lower probability of being terminated if they take risks that fail along with their more generous, hence more comfortable, severance packages (Murphy, 2019, para. 8) should they lose their jobs for taking risks that do not produce favourable results. Murphy further reasons that people who seek more security are more inclined to stay with the same company, possess a higher aversion to risk-taking and as such have a lower probability of leading organizations successfully compared to those who have a lower aversion to risk-taking (Murphy, 2019). Despite acknowledging the role that class status has on one's ability to take risks and by extension to lead successfully, absent in his theorizing about effective leadership, are the roles that power and privilege as determined by the intersection of race, gender and class status have on one's ability to reduce the costs associated with failure and hence on one's appetite for risk-taking. Stated differently, Murphy's theorizing fails to account for how interlocking systems of oppression can work together to prevent marginalized bodies from possessing the same power and privilege as dominant bodies to be able to reduce the costs associated with their failure and thus the same aversion to risk-taking.

Central to the discourse of Black Feminist Thought is the concept of inter-sectionality that took shape to explain why Black women did not feel a connection with White women in the women's movement and with Black men in the Black liberation movement. It also explained why Black women felt compelled to create a separate and distinct space of their own from which to theorize about their oppressive existence at the intersection of race, gender and class status. Elaborating on this sentiment, hooks (2015) writes,

> No one bothered to discuss the way in which sexism operates both inde-pendently of and simultaneously with racism to oppress us. No other group in America has so had their identity socialized out of existence as have black women. We are rarely recognized as a group separate and distinct from black men, or as a present part of the larger group "women" in this culture. When black people are talked about, sexism militates against the acknowledgment of the interests of black women; when women are talked about racism militates against a recognition of black female interests. When black people are talked about the focus tends to be on black *men*; and when women are talked about the focus tends to be on white *women*. (p. 7).

Recognizing how systems of oppression (e.g. racism, sexism and classism) can overlap to create multiple levels of oppression, the concept of intersectionality allows for,

> ... the examination of race, sex, class, national origin, and sexual orienta-tion and how their combination plays out in various settings. These cat-egories – and still others – can be separate disadvantaging factors. What happens when an individual occupies more than one of these categories, for example, is both gay and Native American or both female and black? Individuals like these operate at an intersection of recognized sites of oppression.
>
> (DELGADO & STEFANCIC, 2017, p. 58)

Who are the bodies conceptualized by Murphy, that hold the power and privilege as determined by the intersection of race, gender and class status who are more likely to experience lower costs associated with their failure and as such possess a lesser aversion to risk-taking? Whose reality is more likely reflected in Murphy's presentation and conceptualization of the scientific research data? How do the existing power imbalances as determined by the intersection of race, gender and class status factor into those survey results, one's ability to reduce the costs associated with failure and one's propensity for risk-taking? Are the costs of failure higher for some bodies compared to others on the basis of the intersection of their race, gender and class status? Do the theories conceptualized in Murphy's article reflect the experiences and knowledges of marginalized Black women who have led successfully by navigating their intersecting oppressions with racism, sexism and classism and negotiating their ability to take risks and to reduce the costs of failure? Failing to account for and to interrogate the power imbalances that tend to favour White patriarchal elites, Murphy's proclamations neglect to call out the bodies for whom his theory holds true. When we explore who generally tends to occupy the most senior leadership positions of power and privilege within organizations, we can begin to see how his interpretation of the survey results is biased in favour of the experiences and worldview of dominant White male leaders and against those of marginalized Black women. In doing so, Murphy also fails to account for the ways how Black women might navigate their oppressions at the intersection of racism, sexism and classism and negotiate risk-taking and the cost of failure to go on to lead successfully.

According to Johnson et al. (2016), White men comprise, "... roughly 85% of board members and executives ... [and] 95% of CEOs." (p. 50, word in brackets added). Black women also fall behind their White female counterparts when it comes to advancing to positions of power within organizations. According to Marshall & Wingfield (2016, despite findings that show Black women to be, "... nearly three times more likely than white women to aspire to a position of power with a prestigious title ... white women are about twice as likely as Black women to attain one." (p. 44). At the time of their study, these authors went on to report that, "[r]oughly twenty women helm a Fortune 500 company ... [and that after] the departure of Ursula Burns at Xerox, none of those women will be black." (Marshall & Wingfield, 2014, p. 44, words in brackets added). Since the publication of their study, Ursula Burns is no longer the head of Xerox.

The same dismal findings regarding the advancement of Black women to positons of power within organizations are reflected in Canadian studies that highlight the low representation of visible minorities in the most senior positions of leadership. According to Cukier (2012), "Though female visible minorities account for approximately 25.6% of the GTA population – which is comparable to the proportion of female non-visible minorities (25.8%), ... female visible minority leaders comprise only 2.6% of leaders across [private, public, not-for-profit] sectors compared to female non-visible minority leaders (22.5%)." (Executive Summary, para. 3, words in brackets added). The significantly lower representation of Black women in these most senior leadership positions reflect the reality that while, "[w]omen hit a glass ceiling, ... Black women hit a concrete one ... ." (Catalyst, 2017, para. 5, brackets added). Research has shown that, "Black women deal with some of the workplace's most entrenched hurdles and daunting roadblocks, not least other people's beliefs, attitudes, and experiences – resulting in undue burdens and feelings of constantly being "on-guard"." (Catalyst, 2017, para. 4). When referring to the emotional tax that Black women endure because of their workplace experiences, other studies cite how Black women are left, "... psychologically burdened, feeling like they have to outwork and outperform to compensate for potential discrimination or bias and [to] be seen as equals." (Catalyst, 2017, para 6, word in brackets added).

Black women are not only significantly unrepresented in the most senior positions of power because of the institutional systemic barriers to their advancement, but they do not tend to command the lucrative compensation that Murphy proclaims can reduce a leader's aversion to taking risks. When it comes to earnings, studies have shown that despite their gains in educational achievements in recent decades, "... Black women working full-time earn $0.63 for every dollar earned by white men ..." (Catalyst, 2017, para. 2, brackets added). Given that White men as compared to Black women, tend to overwhelmingly occupy positions of power; positions from which one can realize the privilege capable of reducing the costs of failure as theorized by Murphy, and that these bodies have very different workplace experiences, Murphy's primary reliance on scientific data to prove his theory tends to center the positionalities and standpoints of dominant White men and reify the epistemologies of White patriarchal elites while ignoring those of Black women. According to Hunter (2002), "... racism and power are not outside of the research process at all, and that in fact, they affect nearly every aspect of how researchers conduct their research from the choice of research questions to the interpretation of their data." (p. 119). The way how Murphy takes up the quantitative data to arrive at his theory manifests the epistemology of neo-liberal positivism, as he "... [uses] science to create a reality ..." (Hunter, 2002, p. 129, word in brackets added) that tends to reflect and reify the experiences and knowledges of White male elites of which he is a member. Hunter (2002) writes that, "[p]ositivism is a theory of knowledge that presupposes one absolute truth that is knowable by anyone using the scientific method of inquiry." (p. 128). Hunter (2002) argues that,

> ... [e]pistemologies do not exist outside of the people who construct and use them. Individuals and groups adopt various epistemologies at different points in time to make sense of the world. Epistemologies are also not equal in status, in society at large, ... [and that epistemologies] are situated within political, historical, and economic contexts that can provide power and legitimacy to their knowledge claims. (p. 120, words in brackets added).

Failing to call out his own positionality along with those of the survey participants and the leaders conceptualized in his analysis, Murphy's research falls remarkably short of, acknowledging the power, privilege and biases (Madison, 2005) that favour elite White men in his theorizing about what successful leaders do. Spalek (2005) argues,

> The fallacy of so-called value-neutral or objective research has been exposed and feminists have successfully claimed that the beliefs and behaviours of social scientists influence the perception and documentation of social experience. As a result, it is considered to be important to articulate the often hidden values and characteristics of the researcher and their impact on the research process so as to enable the research to be fully scrutinized.
>
> (EDWARDS & RIBBENS, 1998; HARDING, 1987, as cited in SPALEK, 2005, p. 408)

Through his engagement with scientific data to arrive at his leadership theory, Murphy continues the tradition of using and interpreting seemingly objective and neutral quantitative data to ignore the experiences of those with non-dominant status. Citing Ladner (1973) and other sociologists who, "... were critical of the canonization of sociological research done in the name of objectivity and value-neutrality that confirmed and perpetuated racist assumptions about African Americans ..."(p. 121), Hunter (2002) writes, "[m]ainstream sociology, in this regard, reflects the ideology of the larger society, which has always excluded Black lifestyles, values, behavior, attitudes, and so forth from the body of data that is used to define, describe, conceptualize, and theorize about the structure and functions of American society." (Ladner, 1973, p. xxiii, as cited in Hunter, 2002, p. 121). Relying predominantly on quantitative data to conclude that those most likely to leave an organization are the ones who

are more inclined to take large risks and thus more capable of bringing organizations to success, Murphy's theory intimates that Black women would be
less likely those leaders. According to a 2018 study published by Catalyst, 88%
of Black women surveyed reported that they wanted to remain employed
with the same organization (Catalyst, 2018, p. 10). Using quantitative data in
this manner, Murphy implies a positionality, power and privilege not usually
extended to Black women given their experiences with the matrix of domination and as such develops a leadership theory that can only be taken up by
those dominant bodies already in positions of power of which marginalized
Black women are not apart.

In light of the existing power imbalances that disadvantage Black women
compared to White men, can Black women recover from the costs associated
with their failure the same way how elite White men can? Can we assume that
the cost of failure is different, maybe even higher, for Black women compared
to elite White men? If the cost of failure as defined by a fall in confidence
in one's ability to lead, a negative reputation, the loss of one's job and low
probability to gain similar employment along with its intensity and duration
is determined by the intersection of institutional racism, sexism and classism,
are these costs not outside of a Black woman's ability to control? Stated differently, can Black women even reduce or eliminate the costs associated with
their failure as theorized by Murphy if those costs are perpetuated and sustained by a hegemonic matrix of domination that subjugates Black women?
Are the potential costs of failure, as outlined above, much greater for Black
women than for elite White men given that the former endures oppressions
at the intersection of racism, sexism and classism not endured by White men?
If one's ability to reduce costs associated with failure is dependent upon the
degree of power and privilege provided to them by systems of oppression (i.e.
racism, sexism and classism), then a Black woman's ability to reduce the costs
associated with her failure might extend well beyond her capacity to control.
Furthermore, given the systemic barriers that Black women face, the costs of
failure might be so high and well beyond their ability to reduce or to overcome
on their own, that they might be unable to implement Murphy's theory and
thus risk being seen according to his theory, as those leaders who are incapable of bringing organizations to success. To the extent that elite White men
are more likely the bodies for whom Murphy's theory is intended, his failure
to acknowledge the role that one's positionality at the intersection of race,
gender and class status plays in bringing his theory to fruition, results in the
reification of existing power imbalances that position dominant elite White
men as more naturally suited for bringing organizations to success and for
leadership.

Relying on quantitative methods primarily to prove his theory about effective leadership and risk-taking, Murphy uses science, "... in the service of dominant discourse." (p. 129) thus rendering invisible non-dominant leadership knowledges. According to West (2002) as stated by Hunter (2002), "... powerful discourses have the ability to "produce and prohibit, develop and delimit forms of rationality, scientificity, and objectivity which set perimeters and draw boundaries for the intelligibility, availability, and legitimacy of certain ideas." (West, 2002, p. 49 as cited in Hunter, 2002, p. 129). Researchers who engage with science almost exclusively to develop theories, can, "... make available certain ideas and ... make invisible others." (p. West, 2002, as cited in Hunter, 2002, p. 129). Instead of theorizing about how one should reduce the costs of failure in order to become successful leaders, Murphy's theory should focus instead on how to dismantle the institutional systemic barriers and existing power imbalances that prevent some leaders, such as Black women, from possessing the same privileges as elite White men to be able to reduce the costs associated with their failure and to be regarded by mainstream leadership thought as equally capable leaders as elite White men. To expand the narrative on leadership and risk-taking, maybe we should look at how, despite the costs associated with their failure, Black women have gone on to cultivate strategies that have resulted in their success as leaders. What are the standpoints and epistemologies of some Black women who have taken up risk-taking differently from dominant, privileged White men to go on to lead successfully in a manner not theorized by Murphy? How does a Black Woman's standpoint and experience with the matrix of domination factor into their definition of risk-taking and effective leadership? How do they choose to take up, engage with and be successful with these concepts? These are just some of the questions that do not get positioned prominently nor conceptualized using the data that Murphy relies upon to theorize about effective leadership and risk-taking. In light of the above, his interpretation of the data fails to adequately capture the experiences of marginalized Black women and how they might come to engage with and negotiate risk-taking in leadership roles. In doing so, Murphy's analysis falls short of identifying the multiplicity of effective leadership epistemologies, experiences and strategies of risk-taking and thus upholds the hegemonic discourse that normalizes and renders universal the positionalities and experiences of elite White patriarchy in his contribution to mainstream leadership thought.

Given their experiences with oppression at the intersection of racism, sexism and classism, Black women can develop a standpoint uniquely theirs that can produce knowledge about how to engage with risk-taking and cultivate strategies that can result in their success as leaders. Through her reflection on

Black feminist epistemologies, Collins (2009) supports this notion that within struggles can come different ways of knowing and doing, by stating that, "... the significance of a Black feminist epistemology may lie in its ability to enrich our understanding of how subordinate groups create knowledge that fosters both their empowerment and social justice." (p. 289). When researchers use methodologies that centre the distinct and varied experiences of non-dominant groups, they can develop a variety of leadership theories, add to the body of knowledge about leadership and come closer to the "objective" truths of effective leadership practices. According to Collins (2009), "... those ideas that are validated as true by African-American women, African-American men, Latina lesbians, Asian-American women, Puerto Rican men, and other groups with distinctive standpoints, with each group using the epistemological approaches growing from its unique standpoint, become the most "objective" truths." (p. 290). What are the methodological paradigms that can bring us to greater understanding about how Black women might engage with risk-taking and negotiate the cost of failure to go on to lead successfully? Using methodologies that centre their positionalities, we can reveal the standpoints and epistemologies that can evolve from their experiences with their social location at the axis of their race, gender and class status to learn how some Black women interact with the world. More specifically, the use of these methodologies in our theorizing about effective leadership practices can bring us to understand how these women can take up risk-taking and how they can go on to lead successfully.

4   Using Research Methodologies that Center a Black Woman's Standpoint to Expand the Scope of Strategies about Successful Leadership Practices

To understand how some Black women might practice leadership even in the spaces that are not designed for their success, we need to use methods that Collins (2009) argues,

> ... place Black women's subjectivity in the center of analysis and examine the interdependence of the everyday, taken-for-granted knowledge shared by African-American women as a group, the more specialized knowledge produced by Black women intellectuals, and the social conditions shaping both types of thought. This approach allows [one] to describe the creative tension linking how social conditions influenced a Black women's standpoint and how the power of the ideas themselves

gave many African-American women the strength to shape those same social conditions. (p. 288, word in brackets added).

To conduct research about how Black women might engage with risk-taking and negotiate the cost of failure to go on to lead successfully, we must engage with a variety of approaches to research not necessarily practiced by researchers who, "... control Western structures of knowledge validation, ..." (Collins, 2009, p. 269), but by those who seek to centre the experiences of marginalized and oppressed bodies to reveal how they engage with the world as Black women. (Collins, 2009, p. 269). Supporting this idea that researchers must centre the experiences of Black women in order to understand how they make sense of and come to interact with the world, and by extension develop effective leadership practices, Schreiber (2000) in his argument against ethnocentric bias in research and conclusions, calls for researchers to, "... first ground themselves in the culture's worldview and allow the research program to evolve from this center." (p. 656).

Starting with a critical intersectional epistemology that centers intersectionality into the research practice, researchers not only reveal the systems of domination that make up the experiences of a Black women in leadership, they can de-essentialize notions about Black women leaders because it helps researchers, "... attend to the contradictions entailed within social categories." (Harrington, 2005, p. 292). It can help researchers transcend the notion that there is a monolithic Black woman leader who all too often gets imagined negatively in mainstream discourse about leadership. The importance of engaging with critical intersectional epistemology to study the experiences of Black women who navigate their oppressions, and by extension negotiate risk-taking, cost of failure and successful leadership practices, is reflected in Collins' (2009) argument that, "... Black women have access to the experiences that accrue to being both Black and female, an alternative epistemology used to rearticulate a Black women's standpoint should reflect the convergence of both sets of experiences. Race and gender may be analytically distinct, but in Black women's everyday lives, they work together." (p. 289).

In order to reveal the limitless knowledges and possibilities of effective leadership practices, researchers must account for the power dynamics in the knowledge creation of their participants and can do so if they engage with a critical ethnographic approach. According to Madison (2005), "The critical ethnographer ... takes us beneath surface appearances, disrupts the *status quo*, and unsettles both neutrality and taken-for-granted assumptions by bringing to light underlying and obscure operations of power and control. Therefore, the critical ethnographer resists domestication and moves from "what is" to "what could be". (Carspecken, 1996; Denzin, 2001; Noblit, Flores, & Murillo, 2004, as cited in Madison, 2005, p. 4.)

Allowing one to tell one's story of leadership using her own words, researchers do not allow numbers to continue the legacy of socializing Black women out of existence (hooks, 2015, 7). According to Fraser (2004), narrative researchers use personal narrative,

> ... not only because we wish to delve beneath statistically driven generalizations that are made but also because they have the potential to validate the knowledge of 'ordinary' people, especially 'ordinary' women who are liable to be omitted from many research projects ... , ... the interview is a critical tool for developing new frameworks and theories based on women's lives and women's formulations. (p. 184).

Incorporating one's personal narrative into research about leadership, we can, "... challenge taken-for-granted beliefs, assertions and assumptions, ..." (Fraser, 2004, p. 182) found in the negative controlling images of Black women that reify the supremacy of White elite patriarchy for leadership roles. As stated by Fraser (2004), "... we can only ever speak ourselves into existence within the terms or stories available to us. This means that narrative researchers retain an awareness of social conditions as they consider how culture, and social structures, surface in the stories participants and researchers tell." (Lawler, 2002; Riessman, 1993, 2002, 2003, as cited in Fraser 2004, p. 182).

Using these approaches, researchers can learn how non-dominant bodies intellectualize about their experiences and arrive at the endless possibilities and knowledges that can lead to the multiplicity of ways and diverse worldviews about how to do effective leadership beyond just that of the hegemonic White male privileged way. According to Ladson-Billings (2000),

> The process of developing a worldview that differs from the dominant worldview requires active intellectual work on the part of the knower, because schools, society, and the structure and production of knowledge are designed to create individuals who internalize the dominant worldview and knowledge production and acquisition processes. The hegemony of the dominant paradigm makes it more than just another way to view the world – it claims to be the only way to view the world. (p. 258).

If I were to analyze my responses to the same surveys that Murphy uses to theorize about effective leadership and risk-taking, I would be caste as a person who generally avoid risks, is motivated by security and as such would be considered one of those ineffective leaders according to his theory. In the absence of research that centres my experiences as a Black woman, these responses fail to reveal a Black woman who has led successfully while taking huge risks not by reducing the costs associated with failure, but by conceptualizing strategies that would reduce my chances of failure and that came about from my experiences at the axes of my race, gender and class status. Following is my personal narrative that centres my experiences and epistemologies as a Black woman that will show how I came to lead successfully during a time in my life when I took risks where the costs of my failure brought about by intersecting systems of oppression, were high.

5   My Story on Leadership and Risk-Taking: Transcending the Discourse of Mainstream Leadership Thought

A few years ago, I unexpectedly became a single mother raising a 9-year old daughter while just having returned to the workforce after a two-year sabbatical to complete my Masters' degree. I had just started a new position that, at the time, was my most senior leadership role in my career. When my former partner unilaterally decided to abdicate his parental obligations; a decision that can contribute to the subjugation of single Black female heads of households and the families that they raise, soon thereafter I made significant changes towards establishing a new life for myself and my daughter while having to balance full-time parenting, keeping my full-time job, teaching part-time, advancing in my career and realizing my dreams to return to doctoral studies. Almost immediately I became acutely aware of how my race, gender and new class status as a single Black mother would influence how I would now be perceived and thus come to experience the world. Given our lack of representation in senior leadership roles, the tendency of our earnings to be less than that of our workplace counterparts, and the image of the Matriarch used historically to control and to vilify Black women with single motherhood status, I was aware of the enormity of the risks that I was taking and the equally high costs should my attempts at rebuilding my life fail. The image of the Matriarch, "... supports racial oppression ... (Collins, 2009, p. 85) by labelling Black single mothers as "... aggressive, assertive women ... abandoned by their men, [who] end up impoverished, and are stigmatized as being unfeminine." (Collins, 2009, p. 85, word in brackets added). These images associated with matriarchal status has been used to pathologize Black women and the families that they raise as predisposed to poverty, incompetence, criminality, as abusers of government welfare systems and subject to a life of destitution. Acknowledging this perception of Blackness in the White imagination as depicted in Paul Gilroy's (1987) *There Ain't No Black in the Union Jack: The Cultural Politics of Race and Nation*, Adeji (2013) notes, "... black culture ... is defined as a cycle in which the negative effects of black matriarchy and family pathology wrought destructive changes on the inner city by internally breeding deviancy and of deprivation and discrimination" (Gilroy, 1987, pp. 109–110, as cited in Adeji, 2013, p. 28). Cognizant of these negative stereotypes, I was aware that should my attempts to rebuild a better life for myself and my daughter as a single Black mother fail, the associated costs would consist of an inability to secure another senior leadership role that would allow me to take care of my family on my own and to ensure our self-actualization, the derailment of our life-long dreams, the potential of losing all that I had worked hard to achieve for my family's well-being and the associated emotional and mental impact that goes along with acquiring the negative reputation that got assigned to Matriarchs and their families. Aware that these costs associated with my failure as a single Black mother were outside of my control, instead of seeking ways to reduce or eliminate these costs, I chose to develop the following strategies to reduce my chances of failure as I guided my family on the path to success.

Focusing on the end goal, I cultivated a strong sense of hope in what was to come. I gave permission to myself and to my daughter to dream big and accompanied our ambitions with careful planning, perseverance, and unwavering determination that helped us to focus on the things that we wanted to achieve. While I would allow myself to feel the realness of the situation, I balanced that with focusing on the endless possibilities of what was to come for me and for my family. I was not shy about delegating to my daughter the tasks that would allow her to exercise her leadership skills and to rebuild her internal confidence that got shaken immediately upon learning of her new family status. Building a community of other mothers and other fathers with close friends and family members, I turned to them occasionally for help to look after my daughter during times when my work and school obligations prevented me from doing so. Seeking true allyship/critical friendship with people whom I could trust and for whom I cared and learning to love from afar those who did not have our best interests at heart, we obtained the support that we needed to take this journey towards our liberation. Recognizing when to act and acting fast when the right opportunity presented itself, I was aware of the scarcity of second chances. Tapping into my spirituality, I learned to trust my inner voice, to acknowledge the things that I could not change and to give them up to a higher being so that I could focus on those that were within my power and capacity to execute. Carving out time for self-care, for family and self-reflection on our accomplishments, I made sure to infuse laugher and humour throughout every step of our journey. These strategies helped me and my daughter to become strong, intuitive transformational leaders and presented me with career and academic opportunities that kept us on the path to self-actualization. Most of all, these strategies brought us to happiness, to gratitude, to friendships, to a sense of peace and hopefulness in the future, to a greater connection to a higher power and to success as a family.

6   Conclusion

Leadership researchers must engage with more than just scientific methods that tend to give prominence to the positionalities of an elite White man's worldview and take up approaches to research that can centre the ontological and epistemological struggles of non-dominant bodies in order to understand the multiplicity of ways how one can come to lead successfully. When we take up research methodologies that engage with the principles of intersectional epistemology, critical ethnography and personal narratives, we can decentre theories about leadership that reify the hegemonic notions of White patriarchal elites, and centre those of marginalized Black women who have led successfully. When employers base hiring and promotional decisions on theories that come about primarily from data generated by quantitative research methods that only reflect the perspective of the dominant, they perpetuate the existing power imbalances that position elite White men more prominently in the discourse of capable leaders and overlook the leadership capabilities of those non-dominant and marginalized Black women. To ensure the inclusion of other strategies in the discourse of leadership thought and to come to regard non-dominant bodies as great leaders, researchers must engage with methodologies that position prominently non-dominant stories in order to learn more about what it takes to lead successfully.

References

Adjei, P.B. (2013). When Blackness shows up uninvited: Examining the murder of Trayvon Martin through Fanonian racial interpellation. In Dei, G. J. S. and M. Lordan (eds.) 2013, *Contemporary issues in the sociology of race and ethnicity. A Critical Reader*. New York: Peter Lang.

Carspecken, P.F. (1996). *Critical ethnography in educational research: A theoretical and practical guide*. New York: Routledge.

Catalyst (November 17, 2018). *Women of color in the United States: Quick tale.* Retrieved from https://www.catalyst.org/research/women-of-color-in-th-united-states/.

Catalyst (February 24, 2015). *Profile in disruption: Disrupting the default for women of color.* Retrieved from https://www.catalyst.org/2015/24/profile-in-disruption-disturbing-the-default-for-women-of-color/.

Catalyst (July 31, 2017). *No, Black women still don't earn the same as their White peers. Here's Why.* Retrieved from https://www.catalyst.org/2017/07/31/no-black-women-still-don't-earn-the-same-as-their-White-peers-heres-why/.

Collins, P. (2009). *Black feminist thought: Knowledge, consciousness, and the politics of empowerment.* New York: Routledge.

Cukier, W. et al. (2012). *Diversity leads. Women in senior leadership positions: A profile of the greater Toronto area (GTA).* Retrieved from http://www.ryerson.ca/diversity.

Delgado, R. & Stefancic, J. (2017). *Critical race theory: An introduction.* 3rd Edition. New York: New York University Press.

Denzin, NK. (2001). *Interpretive Interactionism.* Thousand Oaks, CA: Sage.

Edwards, R., & Ribben, J. (1998). Living on the edges: Public knowledge, private lives, personal experience. In J. Ribben & R. Edwards (Eds.), *Feminist dilemmas in qualitative research.* Pp. (1–24). London: Sage.

Gilroy, P. (1987). *There ain't no Black in the Union Jack': The cultural politics of race and nation.* Chicago: University of Chicago Press.

Fraser, H. (2004). Doing narrative research. Analysing personal stories line by line. *Qualitative Social Work* 3 (2): 179–201.

Harding, S. (1987). *Feminism and Methodology.* Milton Keynes: Open University Press.

Harrington, C. (2005). 'Liberating' critical ethnography: Reflections from Fiji garment industry research. *Anthropological Forum* 15 (3): 287–296.

hooks, b. (2015). *ain't i a woman. black women and feminism.* New York: Routledge.

Hunter, M. (2002). Rethinking epistemology, methodology, and racism: or, is White sociology really dead? *Race & Society* 5: 119–138.

Johnson, S.K. et al. (2016). *If there's only one woman in your candidate pool, there's statistically no chance she'll be hired.* Cambridge, MA: Harvard Business School Publishing Corporation.

Ladner, J. (1973). *The Death of White Sociology.* New York: Random House.

Ladson-Billings, G. (2000). Racialized discourses and ethnic epistemologies. In N. Denzin & Y. Lincoln (Eds.). *Handbook of qualitative research* (pp. 257–277). Thousand Oaks, CA: Sage.

Lawler, S. (2002). 'Narrative in Social Research', in T. May (ed.) *Qualitative Research in Action,* pp. 242–58. London: Sage.

LeCompte, M. (2002). The transformation of ethnographic practice: past and current challenges. *Qualitative Research* 2 (3): 283–299.

Madison, D. S. (2005). Introduction to critical ethnography: Theory and method. *Critical ethnography: method, ethics and performance.* Thousand Oaks, CA: Sage Publications, Inc. Retrieved from: http:www.sagepub.com/upm-data/4957_Madison_|_Proof_Chapter_1.pdf.

Mannheim, K. 1936. Ideology and Utopia. New York Harcourt, Brace & World.

Marshall, M. & Wingfield, T. (2016). *Getting more Black women into the C-suite.* Cambridge, MA: Harvard Business School Publishing Corporation. In The Latest Research Diversity. By Harvard Business Review. October 25, 2016.

Murphy, M. (August 13, 2019). *If you want people to be less afraid of taking risks, try reducing the cost of failure.* Forbes.com. Retrieved from: https://www.forbes.com/sites/markmurphy/2019/08/13/if-you-want-your-people-to-be-less-afraid-of-taking-risks-try-reducing-the-cost-of-failure/#6dacbe2f37cf.

Noblit, G. W., Flores, S.Y., & Murillo, E. G. (2004). *Post critical ethnography: An introduction.* Cress, NJ: Hampton Press.

Schreiber, L. (2000). Overcoming methodological elitism: Afrocentrism as a prototypical paradigm for intercultural research. *International Journal of Intercultural Relations* 24: 651–671.

Spalek, B. (2005). A critical reflection on researching Black Muslim women's lives post-September 11th. *International Journal of Social Research Methodology* 8 (5): 405–418.

Riessman, C.K. (1993). *Narrative Analysis.* Newbury Park, CA: Sage.

Riessman, C.K. (forthcoming). 'Narrative Analysis', in *Encyclopedia of Social Science Research Methods.* London: Sage.

Riessman, C.K. (2002). 'Illness Narratives: Positioned Identities', paper presented at Invited Annual Lecture, Health Communication Research Centre, Cardiff University, Wales, May, http:"www.cf.acuk/encap/hcrc/comet/prog/narratives.pdf (consulted Nov. 2003).

West, C. (2002). *Prophesy deliverance!* Louisville, KY: Westminster John Knox Press.

CHAPTER 9

Assessing Math Anxiety in Male Elementary Teachers as Learners and as Teachers

Khulood Agha Khan

1 Introduction

Math surrounds our daily lives, and mathematical skills are crucial predictors for an individual's successful life. Various studies have found that mathematics is considered to be the most challenging subject in school for many adolescents (Attard, 2011; Bales, 2010; Larkin & Jorgensen, 2016). These insecurities, sentiments and attitudes can lead to math anxieties and affect one's attitude towards the subject. Due to math anxiety, math skills are diminished. Many teachers are faced with math anxiety that adversely affects their performance and negatively affect their students. The goal of this research is to understand the male perspective on math anxiety and to improve student's learning, help them build confidence so that a positive student-learning environment is created in the math class. Research on math anxiety has primarily been studied on female primary teachers. Since elementary and primary teachers are predominantly female, this review will include the gendered nature of the previous research, focus on the background knowledge about factors and causes of math anxiety in male teachers and its impact on their students. This chapter will report on some findings from a small qualitative research project how math anxiety can affect teaching instructional strategies, impact their students' learning and achievement. As most of the research has been done on how female teachers feel anxious while teaching math, this study focuses on the links between on male teachers' perspective of math anxiety and their math self-concept* and will contribute to the existing research while extending it in a new direction.

1.1 *Significance of the Study*
This study is intended to be an initial step in addressing the knowledge gap in the literature about the male elementary teachers' perspective on math anxiety. The teacher's anxiety is passed on to their students (Sloan, 2010). There exist gender differences in math anxiety experiences (Bieg, Goetz, Wolter, & Hall, 2015). Most studies have found that females are more likely to have

math anxiety than males (Else-Quest, Hyde, & Linn, 2010; Miller & Bichsel, 2004). But most of the research done to understand math anxiety in elementary teachers is predominantly female that is generalized for all both genders. The primary determinant of student math anxiety is teacher's behaviour and anxiety (Jackson & Leffingwell, 1999; Lake & Kelly, 2014). If there are gender differences between male and female teachers in math anxiety, then there is a need to study the male perspectives separately, as a learner and as a teacher. The recently dropped math scores for Grade 3 and Grade 6 in the EQAO testing (EQAO, 2017) has raised the question of why students are not achieving success in math. The scores for Grade 3 showed that only 49 % students met the provincial standards (that is B grade), a decrease of two percentage point from last year (EQAO, 2017a). On the other hand, the Grade 6 scores show only 37% students at the provincial standard (EQAO, 2017b). Is this drop-in student achievement somehow related to teachers' math anxiety, since most of the teachers in the elementary grades are female? The question was, can we use existing research to assess math anxiety in male teachers based on predominant female data? Is the male teacher's perspective of math anxiety being represented accurately and what are its implications in a classroom setting on student's achievement and student performance? I believe it will be a valuable contribution to the extensive prior research on female math anxiety.

1.2   *Research Problem*
While working in the field of education, I have noticed female teachers have math anxiety that affects their method of instructions. I found many students to be anxious during math classes that were reflective of their teacher's math anxiety. There aren't many male teachers especially in the elementary division, as only 1 in 10 primary, junior teachers (under age 30) is male according to the data collected by Ontario College of Teachers (Jamieson, 2005). This study aims to address the gap in the scholarly literature, as female dominant studies have been generalized for both the genders knowing the fact that gender differences exist in math anxiety (Bieg et al., 2015). This study highlights issues and provides new understanding regarding male teacher's perspective of math anxiety that can be associated with the recent drop in the math scores, student performance and achievement for Grade 3 and Grade 6 in Ontario.

1.3   *Snapshot of the Study*
The purpose of this study is to assess male teachers' perspective of math anxiety and investigate the nature of the relationship among math anxiety, math self-concept, and student performance in mathematics. Based on the research problem, my study aims to understand the existence and impact of math

anxiety in male elementary teachers, as learners and as teachers. By under-standing their perspective, we might be able to find a reason for the drop in students' math achievement as found in the results of the data collected by EQAO (EQAO, 2017).

1.4   *Research Questions*
The specific research questions addressed include:
- Do gender differences exist in the perspective of the elementary teachers for math anxiety?
- What are the implications of math anxiety in male elementary teachers on students' achievement and students' learning?
- What is the male teacher's perspective on math anxiety as a learner and as a teacher?

1.5   *Reflexive Positioning—Engaging in Power*
I had math anxiety as a learner until I took a course in my undergrad and learned how accessible math was. I have two minors in psychology and have always learned about the gender differences that exist in anxiety. As an edu-cator, it is of interest to know the gender differences in math anxiety and what strategies do male teachers use to overcome their anxiety (if they have), how it impacts their pedagogical practices and their students' performance. Understanding this gender gap of perception will provide a direction in pre-vention and treatment for math anxiety and lower math self-concept in stu-dents. By being a female educator in a master's program, I do feel in a position of power because I embody it, literally. Reaching out to male math teachers (as seen in Appendix B via letter), highlights the gendered constructs around teaching a male-dominated subject in a female-dominated profession.

In my research, I seek three roles; an insider, an outsider and an inbetweener that may lead to ethical issues. The identity of the researcher can shift depend-ing on the situation (Arthur, 2010). It is important to identify to which identity my participants refer to because not all of them will consider me an insider or outsider. I claim myself as an insider and an outsider in this research. Insider because I am a member of the community as I am an elementary educator. My self-consciousness enables me to empathize with my participants who will also be elementary teachers. They will share their experiences in response to answering my interview questions. Before I ask them to open up, to share their experiences and feel vulnerable, I will be opening up my experiences and ped-agogy in front of them.

The three teachers sharing their personal narratives gave this research experiential testimony into how male teachers feel about math. Teaching is the power role in a classroom. By speaking with male teachers about a male-dominated subject in a female-dominated profession, this study illuminates power engagement as follows:

There is an ease that men have with math that women commonly do not. Our access to power is that of a fellow teacher but also as a female teacher, because this is one of a selected number of professions is female dominated. I am in a rare role of gendered power, reached out to the socially dominant gender group to examine and gather data about a subject men dominate but maybe that education researchers don't look to them because the focus in largely on females in education.

The gender power in math is still male. Though some of my respondents had no math anxiety as far as teaching the subject goes, one did and that was because he had a terrible woman math teacher. Though women dominate the teaching profession, this study implicitly shows that a woman's anxiety around math does transmit to her students. Women are undervalued in this subject area and maybe unaware their insecurities around math are being taken on by their pupils. From a ontological and axiological perspective, for instance, how are male teachers enjoying teaching math and how does this translate to how math anxiety comes about—or is lessened—with students being affected by teachers' attitudes towards the subject? How would greater study and with a wider sample of male teachers reflect what is at stake in math teaching and anxiety vis-à-vis the reality of how students fare in the subject based on their teacher's confidence level with the subject.

Student success and efficacy in math is attributed to empowering male teachers who teach the subject because they feel confident that they are making choices and choosing teaching methods that effect students 'outcomes and performance positively. From an ontology perspective, this study refutes or provides evidence to my queries into math anxiety with male teachers in Ontario's current education system. Looking at the literature review and existing research, I wondered how to engage my participants given the lack of research in this area. However, based on your results, there was a huge learning as to how male strategies and help female educators to control their math anxiety. From an epistemological point, the design of the study was appropriate to the research because I am an elementary teacher who has experience in the field and my research was specifically geared to my geographical location and to potential male teacher participants who could speak to the research that I am conducting from their own experience as instructors themselves, in schools in the same city/school board.

An ethical issue in relation to power relationship can be confidentiality or privacy. Participants will be informed ahead of time to decide if they want to participate in the study. I will provide them with examples of what to expect in the interview. Starting with some lighter conversation might be useful so my participants can feel relaxed. This will help the participants to decide whether or not they want to partake in the research. By doing so, I will not violate the ethical code of conduct in relation to privacy.

1.6   *Methodology/Design*

Mixed methods of qualitative and quantitative research will be used to collect data through semi-structured interview and survey questions. Qualitative research "emphasizes action, process, perspective and knowledge as they influence the development and completion of acts" (Rothe, 2000). The semi-structured interview allows the flexibility of examining the area to be studied along with the permission to explore the idea that is not initially planned (Rubin & Rubin, 2004). It will permit one to understand the world as seen by the participants (Patton, 2002) and to see the world from participants' perspective (Bryman, Teevan, & Bell, 2009). On the other hand, surveys will allow gathering information through a set of pre-prepared questions to collect data about their opinions and behaviour (Lynn & Flett, 2015).

The researcher contacted the participants via e-mail and in person. These contacting methods are a "combination of convenience sampling and snowball sampling" (Bryman, et al., 2009). The teachers who agreed were interviewed. Three male teachers were recruited from Toronto, Ontario as they belong to the researcher's locality. First preservice teacher (pseudonym: Elvis) was recruited to understand how trained and prepared he feels about teaching math (prepared or not). The second male teacher (pseudonym: Mark) had at least two years of full-time experience in the elementary division. By choosing the experienced teacher, the researcher wanted to know if experience over the years had changed the way to look at math anxiety. The third male teacher (pseudonym: Guru) had at least some months of experience in the elementary division. The researcher added the elementary division to the initial idea of only focusing on primary, as primary had a limited participant pool. The idea was to research if there was any math anxiety element in their perspectives. If so, what strategies the preservice teacher had in mind to deal with it in the future classroom and how the experienced teacher dealt with their math anxiety? What factors play a significant role in feeling anxious/ not anxious about math? To analyze the data coded key themes were identified and mapped across the data from the three teachers to find the interrelated areas of interest (Miller & Glassner, 1997).

The findings from the study are credible as possible because proper research methods were followed including recordings, careful notetaking, attentive listening, double-checking data and revisiting the data for analysis and veri-fication. To confirm the validity of this study, original research question and quotations were used from the interviews. The research questions were care-fully crafted to ensure that they asked what was intended and supported the kind of information meant to research. The participants had a chance to look over the transcripts to ensure that it represents their words accurately. The reliability of the study is limited to the participants' own experiences, beliefs, biases and subjectivity.

There are some ontological, epistemological and axiological questions about this methodology that come to mind, such as: Why has the study of math anx-iety as a gendered issue been overlooked within the context of male teachers and male students' experiences? Why has experiential learning of male teach-ers been accorded less attention in data collection regarding the instruction of a male-dominated subject in a female-dominated profession and its effect on students? Why is empathy not examined in math anxiety if literature in this area demonstrates that students detect their teachers' nervousness when approaching this particular subject? Should personal narratives be given greater importance in researching math anxiety, outside the traditional rubric of using solely a theoretical framework to design methodological rubrics in data collection?

2   Literature Review

In this section, literature will reflect the attempt to provide a background on math anxiety conceptualization and existence in female elementary teachers and its impact on their students. This study is an effort to find the gap between the gender differences of the perspectives on math anxiety and how in turn it affects students' performance and achievement.

2.1   *Math Anxiety*

Math anxiety is defined as: a feeling of nervousness, unease, or tension that interferes with math performance (Chernoff, & Stone, 2014) due to negative emotional reaction (Young, Wu & Menon, 2012), a distasteful feeling students experience while doing assignments or performing the math related daily rou-tine (Ma & Xu, 2004) which accounts for the worrying statistics of academic failure in Mathematics (Iossi, 2007), a "feeling of tension and anxiety that interferes with the manipulation of numbers and the solving of mathemati-cal problems in ordinary life and academic situations" (Ashcraft et al., 2003), a "fear about performing mathematics and is associated with the delayed acquisition of core mathematics and number concepts and poor math competence" (Richardson & Suinn, 1972) and a feeling that makes a person panic, helpless, paralyze, and mentally disorganized when they are asked to solve a math problem (Hunt, 1985).

2.2   *Impact of Teachers' Math Anxiety on Students*

There is a strong connection between teachers' own math anxieties to students' math anxieties and consequently affecting their performance (Sloan, 2010) e.g. math anxiety, math avoidance, lack of self-efficacy and negative attitudes towards math (Beilock et al., 2010). Students may use a variety of avoidance strategies towards academic work based on their negative classroom environment and math anxiety (Patrick et al., 2003). It can lead to avoidance of mathematics and mathematics-related fields (Maloney, Schaeffer & Beilock, 2013). How teachers approach math, leads to positive biases or avoidance (Kawakami et al., 2008).

Math anxiety is closely related to the methods of instruction of a teacher as it can lead to quickly finish the tasks inaccurately to end the stressful situation (Ashcraft & Faust, 1994). A teacher's instructional practices influence the classroom environment (Attard, 2011) and shape students' learning and experience. These practices include implementing curriculum, use to different strategies, and making math engaging (Hargreaves, 1994) or can create a negative environment for students that may be stressful and uncomfortable. It may affect their effort, motivation, persistence, and engagement in the classroom (Patrick et al., 2003). Students internalize their teachers' enthusiasm and motivation when they teach math (Jameson & Fusco, 2014). If teachers' behaviours are negative, they create math anxiety in their students (Jackson & Leffingwell, 1999). Math anxiety leads to poor achievement in mathematics (Finlayson, 2014) and lower grades (Hunsley,1987; Núñez-Peña, Suárez-Pellicioni & Bono, 2013). A teacher' emotional reaction to a given a subject area can have an impact on student achievement (Gunderson et al., 2013). Improving teacher's emotional response to that subject area, can increase the academic achievement of the students in that area (Gunderson et al., 2013).

2.3   *Gender Differences in Math Anxiety*

There is evidence from research about the persistence stereotypes that, females are inferior in ability to males in the field of math (Riegle & Humphries, 2012). It is believed that female teachers tend to have lower math self-efficacy than male teachers (Campbell & Beaudry, 1998; Eccles, 1987). They experience an unpleasant emotional response more than male (Hembree, 1990). On the other hand, math anxiety is less specific in men than women (Liabre & Suarez, 1985).

Males often have a generalized test anxiety for math rather than a specific anxiety related to math (Haynes, Mullins & Stein, 2004). Considering these gender differences there is a need for further investigation about differences in the male and female primary teachers' attitudes towards math and the perceptions of their math anxiety.

"Primary teaching is clearly and evidently a 'female' profession" (Skelton, 2009). Keeping in mind primary division teachers are predominantly female (Beilock et al., 2010) and have math anxiety teaching math. For this reason, in most researches the main participants to measure math anxiety in primary teachers are female (Hembree, 1990; Miller & Bichsel, 2004; Else-Quest, Hyde, & Linn, 2010). For example; a research done by Fennema, Peterson, Carpenter & Lubinski (1990), was to understand success and failure of boys and girls in the classroom. The participants of the research were primary math teachers in U.S.A. and out of 38 teachers, 24 were female. If they had personal negative attitude and gender stereotypes about math, then data can't be generalized to all genders. Female teachers own gendered and stereotypical beliefs about the math abilities, can lead this research into a specific direction.

The research done by Beilock et al., (2010), the impact of female teachers' math anxiety on female students was addressed because more than 90 % of the primary teachers were female. They found an underrepresentation of male teachers in the primary division. In another research to measure the self-efficacy and math anxiety in mathematical problem solving, out of 90 participant preservice teachers, 51 were female and only 19 were male (Hoffman, 2010). Another study, Bernard, Hill, Falter, & Wilson (2004) found that men represented just 10 percent of primary-junior teachers under the age of 30. By 2006, in the same group, men accounted for 11 percent. More specifically, only one in 10 kindergartens, primary and junior qualified teachers (Grades K-6) are men. Of all the teachers in Canada, 30 percent are male teachers which are consistent across all four of the province's publicly funded school systems (Bernard et al., 2004). My research proposes a gap in the voices of both genders when addressing the math anxiety in primary teachers. It also proposes that when the two genders will be equally representative of math anxiety, the results would be different. Female teachers significantly outnumber male teachers that leads us to experience a loss of male teachers' voice in elementary school research. There is a whole area of research on math anxiety in male elementary teachers that needs to be explored and researched. The aim of this research is to find out whether male elementary teachers suffer from math anxiety as a learner and as a teacher. This information can be then used to improve methods of math pedagogical practices and enhance their students' learning and math achievement.

3   Results

The results section presents the data from the interviews with 3 male teacher participants. Their response to the interview questions provided rich insights about their conceptualizations, perceptions of math anxiety and its impact of student performance and achievement.

In response to question about experiencing math anxiety as a student (See Appendix A, Part 2, Q2, a), out of the three participants, two mentioned resiliency factors in having no math anxiety. Only one participant mentioned experiencing math anxiety as a student. Mark mentioned that he "always found math very interesting and never challenging". He also mentioned "knowing my strengths and weaknesses and working on them". Similarly, Guru mentioned that "math was his favourite subject". He was "a strong math student and enjoyed how numbers fit together". He "liked going step - by - step to achieve a final answer". On the contrary to these two participants, Elvis identified "having general uneasiness about math".

> For me anxiety is more situation based. I don't I think .. it could be in my head or probably is in my head, for me I might … it's like I see a problem, and I go like " oh nooo!". That would make me feel like really uneasy, hard to breathe, very nervous and I would stutter. I would be over thinking things.. in general uneasiness.

Elvis claimed that his Grade 9 female math teacher;

> was probably the worst person. She turned me off in math completely. She made me like, essentially it was academic math and I hated this teacher so much that .. I was like is there any other teachers at this time and they said yes … but it's just the applied math. And the little I knew, I said sure whatever. So I switched to the applied math. So I literally fault this teacher, for.. She could have … She essentially limited my whole career, my university career because I hated this teacher.
>
> . … in terms of your question, speaking of, I would say female teachers, I have had for math are more uncomfortable with math than male teachers.

He also stated that his male teacher

> seemed to know what he was talking about unlike some of my female math teachers.

In response to question about experiencing math anxiety as a teacher (See Appendix A, Part 2, Q2, b), out of the three participants, Elvis mentioned that "he didn't feel a hundred percent comfortable with math" whereas Mark and Guru stated that they "never had any math anxiety, as learner or a teacher". Elvis stated that

> I would say female teachers, I have had for math are more uncomfortable with math than the male teachers.

Elvis talked about being "comfortable in teaching math without any anxiety from kindergarten to grade 4". He also mentioned that he "would get a bit uncomfortable beyond grade 4". Mark identified that "the intermediate division is easier to teach without any math anxiety". Guru also associated with "intermediate/senior as the zone with no teaching math anxiety".

In response to question about experiencing math anxiety as a teacher (See Appendix A, Part 2, Q2), Guru mentioned that

> As a teacher, it is really important to know which grade level you work best with because if you are teaching the wrong grade, then you are potentially, hurting I guess, the future of that child. Because they are not learning the way that they needs to, at that grade level. That's our job as a teacher, realizing that each year development learns a certain way.

In response to question about adding something they haven't talked about (See Appendix A, Part 2, Q6), they talked about choosing a division. Elvis mentioned that "even though he feels comfortable with the primary curriculum material, he would still learn the junior curriculum material to work with them". He also said that

> primary students are at the basics of everything ... they can't read ... they can barely count. they don't know their likes ... they like collective one thing e.g. all of them love minions. ... in primary you have to teach school rules.

Similarly, Mark stated that he finds that "primary students are less behavioral and can have more guided and instructional time". Guru also reported that "for primary students one need more patience. Since there is no cap on the student number, it is hard to imagine 32, 8 years old that cry when things don't go their way". He also mentioned that in primary

They still need to be babied. They still call for mommy when things go wrong and I don't have the patience for that, to surround myself with 30 of them. ... I don't have to deal with the paddy little things (with older students). I don't have the patience for that. I had the opportunity of being in a class for like 6 hours a day for about 3 weeks, and I couldn't handle it anymore. Like the kids are cute, you don't get me wrong ... as I like kids, I want my own. I don't want 30.

Elvis stated that

It is easier to deal with junior students in giving the consequences compared to primary students who are more wild. ... junior students, I can personally teach better.

Mark stated that he "prefers intermediate division" and finds that "students in intermediate are more independent and easier to make real world connections." Guru also mentioned that

at intermediate the brains are thinking much deeper. They can go beyond the surface level of any concept. Their cognitive functions are stronger. You can actually have more in depth question. They start to ask questions like or why does the work that way. So start to get to kind of explore something in depth.

In response to question about experiencing math anxiety as a teacher and the roles and responsibilities that comes with it (See Appendix A, Part 2, Q2), Elvis identified his math anxiety and stated that he "would address his students anxiety and make it relatable by sharing personal experience (of how he felt about math)". He would have "conversations, one on one talk, after school help etc to help them boost their confidence". Mark also indicated

it is my role as a teacher to ensure students have manipulatives and sources to help them when they need it e.g. math dictionary where they can take notes.

Guru advocated that;

one thing that people forget about teaching it that we're not just teachers, we are babysitters, we do have to council, and we do have to be the doctor. There is a lot more going on in a day. So when people (and this is a little bit of a side ramp but) when people say "O Teachers get paid so well and they get 2 months off in the summer, that's not fair". I say, come to class and do the job yourself and see what we have to do deal with. It's not that simple. We're exhausted.

He also mentioned that "it is important to know what grades you can teach".

In response to question about approaches to use in the classroom to help engage with your student's math anxiety (See Appendix A, Part 2, Q5), Elvis stated that "there is a need to boost self confidence in our students who encounter math anxiety". All of them mentioned "to make math relatable for students".

Similar to Elvis's response, Mark mentioned "to keep the classroom 'warm and welcoming' for the students". Guru also stated that math should have an:

> application to the real world ... bringing real life problems to my class ... If they can't see the importance of why we are learning a certain topic it is harder for them to get engaged. ... I use relative expressions and slang words that they use ... I try to really embrace their society, and teach it in a way that is relevant to them and that's what engages them.

In response to question about the conceptualization of math anxiety (See Appendix A, Part 2, Q1), Elvis said that It is the fear, of may be failing or feeling uneasy, about math concepts. According to Mark:

As a primary teacher, I saw math anxiety through students choosing to use math manipulatives as a toy, rather than a tool and not asking for help by either staying in their groups silently or sitting at in their areas independently (not asking for assistance).

For Guru, anxiety is

Students who when they see numbers, the 1st thing that happens is they ball up, a wall gets put up they look *scared and anxious, you can see it on their face., tears in their eyes.*

Acknowledgement

This work is dedicated to my family, particularly my husband. Without his ongoing support, none of this would have been possible.

References

Anderson, R., Greene, M. & Loewn, P. (1988). Relationships among teachers' and students' thinking skills, sense of efficacy, and student achievement. *Alberta Journal of Educational Research* 34: 148– 165.

Arthur, L. (2010). "Insider-outsider Perspectives in Comparative Education." Seminar presentation at the Research Centre for International and Comparative Studies, Graduate School of Education, University of Bristol, Bristol.

Ashcraft M. H., Eifert G. H., Hopko D. R., Lejuez C. W., McNeil D. W., Riel J. (2003). The effects of anxious responding on mental arithmetic and lexical decision task performance. *Journal of Anxiety Disorders* 17 (6): 647–665.

Ashcraft, M. H. & Faust, M.W. (1994). Mathematics anxiety and mental arithmetic performance: An exploratory investigation. *Cognition & Emotion* 8: 97–125.

Attard, C. (2011). My favourite subject is maths. for some reason no-one really agrees with me: Student perspectives of mathematics teaching and learning in the upper primary classroom. *Mathematics Education Research Journal* 23 (3): 363–377. doi:10.1007/s13394-011-0020-5.

Bales, A. (2010). Maths: The viewpoint of an ex-student. *The Australian Mathematics Teacher* 66 (3): 2–3.

Bandura, A. (1997). Self-efficacy: The exercise of control. New York: Freeman.

Beckdemir, M. (2010). The pre-service teachers' mathematics anxiety related to depth of negative experiences in mathematics classroom while they were students. *Educational Studies in Mathematics* 75: 311–328.

Beilock, S. L., Gunderson, E. A., Ramirez, G., Levine, S. C., & Smith, E. E. (2010). Female teachers' math anxiety affects girls' math achievement. *Proceedings of the National Academy of Sciences of the United States of America* 107 (5): 1860–1863. doi:10.1073/pnas.0910967107.

Bernard, Jean-Luc., Hill, David., Falter, Pat., & Wilson, Doug (2004). Narrowing the gender gap: attracting men to teaching. Retrieved April 05, 2017, from https://www.oct.ca/-/media/PDF/Attracting%20Men%20To%20Teaching/EN/Men_In_Teaching_e.pdf.

Bieg, M., Goetz, T., Wolter, I., & Hall, N. C. (2015). Gender stereotype endorsement differentially predicts girls' and boys' trait-state discrepancy in math anxiety. *Frontiers in Psychology* 6: 1404. doi:10.3389/fpsyg.2015.01404.

Brady, P., & Bowd, A. (2005). Mathematics anxiety, prior experience and confidence to teach mathematics among pre-service education students. *Teachers and Teaching: Theory and Practice* 11: 37–46. doi:10.1080/1354060042000337084.

Bryman, A., Teevan, J., & Bell, E. (2009). *Social research methods* (2nd Canadian ed.). North York, ON, Canada: Oxford University Press.

Campbell, James R. and Jeffrey S. Beaudry. (1998). Gender Gap Linked to Differential Socialization for High-Achieving Mathematics Students. *The Journal of Educational Research* 91 (3): 140–53.

Chernoff, E. J., & Stone, M. (2014). An examination of math anxiety research. *Gazette - Ontario Association for Mathematics* 52 (4): 29–31. Retrieved from http://ezproxy.lib.ryerson.ca/login?url=http://search.proquest.com/docview/1563633518?accountid=13631.

Else-Quest N. M., Hyde J. S., Linn M. C. (2010). Cross-national patterns of gender differences in mathematics: A meta-analysis. *Psychological Bulletin* 136: 103–127.

Education Quality and Accountability Office. (2017). Annual Reports: 2016–2017. Author. Queen's Printer for Ontario.

EQAO. (2017a). Achievement Results: Primary Division. Retrieved October 13, 2017, from http://www.eqao.com/en/assessments/results/assessment-docs-elementary/provincial-report-primary-achievement-results-2017.pdf.

EQAO. (2017b). Achievement Results: Junior Division. Retrieved October 13, 2017, from http://www.eqao.com/en/assessments/results/assessment-docs-elementary/provincial-report-junior-achievement-results-2017.pdf.

Eccles, J. S. (1987). Gender roles and women's achievement-related decisions. *Psychology of Women Quarterly*, 11, 135–172.

Fennema, E., Peterson, P. L., Carpenter, T. P., & Lubinski, C. A. (1990). Teachers' attributions and beliefs about girls, boys, and mathematics. *Educational Studies in Mathematics* 21 (1): 55–69. doi:10.1007/BF00311015.

Finlayson, M. (2014). Addressing math anxiety in the classroom. *Improving Schools* 17 (1): 99–115.

Garvis, S. (2013). Beginning generalist teacher self-efficacy for music compared with maths and english. *British Journal of Music Education* 30 (1): 85. doi:10.1017/S0265051712000411.

Griggs, M. S., Rimm-Kaufman, S., Merritt, E. G., & Patton, C. L. (2013). The responsive classroom approach and fifth grade students' math and science anxiety and self-efficacy. *School Psychology Quarterly* 28 (4): 360–373. Retrieved from http://ezproxy.lib.ryerson.ca/login?url=http://search.proquest.com/docview/1415593692?accountid=13631.

Gunderson, E. A., Ramirez, G., Beilock, S. L., & Levine, S. C. (2013). Teachers' spatial anxiety relates to 1st- and 2nd-Graders' spatial learning. *Mind, Brain, and Education* 7 (3): 196–199. doi:10.1111/mbe.12027.

Hargreaves, A. (1994). Changing teachers, changing times: Teachers' work and culture on the postmodern age. London: Cassell.

Haynes, A. F., Mullins, A. G., & Stein, B. S. (2004). Differential models for math anxiety in male and female college students. *Sociological Spectrum* 24 (3): 295–318. doi:10.1080/02732170490431304.

Hembree, R. (1990). The nature, effects, and relief of mathematics anxiety. *Journal for Research in Mathematics Education* 21: 33–46.

Hoffman, B. (2010). I think I can, but I'm afraid to try: The role of self-efficacy beliefs and mathematics anxiety in mathematics problem-solving efficiency. *Learning and Individual Differences* 20 (3): 276–283. doi:10.1016/j.lindif.2010.02.001.

Hunsley, J. (1987). Cognitive processes in mathematics anxiety and test anxiety: the role of appraisals, internal dialogue and attributions. *Journal of Educational Psychology* 79 (4): 388–392.

Hunt, G.E. (1985). Math anxiety- Where do we go from here? *Focus on Learning Problems in Mathematics* 7 (2): 29–40.

Iossi, L. (2007). Strategies for reducing math anxiety in post-secondary students. In S. M. Nielsen & M. S. Plakhotnik (Eds). *Proceedings of the Sixth Annual College of Education Research Conference: Urban and International Education Section* (pp. 30–35). Miami: Florida International University.

Jackson, C. D., & Leffingwell, R. J. (1999). The role of instructions in creating math anxiety in students from kindergarten through college. *The Mathematics Teacher* 92 (7): 583–586.

Jameson, M. M., & Fusco, B. R. (2014). Math anxiety, math self-concept, and math self-efficacy in adult learners compared to traditional undergraduate students. *Adult Education Quarterly* 64 (4): 306–322. doi:10.1177/0741713614541461.

Jamieson, B. (2005). Where have all the male teachers gone? Narrowing the gender gap: Attracting men to teaching]. *Education Today* 17: 12–15. Retrieved from http://ezproxy.lib.ryerson.ca/login?url=https://search-proquest-com.ezproxy.lib.ryerson.ca/docview/218630738?accountid=13631.

Jones, MG. & Carter, G., (2007) Science teacher attitudes and beliefs. In: Abel S (ed) *Handbook of research on science teaching*. Mahwah, NJ: Lawrence Erlbaum.

Kawakami, K., Steele, J. R., Cifa, C., Phills, C. E., & Dovidio, J. F. (2008). Approaching math increases math = me and math = pleasant. *Journal of Experimental Social Psychology* 44 (3): 818–825. doi:10.1016/j.jesp.2007.07.009.

Lake, V. E., & Kelly, L. (2014). Female preservice teachers and mathematics: Anxiety, beliefs, and stereotypes. *Journal of Early Childhood Teacher Education* 35 (3): 262–275. doi:10.1080/10901027.2014.936071.

Larkin, K., & Jorgensen, R. (2016). I hate maths: Why do we need to do maths? Using iPad video diaries to investigate attitudes and emotions towards mathematics in year 3 and year 6 students. *International Journal of Science and Mathematics Education* 14 (5): 925–944. doi:10.1007/s10763-015-9621-x.

Levine, G. (1996). Variability in anxiety for teaching mathematics among pre-service elementary school teachers enrolled in a mathematics course. Retrieved 12 February 2017, from http://gateway.library.qut.edu.au:2127/Webstore/CommonSearchResults.asp?.

Liabre, M. Mana & Eduraho, Suarez. (1985). Predicting math anxiety and course performance in college women and men. *Journal of Counseling Psychology* 32: 283–87.

Lynn, P., & Flett, B. (2015). What are surveys? London: Sage Publications Ltd.

Ma, X. & Xu, J. (2004). The causal ordering of mathematics anxiety and mathematics achievement: a longitudinal panel analysis. *Journal of Adolescence* 27: 165–179.

Maloney, E. A., Schaeffer, M. W., & Beilock, S. L. (2013). Mathematics anxiety and stereotype threat: Shared mechanisms, negative consequences and promising interventions. *Research in Mathematics Education* 15 (2): 115–128. doi:10.1080/14794802.2013.797744.

Miller, H., & Bichsel, J. (2004). Anxiety, working memory, gender, and math performance. *Personality and Individual Differences* 37 (3): 591- 606. https://doi.org/10.1016/j.paid.2003.09.029.

Miller, J. & Glassner, B. (1997). The 'inside' and 'outside': Finding realities in interviews. In D. Silverman (Ed), *Qualitative research: Theory, method and practice* (pp. 99–112). London: Sage Publications.

Newstead, J. (1998). Aspects of children's mathematics anxiety. *Educational Studies in Mathematics* 36 (1): 53–71.

Núñez-Peña, M. I., Suárez-Pellicioni, M., & Bono, R. (2013). Effects of math anxiety on student success in higher education. *International Journal of Educational Research* 58: 36–43. doi:10.1016/j.ijer.2012.12.004.

Pajares, F., & Graham, L. (1999). Self-efficacy, motivational constructs, and mathematics performance of entering middle school students. *Contemporary Educational Psychology* 24: 124–139. doi:10.1006/ceps.1998.0991.

Pajares, Frank & Kranzler. John. (1995). Self-Efficacy beliefs and general mental ability in mathematical problem-solving. *Contemporary Educational Psychology* 20: 426–43.

Patrick, H., Turner, J. C., Meyer, D. K., & Midgley, C. (2003). How teachers establish psychological environments during the first days of school: Associations with avoidance in mathematics. *Teachers College Record* 105 (8): 1521–1558. doi:10.1111/1467-9620.00299.

Patton, M. Q. (2002). *Qualitative research and evaluation methods* (3rd ed.). Thousand Oaks, CA: Sage.

Reyna, C., & Weiner, B. (2001). Justice and utility in the classroom: An attributional analysis of the goals of teachers' punishment and intervention strategies. *Journal of Educational Psychology* 93: 309–319. doi:10.1037/0022-0663.93.2.309.

Richardson F. C., Suinn R. M. (1972). The mathematics anxiety rating scale. *Journal of Counseling Psychology* 19: 551–554.

Riegle-Crumb, C., & Humphries, M. (2012). Exploring bias in math teachers' perceptions of students' ability by gender and race/ethnicity. *Gender and Society* 26 (2): 290–322. doi:10.1177/0891243211434614.

Ross, J. A. (1992). Teacher efficacy and the effects of coaching on student achievement. *Canadian Journal of Education* 17: 51–65.

Rothe, J. P. (2000). *Undertaking qualitative research: Concepts and cases in injury, health and social life*. Edmonton, AB: The University of Alberta Press.

Rubin, H. J., & Rubin, I. (2004). Qualitative interviewing: The art of hearing data (2nd ed.) Thousand Oaks, CA: Sage.

Sargent, P. (2001). *Real men or real teachers? Contradictions in the lives of men elementary school teachers.* Harriman, TN: Men's Studies Press.

Skelton, C. (2001). *Schooling the boys: Masculinities and primary education.* Buckingham: Open University Press.

Skelton, C. (2009). Failing to get men into primary teaching: A feminist critique. *Journal of Education Policy* 24 (1): 39–54. doi:10.1080/02680930802412677.

Sloan, T. R. (2010). A quantitative and qualitative study of math anxiety among preservice teachers. *The Educational Forum* 74 (3): 242–256. doi:10.1080/00131725.2010.483909.

Stipek, D. J., Givvin, K. B., Salmon, J. M., & MacGyvers, V. L. (2001). Teachers' beliefs and practices related to mathematics instruction. *Teaching and Teacher Education* 17: 213–226. doi:10.1016/S0742-051X(00)00052-4.

Swetman, D., Munday, R., & Windham, R. (1993). Math-anxious teachers: Breaking the cycle. *College Student Journal* 27: 421–427.

Young, C. B., Wu, S. S., & Menon, V. (2012). The neurodevelopmental basis of math anxiety. *Psychological Science* 23 (5): 492–501. doi:10.1177/0956797611429134.

Connecting the "Here and Now" with "What Could Be"

A Critical Analysis of Imagination as Method Engaging Queer Futurities

Katie Bannon

1   Introduction

Research orientated or aligned with social justice often expresses goals of contributing to a more just future. Department in academia that centre on engaging in social justice often include acknowledging and addressing forms of oppression with expressed commitment. For example, Brock University demonstrates through their Social Justice Research Institute's statement their primary mission is "to create and mobilize knowledge that addresses contemporary social problems, opens pathways to progressive social change, and ultimately, helps to build a more just society" (Brock Univeristy, 2020). What is absent from this statement is the need to shift the source of where the majority of epistemological perspectives are sourced from, particularity in social justice. Without an expressed commitment to elevate and map voices that belong to marginalized identities (including racialized, Indigenous, those belonging to LGBQT+, disability, and migrant communities), there is erasure of academia's history of failing to map and centre these knowledges. Engaging and executing research projects oriented towards a goal of contributing to social justice so that the research is aligned with elevating and mapping the voices of marginalized identities onto political landscapes. Engaging in the concept of Imagination supports the process of mapping the knowledge and voices of marginalized identities onto political landscapes contributes to create a more just society (Khasnabish, 2014). "Imagination as Method" is a tool to incorporate this process into the method of qualitative research in the aim of contributing to more just society (Hayes, Sameshima, & Watson, 2014).

This chapter provides a critical analysis of the qualitative research method "Imagination as Method" beginning with a brief orientation to the concept of Imagination in theory. Following an orientation to the concept of Imagination, the components that structure "Imagination as Method", including "Play of Signs", "Mythopoesis", and "Values", is explored. This chapter addresses limitations and considerations of Imagination and concludes by exploring how

Imagination as a methodology may be used in qualitative research with the goals of enacting a "more just, abundant and connected global" (Hayes, Sameshima, & Watson, 2014) that centers knowledge from historically marginalized communities.

2   A Brief Genealogy of Imagination

In this chapter, the concept of Imagination is drawn on by the works of Arjun Appadurai who shapes Imagination as a "faculty that informs the daily lives of ordinary people in myriad ways" rather than a "matter of individual genius, escapism from ordinary life, or just a dimension of aesthetics" (2000, p. 6). While Imagination is a system used to maintain control and discipline over citizens through structures such as the states and markets, Imagination also has the capacity to produce the local as a spatial fact and motivate social movements that span national borders (Lee, 2011). In this capacity, Imagination may be engaged in to "consider migration, resist state violence, seek social redress, and design new forms of civic associations and collaboration, often across national borders" (Appadurai, 2000). The Black Lives Matter (BLM) movement that has developed into global protests and action is an example of engagement in Imagination as a tool of social justice that transcends the spatial of the local and manifests globally. The movement originated in the United States in 2013 and momentum accelerated following police violence that resulted in the murders of Breanna Taylor, Nina Pop, Tony McDade and George Floyd in 2020 (Black Lives Matter ™, 2020; The Okra Project, 2020). The social media hashtag, "#BlackLivesMatter" or "#BLM" that the movement developed from transcends the face value of meaning of the phrase, and instead invites the engager to imagine a world where Black liberation exists and the power structure of white supremacy are eradicated (Black Lives Matter ™, 2020).

Imagination has been theorized as a concept; Imagination as Method (hereafter referred to as IAM) builds upon the concept of Imagination to explore how this concept may be utilized as method in ethnographic research to imagine a more "just, abundant and connected future" (Hayes, Sameshima, & Watson, 2014; Appadurai, 2000). IAM guides the researcher in structuring their methodology to explore "what could be" in order to transcend an over saturated production of "what is" or "desert of real" that ethnographic research is often limited within (Zizek, 2002; Hayes, Sameshima, & Watson, 2014). Identifying a gap in ethnography to explore "what could be" in contrast to an over saturated production of "what is", IAM enables the researcher to reframe the nature of method. Ethnography has a tradition of restricting participants

to the role of subjects, "rarely considered worth citing as part of one's intellectual grounding" (Cruz, 2008). Situating research within "what is" maintains a
complicity to continue engaging in dominating social and political systems of
power. Engaging in ethnographic futurities involves the researcher engaging in
a continuing process of grappling with what constitutes knowledge and evaluation of epistemologies (Cruz, 2008). Shifting research and research method
to frame "what could be" using IAM has the capacity to invest in futurities that
imagine a more "just, abundant and connected future" (Hayes, Sameshima, &
Watson, 2014).

A gap in mapping futurities that centre the knowledges of those who
Imagine a more "just, abundant and connected future" for marginalized identities is resistance from those who wish to uphold the status quo. Black theorists
such as Angela Davis and Robyn Maynard have called for defunding or abolishment of the police and prison systems as these systems are disproportionally
violent towards Black people, as well as Indigenous identities and people of
colour (Maynard & Palmater, 2020; 8TOABOLITION, 2020). Many politicians,
in particular white politicians and their followers, have opposed these ideas as
they connote the idea of the abolishment of these institutions as a threat to
their own safety, or deny systemic racism and anti-Indigeneity entirely (Davis,
2020; Palacios, 2016; Maynard & Palmater, Robyn Maynard on Police Anti-Black
Racism and Violence, 2020). Police and prisons are a product of white, colonial
imagination and through the demonstrated resistance to explore defunding or
abolishing police, there is a failure to map the epistemological perspective of
Black theory and knowledge, or Black Imagination onto political landscapes
(Palacios, 2016). Simultaneously, this also reflects the depth of white supremacy in political and social systems, and both the resistance to elevate Black
(or Indigenous and racialized identities) epistemological perspective and
Imagination while clinging to the status quo of white supremacy, settler colonial, capitalist power structures (Palacios, 2016).

In developing the methodology of Imagination, the authors look at
Imagination in research as a concept providing a context for understanding
of culture and society. As researchers, the authors provide an idea of a "Global
Socius", encouraging exploration of ways to look at society in reaction to the possibility of a shift in global consciousness. The global socius is a set of ideas that
support and create the possibility to understand and imagine an individual's
place within the nature of the global rather than limiting futurities or action to
the local or national. This positions a counter discourse to dominating epistemological perspectives on Imagination through mapping epistemological perspectives globally, rather than centering the global North. While movements
that action for social justice issues such as human rights and labour rights may

manifest at a local level, the motives or actions of these movements encapsulate social issues that transcend local or national borders. Many Black and Indigenous historians have recorded genealogies both locally and in diasporas. These knowledges and counter discourses exist, but there is resistance by dominating powers of white supremacy, settler-colonialism and capitalism to map Black, Indigenous and Migrant knowledge onto political landscapes (Maynard & Palmater, Robyn Maynard on Police Anti-Black Racism and Violence, 2020; Foucault M., 2003). Engaging in Imagination as a tool of social justice positions the researcher to explore mapping Black, Indigenous and Migrant knowledges on the political landscape not just at a local level, but globally.

In this critical analysis of Imagination of Method, the Queer of Colour critique (as coined by Roderick Ferguson in *Aberrations in Black: Toward a Queer of Colour Critique* (2004)) is employed to provide a critique around the concepts of "Utopia" and "Global Socius", which are identified by Hayes, Sameshima, & Watson (2014) as a potential outcome from employing IAM. Queer of Colour critique (Ferguson, 2003) is implemented through engagement with work developed by Queer theorists of colour such as Sara Ahmed's *Queer Phenomenology* (2006), Jose Esteban Munoz's *Disidentifications* (1999) and *Cruising Utopia* (2009) and Christina Sharpe's *In the Wake: On Blackness and Being* (2016) The authors mentioned do not connect to ideas of "Queer Utopia" in their work on IAM; and in order to centre ideas, writing and voices that have historically and continue to be marginalized in academia, this chapter centres Black, Indigenous and Queer of Colour scholarship and theorization.

In their article outlining IAM, Hayes, Sameshima, & Watson (2014) reframe several components about the nature of method using Imagination through challenging methodologies and epistomologies in qualiative research. Components of IAM delineated include "Play of Signs", "Mythoposies and Ethnographic Narratives", and examination of "Values" that researchers bring to work. These three introduced concepts around methodology and epistemology as fundementals to executing IAM will be explored and critqued using Queer of Colour theory (Ferguson, 2004).

Labels such as, but not limited to "Queer", have historically been used to mark bodies that transcend hegemonic identity markers such as white, male, cis, hetero, able, and financially secure. Identity labels are engaged as a method of classification, but also weaponized against identities to mark this transcending from hegemonic identity, however, marginalized identities have reclaimed and repurposed these labels as a way to engage in "reverse discourse"-discourses that are formed as constructions against dominant discourses (Foucault, 1980). "Queer" research methods are inherently queer in the way they are applied, or "query" the method or research rather than being developed under a label of "queer" (Brown & Nash, 2016, pp. 4,8), and engaging with queer theorists of colour not only centres voices that have historically been silenced in academia, but also brings an encompassed perspective to theory which cannot be provided by voices that have been traditionally centred in academia. This also aligns with the orientation of IAM, to imagine "a more just, connected and abundant future" (Hayes, Sameshima, & Watson, 2014), which suggests that we approach a global collective action through mapping marginalized knowledge, realities and culture onto political landscapes (Khasnabish, 2014).

Although IAM as a research method does not overtly situate itself under the label of "Queer", this critical analysis posits that the application and approach of this method is an inherently queer epistemology as it transcends heteronormative, colonial research methods and markers of evaluation. For the purpose of this critical analysis, discussions of epistemology are focused on the philosophical investigation of issues in over-arching theories of knowledge (Hill-Collins, 2003) that relate specifically to method. Imagination supports the mapping of marginalized knowledges and realities on political landscapes (Khasnabish, 2014); it also supports transcending hegemonic colonial methods of development, application, and evaluation which elude queerness as inherent to development of this research method. Using a Queer of Colour theory (Ferguson, 2004) to apply critique to IAM supports the application of an intersectional approach that maps traditionally marginalized knowledges. Without using Queer of Colour theory (Ferguson, 2004) there is a tendency to maintain the interests of colonial culture and this fails to orient futurities that align with the concept of the global socius.

3   Methodology and Epistemology

Methodology refers to "the broad principles of how to conduct research and how interpretive paradigms (encompassing interpretive frameworks used to explain phenomena) are to be applied" (Hill-Collins, 2003, p. 252). The authors of IAM explicate "methodologies and epistemologies" of ethnography have guided a mythos situated in the scientific tradition. This draws attention to examining practices in scientific and research fields to consider the ways in which discourse guides researchers to determine the development or structure and finding of their work and the biases that effect execution and finding (Hodges, Martiminakis, McNaughton, & Whitehead, 2014). While this critical analysis does not delve deeply into Foucauldian analysis, it is relevant to consider the way discourse around research and genealogy of research often determines how research is executed. Discourse around research and genealogy of

research implicate the means through which data is interpreted and how findings are presented (Hodges, Martiminakis, McNaughton, & Whitehead, 2014).

In academia, methods and prescribed techniques or strategies for gathering, organizing and analysing data are traditionally structured, rigid in process
and influenced by white, settler-colonial values through dominating discourse.
Power plays an important part in the distribution of knowledge, not only in
who can access knowledge, but whose knowledge is considered valuable
(Torres & Nyaga, 2016). A method of enacting colonial violence is manifested
through the refusal to map marginalized knowledge onto political landscapes
through the action of erasure.

Those executing the research and analysis of data are not neutral figures;
the identity of researches influences imposition of values, experience and
engrained structural perspectives that vary based on components of intersectional identities (Hayes, Sameshima, & Watson, 2014). Decolonizing, queering,
Indigenizing and untethering oneself from whiteness embedded in epistemologies embedded in research methods is an on-going grappling with what constitutes knowledge and what are the methods used to collect knowledge and
have it established as fact (Cruz, 2008).

Science and research are socio-political acts (Hayes, Sameshima, & Watson,
2014, p. 40). Research is often conducted within academia with the intention of
improving social conditions. However, we must consider that the institutions
funding research projects are inherently political as academic institutions are
extensions of the state, and have been constructed and are rooted in white,
settler-colonial values. Although academic institutions often have departments
or faculties that focus on working towards social justice, the state can use work
executed by these factions as a tool to pacify acts of revolution that stem from
marginalized groups who experience oppression from the current structure of
state which favors, white, western, colonial, heteronormative and patriarchal
identities and values (Lorde, 1984; Todorova, 2019). In reaction to acts of revolution and activism, the academic institutions performatively embrace diversity,
equity or social justice, when in fact they are folding these movements under
the umbrella of the hegemonic (Ahmed, Equality and Performance Culture,
2012). Although the authors provide the reader with ways to approach method
which promote imagination in research, they suggest that these methods not
be utilized as separate techniques and strategies, or to place them in an spec-
ified order, but to "ferment the ways of being in the world that are unique to
ethnography" (Hayes, Sameshima, & Watson, 2014, p. 40). This suggestion circles back to an earlier statement, identifying the action of "queering" research
to subvert the traditional structured and rigidness of process that research
method traditionally follows.

4   Play of Signs

In efforts to support thinking differently about the nature of method, the concept of orientating ourselves to signs is essential. IAM "Play of Signs" suggests for researchers to play with the "phenomenon by which the sign and the signified integrate consciousness with the material world" (Hayes, Sameshima, & Watson, 2014, p. 41). In IAM, a sign is described as consisting of two parts- a provided example is an "Open" sign that a shop might use, with the word "Open" consisting as the "signifier" and the "signified" being that the shop is open for business (Hayes, Sameshima, & Watson, 2014, p. 41). Signs do not have to be words however, a traffic light is also an example of a sign in the colours (yellow, green, red) being the signifiers and the movement of traffic (yield, go, stop) representing the signified. Or perhaps an open door signifies that we are to enter with the position of door being signifier and openness of the position that we are to enter, which also indicates that we are to enter. The authors of IAM identify that there is "slippage" or "play" that already exists between the signifier and signified and allows the possibility of multiple interpretations, but that this liminal space "play" is limited through ethnographic discourse and genealogy – this limitation is a fertile opportunity to implement IAM.

Rather than taking for granted the signifiers that come from objects that signify as dictated by a static cultural-associated data or meaning, "Play of Signs" asks researchers to untether themselves from the engrained culturally data that we associate with signs. Signs are described as a "reduction of being, the life-world of experience, into symbols"; those who encounter signs "rationally categorize and organize" (Hayes, Sameshima, & Watson, 2014, p. 41) and anchor cultural association with signs. In IAM, it is suggested that researchers move play to the foreground of method and loosen associations to signs in order to promote an "imaginative reworking and re-articulation of signs" (Hayes, Sameshima, & Watson, 2014, p. 41). Through approaching or re-orienting the self to signs through "play" the ethnographer may re-imagine or integrate imagination into method that supports constructing "what could be" rather than re-establishing the reality of already existing phenomenon.

Mila Jam, an artist and Trans rights activist launched a campaign to initiate action and awareness to the issue of murder and violence against Black Transgender women. Jam initiated a campaign through her music video, "Masquerade" (2019) and various social media posts. In images and videos Jam is standing naked in various locations and has written "Stop Killing Us" multiple times over her body. Engaging with "Play of Signs" from IAM, both Jam's choice of using her body as a medium and the text "Stop Killing Us" consists of the "signifier"; the "signified" being that action must be taken to stop the

murder and violence against Black Trans women. Loosening oneself from culturally engrained association may be employed through the medium of Jam's
naked body. Black women have documented in academia that in experiencing
racial discrimination and violence, their bodies and existence are inherently
sexualized; one form of violence does not manifest without the other (Kalof,
Eby, Matheson, & Kroska, 2012). Jam's choice of medium contrasts western-
cultural interpretations of Black Trans femme bodies and repositions this
medium as resilience, beauty and power. Without her choice of medium or
playing with signs the signifier would not express the same magnitude of what
is signified. For another medium with Jam's message "Stop Killing Us", "Us"
representing Black Trans women, the signified would not also connotate what
Jam has done with re-orientating the symbol of a Black Trans femme body to
signify resilience, power and of beauty.

One of the reasons ethnographies might struggle with re-orientating and
re-conditioning oneself to objects and signs is that there is a paucity of queering of method among ethnographic research. Sara Ahmed's work on *Queer
Phenomenology* (2006) can assist in drawing parallels, support understanding
and determine limitations with the concepts of "reorientation" and "play of
signs" as ethnographic method. Much like the authors of IAM elucidate that
we anchor meaning to signs (through culturally engrained process of signified
and signifier), Ahmed suggests that we orient ourselves to objects. However,
our orientation to objects is not something that is engrained through culture,
but that race, gender, ability and class impact how an individual orient themselves to objects and affects the neutrality of objects. Ahmed (2012) uses an
example from Edmund Husserl's work on phenomenology where he theorizes
orientating oneself to objects in a room, such as a writing table. Husserl considers a writing table a neutral object in the room. Ahmed contrasts the neutrality of the writing table through theorizing that a person's orientation to the
table varies based on their identity. Traditionally women are the caretakers of
homes or offices, the writing table actually represents labour in terms of setting up the room so that Husserl (a cis man) can access the table, cleaning the
table and keeping the table stocked. From a class perspective, Husserl does not
consider the labour that went into constructing the table. From a race perspective, Husserl has the privilege of accessing the writing table as education has
historically and continues to be accessible to white identities. From an ability
perspective, the table is orientated to those who are "able" bodied and therefore signifies that it is the able bodied who may participate in academia.

Parallels can be drawn in the process of engaging in disorientation and "play
of signs". Our associations and relationship to objects and signs are culturally
embedded (as signs are often objects themselves or appear on objects). Just as

identity politics and power relations are structured into hegemonic culture, there is reason to consider identity and power dynamics in situating relationship to signs and objects or engaging an intersectional lens. Phenomenology within queer studies supports emphasizing the lived experience of queers, the "intentionality of consciousness, the significance of nearness or what is ready at hand and the role of repeated and habitual actions in shaping bodies and worlds" (Ahmed, Queer Phenomenology, 2006, p. 2). Emphasis of the lived experience creates considerations for an ethnographer engaging in playing of signs. It is difficult for a white, cis-hetero, able bodied person to transcend engrained anchored "signed" and "signified" components of signs when they are unable to grasp the ways slippage antecedent through power relations directed out of a white, western colonialist rule. This necessitates considerations to who will be developing method in research as academia is an extension of a white colonial state structure and centres white, western colonial knowledge which are maintained structurally in academia and research. Research will need to shift to represent identities whose knowledge and culture has not been centred in academia and shift away from dominance of a white colonial lens to promote the global collective.

5   Mythopoiesis and Ethnographic Fiction

Mythopoiesis are the purpose and outcome of "play of signs". Using the definition from researchers Leonard and Willis in Hayes, Sameshima, & Watson (2014), Mythopoiesis are defined as actioning the construction of stories and narratives through "activating the imagination within an ethical movement to define and provide meaning to our place in the world" (p. 42). Mythopoiesis are introduced as a method to action the gap in imagining futurity that transcends the dominant narratives. In partnership with Ethnographic Fiction, Mythopoiesis provide the ability to imagine new myths and come up with stories and narratives to share, in action of contributing hope. The authors of IAM argue that what is missing in ethnography is the "potential to generate new ethnographies that offer the promise of a world that is abundant, just and connected" (Hayes, Sameshima, & Watson, 2014).

   In the process of creating new mythopoesis ethnographers are engaging in "play of signs" along with developing narratives and stories in a "generation of a place not yet, or a space other than but intimately connected to the here and now" (Hayes, Sameshima, & Watson, 2014, p. 42). The point of connecting to new narratives to "the here and now" is significant in developing queer futurities. In an essay *Queer Sociality and Other Sexual Fantasies* (2011), author Juana

María Rodríguez focuses on theory developed by José Muñoz that in working towards Utopia there must always be casting of ideas in cohesion with a critique or constant analysis of the present . Reflecting on the argument from the authors of IAM, ethnography is saturated in "the desert of real" suggesting that ethnography has done enough of what has been or what is, and instead needs to develop what could be. However, because hegemonic narratives and academia have traditionally mandated a "white possessive" (Moreton-Robinson, 2015) over what is, has been and could be, there must be consideration that perhaps "the desert of real" is restrictive to a white (or white-adjacent) "desert" of real. In order for Mythopoiesis to emerge, we are imagining a future of a "place not yet" that is still intimately connected to the here and now; and a deeper understanding of the here and now (and past) that is narrated outside the white possessive requires further development.

Ethnographic fiction works with mythopoesis to disrupt personal stories and identify discrepancies in what is taken as granted for truth. Identifying discrepancies in taken for granted truths can provide tools to imagine what it yet to come and can drive revolution. Through media we are constantly exposed to narratives that imagine impending societal global doom. Engaging IAM in creating and developing new myths through troubling dominant narratives positions us to question what could be in contrast to these dominant narratives and creates futurities that are driven by hope.

Black, Indigenous and Queers of Colour have already engaged in this process as theorized by Jose Muñoz in his book, *Cruising Utopia and Disidentifications* (2009). The artists and performers Muñoz features in his book counter white imagination not by rejecting or aligning with or against the exclusionary white imagination but through renegotiating the signs, mythopoesis and values of white or hegemonic imagination. In this process of reimagining or renegotiating orientation to hegemonic culture, the featured performers and producers of art in Muñoz's book are imagining possibilities of what could be (specifically in terms of race, citizenship, gender and sexuality) in moving towards a more just, abundant and connected planet.

Christina Sharpe's work, *In the Wake: On Blackness and Being* (2016) reflects a work that provides narrative outside the hegemonic or white imagination of Black being in the "wake" of slavery in past and current contexts. Using slippage, Sharpe approaches "wake" as a sign and uses the various definitions: in the wake of a ship, in vigil and to rise from slumbers to shape the narrative she provides framing what survives despite a "climate" of white supremacy and antiblackness. In the development of mythopoesis, Sharpe uses ethnographic fiction to challenge what is taken for granted in order to drive forward new possibilities through situating anti-Blackness and white supremacy as a climate which normalizes the de-valuation of Black lives. This narrative might be described by the authors of IAM as "the desert of real", however the narrative produced by Sharpe counters dominant narratives and creates positions for emerging mythopoesises. This circles back to Muñoz's thought that in working towards Utopia and in casting ideas of what could be, there must be cohesion with a critique and constant analysis of the present. If "the desert of real" is dominated by white, colonial, narratives from the global North then there is a difficulty in casting ideas of what could be without an analysis that challenges dominant narratives we take for granted. Sharpe's construction of "the wake" as a narrative and addressing "wake work" (such as Black annotation and Black reduction as orthographies) as "sites for artistic production, resistance consciousness and possibility" in the Black diaspora (2016, p. 126) offers imagination of ways forward and of being that promote a 'just, connected and abundant future'. Sharpe's work exemplifies that in casting new mythopoesises there is a need to connect to the past, here and now in casting Queer of Colour futurities.

6   Values

In execution of their work, researchers and ethnographers bring values and bias into method, execution and analysis of research. This is unavoidable, and the authors of IAM identify that ideally the researchers engage in reflecting on and identify values they bring and resulting biases that will impact the research process. Ethnography as practiced through IAM transcends acts of interpretation and research and instead suggests the researcher engage in the service of imagining and generating a world we wish to live in. The authors of IAM express that in engaging in IAM there needs to be a standard for researchers to interrogate the biases and values they bring to the research project. In this assessment of "Values" as a component of IAM, there is potential to develop an analysis or overview of the reflection of values in IAM so that that researchers are engaging in on-going reflexivity. Reflexivity tools, such as the Social Identify Map developed by Danielle Jacobson and Nida Mustafa (2019), position researchers to "explicitly identify and reflect on their social identity" and provide a guide for researchers to methodologically reflect and be reflexive on their social location and the cultural values and biases that are often integrated in relation to social location and position (Jacobson & Mustafa, 2019). In order to maintain an interrogation of values, researchers need to engage in self-reflection to address culturally engrained biases and values, and instead contribute values that align with "the kind of world we wish ourselves to be in" (Hayes, Sameshima, & Watson, 2014).

The authors of IAM suggest that there is no prescribed set of values that researcher should bring into their research but that researchers should bring values that are conductive to an abundant, hopeful and vibrant society and that critical ethnography proceeds from values of social justice, activism, equity and solidarity with mentions of prioritized values from other theorists such as autonomy, freedom, community, compassion and activism (Hayes, Sameshima, & Watson, 2014, p. 42). As much of the world is exposed to white, settler-colonial, capitalistic structures, if researchers have not already spent significant time exposing selves to knowledges, ideas and cultures that counter these systems it will create barriers to imagining what could be as unlearning hegemonic culture and white supremacy that comes along with these narratives requires long-term cognitive curriculum (DeGue, et al., 2014). Reflecting on values and biases that researchers bring to study is an action that will always remain as a necessity on the horizon in research. Taking time to unsettle oneself from what they believe to be true or valuable will contribute to an expansion of ideas and compassion towards others. Research and ethnography are saturated with white, settler-colonial, capitalistic ways of being. The voices of those historically marginalized in academia are continually advocating for authenticity of knowledge and knowledge production indicating that academia and higher-education institutions continue to value knowledge production that falls in line with values of the institution.

7   Limitations and Considerations

Centering voices that belong to identities of traditionally marginalized groups is at the foreground of enacting IAM in ethnography to explore a future in the global socius. However, a challenge remains in centering these voices. The authors of IAM state that ethnography is stymied in a "desert of real" and that ethnography needs to start imagining "what could be". A limitation to this argument is that the "desert of real" does not transcend a colonial lens. Colonialism has actively and passively suppressed knowledges and knowledge production of Black, Indigenous and migrant identities as a tool of colonial violence. Identities of traditionally marginalized groups and those that have encountered colonial violence for several past centuries may not have the luxury of a saturated ethnographic research pool. Imagining "what could be" could simultaneously occur while exploring "what is" or "what was", and the possibility to create mythopoesis and engage in ethnographic fiction supports ethnography to explore "what could be". Sharpe, Muñoz and Rodriguez's works explore Black, Indigenous and Queer of colour knowledge and lived realities in past and in present tenses so that Black, Indigenous and Queer of colour futurities can take shape.

White, western-European, colonial hetero-patriarchal structures and systems have passively and actively suppressed languages, history, narratives and culture from Indigenous, Black or migrant identities under structures of colonial violence in order to maintain a white-supremacist colonial rule. For example, this form of colonial violence takes shape through academia, where the "desert of real" continues to suppress the voices of marginalized identities in the academy. While higher-education institutions have departments or faculties that focus on colonial violence, social justice or "white-studies"; colonial knowledge is still centred across higher-education institutions continuing the process of suppressing knowledge from Black, Indigenous and theorists or researchers of colour (Hill-Collins, 2003).

Displaced or lost narratives as a result of colonial violence contribute to a genealogical gap that would inform Indigenous ethnographies at the local and in the diaspora (Moreton-Robinson, 2015; Sharpe, 2016). Futurities are theorized and explored by Black and Indigenous and theorists of colour, but an ethnographic "desert of real" under a colonial lens, combined with on-going colonial violence stifles and suppresses mythopoesis, narrative and futurities that centre Black, Indigenous and Queer of Colour theory:

> Futurity has never been given to queers of color, children of color, or other marginalized communities that live under the violence of state and social erasure, a violence whose daily injustices exceed the register of a politics organize solely around sexuality, even as they are enmeshed within a logic of sexuality that is always already racialized through an imagined-ideal of citizen subject.
>
> (RODRÍGUEZ, 2011, p. 333)

Indigenous and diaspora narratives, mythopoesises and ethnographic inquiries may still need space and time to develop as futurities and are easier to imagine once the past and "here and now" have been explored and unpacked in further depth.

Further consideration of academia and colonial institutional roles in research expand past a saturated "desert of real" under a colonial lens, and into considerations of standards around knowledge production. Researchers and their research are not only associated with institutions, studies are executed based on approval of the ethical guidelines or boards of the academic institutions and a reflection of the values of the institution. Higher-education institutions are often dependant on state funding to maintain existence; compelling higher-education institutions to align with the values of the state. Western-European colonization has systemically rooted power in academia throughout the global South and North, and manifested a global standard for what consists of "academia" (Cruz, 2008). This is not to suggest that researchers whose work is produced through higher-education institution is of a colonial lens, but rather that there are barriers in bringing authenticity to knowledge and realities that escape western euro-centric colonial standards.

8   Employing Imagination as Method in Research

Mila Jam, whose work was explored earlier in this chapter, reflects on Black trans identity in an interview with *Advocate Magazine* (2020). She frames trans-identities as being a gift and poses a question that asks the reader to reflect on "what could be"; "Queer and trans people, we really do have something that's a gift, that we can share about the human experience. Why can't our culture celebrate that?" (Jam, 2020). This question not only exemplifies "what could be" but simultaneously challenges ethnographic fiction and engaging in new mythopoesis. *Advocate Magazine* (2020). She frames trans-identities as being a gift and poses a question that asks the reader to reflect on "what could be": "Queer and trans people, we really do have something that's a gift, that we can share about the human experience. Why can't our culture celebrate that?" (Jam, 2020). This question not only exemplifies "what could be" but simultaneously challenges ethnographic fiction and engaging in new mythopoesis.

Situating questions that dislodge colonial knowledge and imagine futurities that usurps colonial violence have been posed for the past several decades. Indigenous scholar Brooks directly engages IAM by challenging knowledge producers to reflect "what happens when indigenous narratives are not just present but prioritized?" (Brooks, 2008). While euro-centric colonial higher-education institutions have the tendency to implement diversity policies or equity offices, these are often performative measures and do not actually unsettle whiteness, colonialism and heteronormativity within these institutions (Ahmed, Equality and Performance Culture, 2012). Brook's question reflects a challenge for academia and scholarship to go beyond performative equity and centre Indigenous knowledges in the academy while simultaneously pivoting towards the process of IAM to imagine what could be through employing creation of mythopoesis.

Questions inspired by futurity that are executed through IAM can take form through transnational literacy. "Transnational literacy" is a concept that has capacity as a critical and pedagogical methodology to "grasp contemporary cultural phenomena, termed globalization and transnational" through comparative literacy and cultural studies (Lee, 2011). Transnational literacy can support imagination as a social force that transcends national boundaries to foster global communities. The influence of academia produced in the Global North globally results in limiting the development of new ideas or futurities. Transnational literacy positions researchers to explore knowledge not just from the Global North or South, but to orient themselves to an array of global knowledges and to centre knowledges or research enacted by the most marginalized voices. A relevant consideration to address is that knowledge production and discourse exists in forms beyond academic literacy and that research cannot just rely on critical analyses that is produced at an academic level, but that also with knowledge production beyond academia.

Theorists and practitioners in the late 1970s-90s moved beyond action research into an explicit analysis of the relation of science to social inequality and radical social change. Action in research shifted toward transformation of reality and to orient researchers not exclusively towards "what is" but towards "what could be" while encompassing social justice goals through Participatory Action Research (PAR) (Fine, et al., 2004). In a research essay that outlines a PAR project titled, "Participatory Action Research: From Within and Beyond Prison Bars" (Fine, et al., 2004), IAM is encapsulated through the partnership of authoring and executing a research project that centres the knowledges and realities of women in incarceration institutions. The partnership takes place between educational leaders within and outside the incarceration facility. IAM is enacted is through the centering and promotion of knowledge that expands beyond the credentials attributed by dominating systems of academia. The PAR project explored the development of a college program within an incarceration facility in the United States that had seen its previous program cancelled by the Clinton era. The women detained in the incarceration facility designed and executed their own academic program so that participation from every constituency was a core element. The motivation behind this was to simultaneously emphasize the value and fragility of the program (Fine, et al., 2004). The result is that women who participated in this program re-imagined themselves as agents who make choices and engage in action as makers of change and designers of the future. The project actions incorporating the values, beliefs and behaviours of communities that are marginalized in academia into praxis and methodology (Fine, et al., 2004). IAM is evoked through PAR in that there is a reciprocation of exchange in knowledge and a collective partnership in developing and enacting futurities. Regardless of the researcher's status in academia, knowledge brought to the project is regarded as legitimate and the marginalized knowledge is centered. This was actioned in the study through centering leaders of academia detained in the incarceration facility in development and as authors of the research project. In exchange for participating in the study, the researchers and participants were equipped with tools to continue to create and develop a "legacy of inquiry, process of change and material resources to enable transform(action)" (Fine, et al., 2004) that is developed by and centre's marginalized knowledge, culture and way of being.

9   Moving Forward

As this chapter has been written, a global pandemic as a result of COVID-19 has occurred that has profoundly shifted our ways of being and social interaction. In aims to flatten the curve of infection and promote the safety of the most vulnerable identities, calls have been made for people to severely limit physical interaction with one another, often resulting in isolation or quarantine with those who share a household. This has not only affected our intimate social relations, but the way we enact and engage in social justice actions and advocacy. Action by the state has manifested in a way that prioritizes the well-being of those who identity and values align with colonial values and interests of the economic institutions. The actions of the state differ from actions of grassroots organizations such as Maggie's Sex Worker Action Project, ClimateJusticeTO™ and RisingTideNA™ who have adjusted the direction of the collectives to align action in the interests of the global socius. The concept of the global socius consistently moves, shifts and transcends boundaries and functions as a self-organized collective movement. While uncertainty is abundant and isolation can be lonely, these grassroots organization have taken this opportunity to create new mythopoesis of hope, abundance and connection that counter narratives saturating dominant media. Reflecting on the values of the organizations, grassroots collectives have altered courses and mediums of action in order to centre the well-being of the most marginalized while continuing actioning for causes whose attention have been eclipsed in the wake of the pandemic, on a global scale. As a result of continuing colonial and white supremacy violence against Black lives, the Black Lives Matter movement and supporters have asserted that the public health crisis of anti-Black racism is in need of critical intervention. Global action in solidarity, and narratives of Black liberation that eradicate white supremacy have placed pressure on social and political structures to being mapping Black theory onto political landscapes. Employing the principles of IAM as an ethnographic method of research in examining the actions of the fore mentioned grassroots organizations during this time exemplifies imagining what could be in "a more just, abundant and connected future" while grounding and reflecting on the "here and now" in a way that centres the well-being of a collective.

References

8TOABOLITION. (2020). *Abolitionist policy changes to demand from your city officials.* Retrieved from 8TOABOLITION: https://www.8toabolition.com/why.

Ahmed, S. (2006). *Queer phenomenology.* Durham, NC: Duke University Press.

Ahmed, S. (2012). Equality and performance culture. In S. Ahmed, *On being included: Racism and diversity in institutional life* (pp. 83–112). Durham, NC: Duke University Press.

Appadurai, A. (2000). Grassroots, globalization and the research imagination. *Public Culture* 12(1): 1–19.

Black Lives Matter ™. (2020). *About.* Retrieved from Black Lives Matter ™: https://black-livesmatter.com/about/.

Brock University. (2020). *Social justice research institute: Home.* Retrieved from Brock University: https://brocku.ca/social-justice-research-institute/.

Brooks, L. (2008). *The common pot: Recovery of land in the North East.* Minneapolis, MN: University of Minnesota.

Brown, K., & Nash, C. J. (2016). Intoduction. In K. Brown, & C. J. Nash, *Queer methods and methodologies: Intersecting queer theories and social science research.* Milton Park, Abingdon, UK: Routledge.

Cruz, M. R. (2008). What if I just cite Graceiela?: Working toward decolonizing knowledge through critical ethnography. *Qualitative Inquiry* 14 (4): 651–658.

Davis, A. (2020, June 12). Angela Davis on abolition, calls to defund police, toppled racist statues & voting in 2020 election. *Democracy Now*, https://www.democracynow.org/2020/6/12/angela_davis_on_abolition_calls_to. (A. Goodman, Interviewer).

DeGue, S., Valle, L., Holt, M., Massetti, G., Matjasko, J., & Tharp, A. (2014). A systemic review of primary prevention strategies for violence perpetration. *Aggresion and Violent Behavior* 19 (4): 346–362.

Fine, M., Torre, M. E., Boudin, K., Bowen, I., Clark, J., Hylton, D., Martinez, M., Missy, Roberts, R. A., Smart, P., & Upegui, D. (2004). Participatory action research: From within and beyond prison bars. In P. Camic, J. Rhodes, & L. Yardley (Eds.), *Qualitative research in psychology: Expanding perspectives in methodology and design* (pp. 173–198). Washington, D.C: American Psychological Association.

Ferguson, R.A. (2003) Abberations in Black: Toward a Queer of Color critique. Minneapolis: University of Minnesota Press.

Foucault, M. (1980). *The history of sexuality (vol 1)*. New York: Vintage.

Foucault, M. (2003). Nietzsche, genealogy, history. In P. Rabinow & N.S. Rose. (Eds.), *The essential Foucault: Selection from the essential works of Foucault* (pp. 43-57). New York: The New York Press.

Hayes, M. T., Sameshima, P., & Watson, F. (2014). Imagination as method. *International Journal of Qualitative Methods* 14 (1): 36–52.

Hill-Collins, P. (2003). Toward an Afrocentric feminist epistemology. In Y.S. Lincoln, *Turning points in qualitative research* (pp. 47–72). Walnut Creek, CA: Altimira Press.

Hodges, B., Martiminakis, M., McNaughton, N., & Whitehead, C. (2014). Medical education. ... meet Michel Foucault. *Medical Education* 48 (6): 563–571.

Jacobson, D., & Mustafa, N. (2019). Social identity map: A reflexivity tool for practicing explicit positionality in critical qualitative research. *International Journal of Qualitative Methods* 18: 1–12.

Jam, M. (2019). Masquerade (Single).New York, NY: Midas Music Inc.

Jam, M. (2020, March 10). Singer Mila Jam on dating, New music, and why being trans is a gift. (J. Masters, Interviewer).

Kalof, L., Eby, K., Matheson, J., & Kroska, R. J. (2012). The influence of race and gender on student self-reports of sexual harassment by college professors. *Gender and Society* 15 (2): 282–302.

Khasnabish, A. (2014). Subterranean currents: Research and the radical imagination in the age of austerity. *Studies in Social Justice* 8 (1): 45–65.

Lee, E. Y.-H. (2011). Globalization, pedigogical imagination, and transnational literacy. *CLCWeb: Comparative Literature and Culture*, <https://doi.org/10.7771/1481-4374.1705>.

Lorde, A. (1984). The master's tools will never dismantle the master's house. In A. Lorde, *Sister, Outsider* (pp. 110–113). New York: Crossing Press.

Maynard, R. (2017). *Policing Black lives: State violence in Canada from slavery to the present.* Black Point, Nova Scotia: Fernwood Publishing.

Maynard, R. (2020, June 8th). Robyn Maynard on police anti-Black racism and violence. *Warrior life by Pam Palmater.* (P. Palmater, Interviewer).

Maynard, R. (2020, June 8). Robyn Maynard: Police violence is a legacy of Canada's history of racial and economic injustice. (H. Samphir, Interviewer).

Moreton-Robinson, A. (2015). *The White possessive.* Minneapolis, MN: University of Minnesota.

Muñoz, J. E. (1999). *Disidentifications: Queers of color and the performance of politics.* Minneapolis, MN: University of Minnesota Press.

Muñoz, J. E. (2009). *Cruising utopia.* New York: New York University Press.

Ontario Institute for Studies in Education. (2020). *Mission statement.* Retrieved from Social Justice Education: https://www.oise.utoronto.ca/sje/About/Mission_Statement.html.

Palacios, L. (2016). Challenging convictions: Indigenous and Black race-radical feminists theorizing the carceral state and abolitionist praxis in the United Staes and Canada. *Meridians* 15 (1): 137–165.

Rodríguez, J. M. (2011). Queer sociality and other sexual fantasies. *GLQ: A Journal of Lesbian and Gay Studies* 17 (2–3): 31–348.

Sharpe, C. (2016). *In the wake: On Blackness and being.* Durham, NC: Duke University Press.

The Okra Project. (2020). *Home.* Retrieved from The Okra Project: https://www.theokraproject.com/.

Todorova, M. (2019, September 25). Theorizing violence, power and education. Toronto: Cont.

Torres, R. A., & Nyaga, D. (2016). Discussion of power through the eyes of the margins: Praxis of post-Colonial Aeta indigenous women healers in the Philippines. *International Journal of Asia Pacific Studies* 12 (2): 31–56.

Zizek. (2002). *Welcome to the desert of real.* New York: Verso.

CHAPTER 11

Black Afrocentric Methodologies

Beyond Colour-Coated Investigation

Dionisio Nyaga

1   Introduction

This chapter seeks to engage with Blackness and the art of doing research among/with Black communities. While a lot has been written on Black and Blackness (Dei, 2018; Gilroy, 1993, 2010; Hall & Ghazoul, 2012; McKittrick, 2006; Mercer, 1994; Nyaga, 2019; Walcott, 2003), little has been discussed on "how" research is done among Black communities. While available literature places Black research within an Afrocentric framework/canon (Hlela, 2018; Reviere, 2001), little is discussed beyond the canonization of African-centred research. I argue that canonization operates within a gendered framework of knowledge creation. While systems of canonization bring order on the "how" of Black and Afrocentric research, this article engages with canons as the colonial, gendered operation and manipulation of Black bodies. Black and Blackness is complex and complicated and at no one time can the tools and theories of investigation unravel the mystery of the jungle that is Black. I argue that to do Black studies is to engage with its complexities beyond colour coating the "how" of research.

This chapter therefore is an engagement with how Black experience can affect research and subsequently policy. I submit that Black research is temporal, unending, and an exercise that more so acknowledges Black historical experiences rather than understands their pain. To understand Black pain is itself a placement of knowledge before ethics. This chapter seeks to underline that Black research is more of an ethical prerogative that it is about sifting for a truth into Black experience. Since the rationale for research continues to be policy oriented, Black research should not be just about policy but rather placed within community development. Results of any Black research should not only be for policy change but also be returned to communities to help them reflect on themselves based on what they provided. From this perspective, research becomes a critical reflexive exercise and for which real social change can be found and established (George, 2017).

I argue that Black research for policy should break away from its instrumental orientation and instead be a process of mental insubordination. I argue that

research should be a process of breaking colonial mental walls that are meant
to mark Black and Blackness inferior and are unable to tell its story (Mbembe,
2016; Wehbi, 2017). If research is about the search for knowledge, then studies on Black/African bodies have never been a process of knowledge production but a presentation of difference between the West and the Global South
(Wehbi, 2017). Speaking of Western studies on Africa, Shipley et al. (2010) say

> One of the dominant ways of accounting for the African present was pre-
> sentism. Presentism was neither a method nor a theory. It was a way of
> defining and reading African life forms that relied on a series of anec-
> dotes and negative statements or simply turned to statistical indices to
> measure the gap between what Africa was and what we were told it ought
> to be. This way of reading always ended up constructing Africa as a patho-
> logical case, as a figure of lack. It was a set of statements that told us what
> Africa was not. It never told us what it actually was. In that sense—and
> this the second point—presentism was not a form of knowledge as such;
> rather it was a model of misrecognition and dis figuration. It operated by
> segmentation of time, excision of the past and deferral of the future. It
> was not interested in the points of articulation between different layers
> of African social existence. In short, it was as if to theorize the African
> present required, paradoxically, a shrinking of the social and the political
> and not an expanded idea of these terms or categories. When the social
> was taken into consideration at all, it was always defined as "custom" and
> "tradition"—the routine logic of difference (they are not like us; we are
> not the same) and repetition (they have been and will always remain the
> same) and the foreclosure of the present as such. In short, the belief that
> when it comes to Africa, there is, strictly speaking, nothing to theorize.
> (pp. 656–657)

Knowing that research has been used for misrepresentation (Smith, 2012), this
chapter calls for a misrepresentation of colonial narratives that continue to
mark Africa and Black bodies as Blank slate. African bodies and spaces manifest a conglomerate of histories, cultures, values, and ways of being that needs
to be invested in any research that claims Blackness as its orientation. Black
research should not only be a re-righting of past and present misrepresentation of Blackness but also a process that is steeped in Black histories, values,
and ways of life. I must be cautious to say that while I accept cultures (ways of
life) as fundamental in Black studies, one should not assume that various Black
arts are all the final representation of Blackness. That would be considered
colonial as it has been noted as conserving Black and Blackness. It would also

mean any Black bodies that do not "wear" such cultures are not Black enough, and which would simultaneously mean that such bodies are pathologies. In a nutshell, Black research is not about instrumentalization of knowledge production but rather emotional and ethical engagement with complexities that is Blackness.

Research should not be an art of colonial policy but rather a process of emancipating the psychic self. To do this, research will have to return to its authors. As such, Black and Blackness in research inaugurates a new orientation of the "how" of serving Black communities steeped in Black experiences (with their complex ways). My take on policy goes beyond the current fixed orientation on solving Black people's problems. Such a direction in research and policy problematizes Black communities, reducing them to a solvable "mathematical equation." Such a form of problem solving (read also saving) collapses "Black skin" into templates of knowledge creation rather than engaging the Black communities. To speak of "collapsing" is metaphorical of the ways in which Black storied lives continue die under a neoliberal concept of producing the other as a security problem that needs to be eradicated. Such an eradication is material and symbolic, if the current discussion of Black Lives Matter are anything to go by. This chapter argues that Black research should identify diverse values and ways of being without necessarily arriving at a fixed point as inculcated by "cultural competence."

While cultural competence has defined the "how" of research in multicultural systems (Liu et al., 2004; Worthington et al., 2007), Pon (2009) has critiqued it as steeped in Whiteness, and subsequently an "ontology of forgetting." Paul Gilroy's work reminds us to break beyond traditional colour-coated race-based orientation (read cultural competency) and imagine how current trends informed by technology inform racial bias. If Gilroy's and Pon's findings are anything to go by, the question of Black research should move beyond its traditional "competency sense making" and inscribe the work of technology in discussing Blackness and research. In the age where technology has become the norm in imagining the "how" of making knowledge, it is equally important to be futuristic in imagining Black research. Technology continues be used in analyzing text in major research projects. This has helped save time and labour while simultaneously destroying community lives. Collapsing of human storyline into one truth using research analytical software should be considered an art of genocide, to which scientific research continue to be implicated.

To that end, culturally competent research is a technology of modern-day racism that seeks to look at cultures as fixed problems needing perpetual and stable solutions. Such a culturally fixed operation of research collapses Black bodies through simplification of people's narratives into one universal truth (Danso, 2015). The art of Black cultural reduction and simplification when inducted in an already simplistic Western science is a stark reminder of Black imprisonment (Walcott, 2003). My argument is: If research is to operate under its current colonial grounds that continue to mark Black stories as raw material for capital accumulation, then Black lives will remain ungrievable. The process of grievability is an essential process of engaging with the history of Black lives within and without the contemporary context. To grieve becomes a process of sitting within the discomfort of past ghosts in the present ways of understanding the other (Butler, 2001). To grieve is a process of recognizing the Black bodies as complicated beings that cannot be preserved or reduced to statements or numbers. To grieve Black lives becomes a process of accounting for what has been discounted in research. This is the art of messiness (read messy methodology) that Black research brings to contemporary, fixed, culturally competent research. Black life continues to exist because of its storied self. To erase Black people's stories and praxis in its material and symbolic sense under such a market-based rationalized research regime is genocidal and a testament of ungrievability of Blackness.

This chapter is an Afrocentric Black reflexive exercise on the "how" of doing Black research. The "how" of Black research is not an end of knowing Black research, but instead it is "cyclical" in its orientation and does not provide fixed answers and solutions. The chapter looks at complexities and contradictions of doing Black research/studies while paying attention to Afrocentric research and its prevailing limitations and contradictions. Finally, the chapter concludes with a quick discussion of Black and Blackness in research. The chapter is not a "step by step" way of doing Black research; rather, it attempts to provide some reflexive questions that can help Black researchers Blacken research. To paint research Black is a transformative practice that makes Western research come to terms with Black communities and the atrocities they continue to face under the current colonial research regimes. The death of Black populations the in race-based Tuskegee syphilis experiment is a testament of raced-based research and explains why we need to change how we come to know what we know (Sharma, 2010; Washington, 2006). The chapter breaks away from a normalized conceptualization of Blackness (Walcott, 2003) and transforms what is "Black" ' a research. What we currently have in research is a "Black" culturally informed processed research (simplified story; dead data) which continues to replicate and imprint pain on Black communities (Rusert, 2009). What you expect from "dead data" in terms of policy are solutions that are "dead." Subsequently, what this chapter provides is a deeper and critical discussion beyond the current Black research.

2   Research as an Industrial Complex

In modern day society, the research process among Black communities is covered with blood oozing from simplification of Black communities and their narrative (Washington, 2006). As an educator, I fondly like using the metaphor of meat grinder to make sense of how we distill, refine, and purify Black knowledge and simultaneously commit cultural genocide in Black communities. The current market-oriented research methodology organizes knowledge production like meat production. I apply this metaphor to argue that being a Black man from Africa, my stories line will continuously be reduced to nature and for them to exist and be considered as a sentence they will have to die in the process of becoming. The Black African body's stories are emotional and fall below rational human thinking. According to Mbembe (2016),

> The Negro ... exhibits the natural man in his completely wild and untamed state. We must lay aside all thought of reverence and morality—all that we call feeling—if we would rightly comprehend him. There is nothing harmonious with humanity to be found in this type of character. Hegel then promises himself not to ever mention Africa again, for "it is no historical part of the World; it has no movement or development to exhibit." What we properly understand by Africa, he concludes, "is the Unhistorical, Undeveloped Spirit, still involved in the conditions of mere nature." (p. 91)

My claim is that in the current research process, Black blood must be streamed for knowledge to be produced and for the Black body to have a spirit and a name. The current industry complex depends on Black blood to survive.

I argue that grinding of meat is a process of simplification through the taking away of Black life (read water as life). Of course, blood is made of water (life) but let us imagine the role of "red" in the humanization of the Black other. To think of Black as human is to agree that Black is the new "red" in research. Research for social change is a claim of humanizing how we come to know what we know. This claim means humanizing research to reach the desires of the human in their context. This means returning blood into the mincemeat in ways that give life to our epistemological process of knowledge production. In a nutshell, by grinding (read reduction or simplification as fundamental in scientific/quantitative research) the meat loses life (water is life) and its human side. My wager is that the mincemeat is dead, and which is a fundamental requirement of the neoliberal market.

This chapter argues that the process of knowledge production currently operated in the academy is covered with "Black blood" and claiming cultural competence in such a dark moment of Black history is an implication to Black erasure in research. Note that cultural competence in its current form is marked with Black atrocities. I also look at the academy as the industrial complex that produces knowledge through obliteration and annihilation of Black communities. If you think of quantitative research and the current reliance of software like Statistical Package for the Social Sciences (SPSS) as a form of statistical analysis, then the analogy of the meat grinder makes sense. Recognizing narratives as part of being Black and as an ontological and epistemological requirement, applying such a statistical prerogative in analyzing Black lives is genocidal and has eradicated the blood and water (read life) of Black communities. It is equally interesting how the researcher who may be expected to be the expert in Black research also disappears from the process of knowledge production when the software is applied. This claim helps look at knowledge production as isolating to the researcher as he tried to become the expert while simultaneously obliterating the Black participants. To invoke such a sense is to claim that research within the current neoliberal regime is a form of labour that alienates the self from others, self, the analysis (which is the fundamental place of becoming human), and from the result (Read Karl Marx on labour and alienation). To argue that the software is culturally competent to Blacks and Blackness is epistemologically anti-Black, and colonial. To make sense of this claim, I engage with Marx's alienation of labour (read research).

3 Social Research as an Estrangement

To claim that research is alienating means that the researcher cannot relate with the research subject matter. In phenomenological studies, bracketing is used to distance oneself from the subject matter, in what is assumed as a means of being objective (Padgett, 2017). In a nutshell, we have researchers who want and others who do not want to be connected to what they are researching. There are those who claim objectivity as a fundamental research practice while others believe in subjectivity as a research strength. My wager is that this scholarly conundrum existing in research makes one see the ways in which we are distanced from research and either want to expand the length or shorten the distance.

For a while now, studies have not identified ways in which researchers working in a neoliberal system continue to be objectified and how by internalizing that they eliminate participants from the process of knowledge production. The claims on estrangement help look at research as external to the researcher. To claim that research is a form of labour is to argue through Marx that research is an industrial project in which the researchers lose themselves (read corporately lose) with every production of knowledge. The researcher is framed as a necessary "glue" (read objectified) towards the becoming of his master (read the corporatization of knowledge production). To claim that the researcher is labouring is to identify the ways in which he disappears by allowing himself to become the graveyard of the master's reality. In this instance, the researcher as a labourer is a claim that he is an infrastructural necessity (read means of production) for the exultation and existence of the master. While research alienates the researcher, it exults the profits.

Research as an alienating labour is classed, raced, and gendered. There is a sense in which research interlocks with these social constructions in ways that are symbolically and materially advantageous to the capital. To take such a claim beyond the Marxist analogy of classed labour is to affirm the place of the slave plantation in research. To claim that research (read also labour) alienates the researcher (read worker) from the process means that the current statistical analysis of the data is alienating and not meant to make the researcher as engaging and creative (read deskilling the researcher). To be alienated to this process of making knowledge is to claim that research dehumanizes the researcher by eliminating creativity of the researcher. This claim of dehumanization borrows from Aristotelian conception of a thinking human being.

While thinking has fundamentally been placed within the mind, I argue that it also has a place in the body and that the body exists in the mind. Subsequently, the right to be human is not just the business of the mind but also of the body. This aspect of reclaiming the self from capital death is psychic and continues to be affirmed as a point of research reformation.

This means that while the right to be human sits within a White narrative of being human, I claim that to be alienated in this form of neoliberal research is to lose oneself. This is a corporate death that does not imagine the researcher as creator but rather a ground place of exulting the master. To be lost in this way is also to cease to exist. Your mind and body are replaced by the software (read the master) and in the process the researcher disappears. I also argue that the interface between the body and the mind remain trapped within the prison of the rational and hence objectified, making the process of production of knowledge rationalized and detached from emotions. If that is the case, could this become our point of becoming? Could this form of alienation form our place of return—our inconsolable point of breaking away? My wager is that such a form of return is not self-instigated. It remains within the dictates of grand narratives meant to confirm the master through dissolving our place in knowledge production. Such a form of return will work for the master rather than inform our becoming. Key in this breaking away is to understand the methodology of returning.

To be Black is complex and complicated and cannot be simplified and reduced but rather verbed. Black is fluid (Walcott, 2003) and keeps moving and changing based on time and space (Gilroy, 1993, 2004a, 2004b; Mercer, 1994). The gap that prevails in research is the application of market in Black research. The assumption is that Black is fixable and a fixed thing that can be introspected and made to make sense. There is not a place in the current research regime where Black can make sense based on its context (Mbembe, 2016). The Black must disappear to become part of the dominant grammar of knowledge. To imagine research as a marketplace is to look at the "how" of research as racially devaluing Black bodies as logically broken. Black histories have been and continue to be denied and misplaced as "unbelievable" and as such are dangerous in knowledge production (McKittrick, 2006). The speaking histories of Blackness is a misnomer and unnecessary in knowledge production since it will stretch the margin of what we know and how we know what we know; which in itself is not efficient and economical in the prevailing market rationalities of neoliberal research.

To de-industrialize such a research process is to engage in a reflexive process of disengaging universal rationalism in knowledge production. In social science research, location of self is a fundamental aspect of research that helps researchers to connect with the study they are undertaking, and this reduces this estrangement. But while that is the case, more has been done in terms of critical self-reflection and reflexivity as a place of implicating the self with the research. It is assumed that by attending to the interlocking aspect of oppression and privileges, one can connect more with the study (Thomas, 2008).

To claim that research needs to be Black is to call out the modalities of market (read meat mincer) by inscribing Blackness as a fundamental research methodology. To speak of Blackness and research is to seek to verb research beyond its present market rationalities—and instead, include Black emotions as a fundamental ontological place of knowledge production. To pay attention to emotions as fundamental ontological Black research methodology is to recognize the place of histories of slavery and colonization as a precondition in the research process. It is imperative as a Black researcher to "allow" such histories to speak. Our role is to facilitate such speakability of the unsayable through actively listening to their presentation. Speaking of

Black historical speakability is to find a place within ourselves and studies where Black knowledges and histories come to be considered as unintelligible to speak.

When we speak of Black histories as speaking subject, we also need to ask under whose environment is such speaking made manifest. We need to ask who allows such histories to speak and what are the modalities/methodologies of such permission/s. Such reflexive places of speakabilities of Blackness in research help conceptualize Black research as political in its fluid and contextual histories. The question to Black researchers is "how" to account these Black sensibilities/traumas without ever reducing and simplifying them. Black research will have to seek whose context and knowledge counts in a research regime that works towards the elimination of the Black other. This means a coming to terms with the current colonial and imperial climate dictating the "how" of research and asking a reflexive question of whose research (read life) matters. This epistemological questioning will have to define the "how" of Black research so that those histories of colonialism, slavery, assault of Black bodies, Black racial profiling, and other forms of colonial brutality become the demonic grounds (McKattrick, 2006) of Blackening research. Such histories and their present manifestations will have to be central for any Black research to be considered decolonial and reflexive.

To speak of Black reflexivity in research is to imagine a fundamental and transformative philosophical reorientation of market-oriented research. These assumptions continue to define research among Black communities and beyond and this chapter seeks to push beyond their canonization and instead calls for entrenchment of a different form of Black emotion that continues to be footnoted. This chapter looks at Afrocentricity and the place of canons in Black research. The chapter seeks to define Afrocentricity and Afrocentric research, and open deeper philosophical assumptions of Afrocentric methodologies in ways that bring other possibilities beyond the current canonization of African-centred research. In a nutshell, this chapter seeks to de-industrialize (read industrial complex or the market) the current rationalities hiding behind the colonial progressive Black research process. I call upon a redefinition of Black research to understand Black diversity through time and space in ways that find comfort in discomfort, more so when histories of Black atrocities come to define the how of doing Black research. This chapter calls for a reimagination of love and the philosophy of forgiveness as a necessary reflexive point of undertaking research among Black communities. To do this, I plan to delve into Afrocentric research methodology and the place of love and forgiveness and then look at Blackening research as de-industrialization of knowledge and finally conclude.

4   Afrocentric Research

According to Asante (2009), Afrocentricity is a paradigm that centralizes African histories, context, values, realities, and ways of being in the world that still operates under a colonial platform. Afrocentricity, as a paradigm, shifts the way we see the world by bringing on board African ways of knowing as fundamental in organizing how we think and act. According to Reviere (2001),

> A principal advantage of an Afrocentric approach is that it compels the researcher to challenge the use of the traditional Eurocentric research criteria of objectivity, reliability, and validity in the inquiry process. The researcher is expected to examine and to place in the foreground of the inquiry any and all subjectivities or societal baggage that would otherwise remain hidden and, hence, covertly influence the research activity. (p. 710)

The fact that one has to be open and transparent in their subjectivities in Afrocentric research speaks of critical reflection of the self. This flames Afrocentric research as decolonial and critical, which is the foundation of any qualitative study.

The Afrocentric research paradigm questions the ways knowledge is produced by asking the "how" of truth making. It seeks to look at knowledge production as a subjective process that relies on the context under which that knowledge is produced. Context remains the fundamental place of knowing and producing knowledge in African-based knowledge making. This orientation that is African centered questions reliability and validity as a colonial practice of discarding other ways of knowing as broken and unnecessary since they cannot be trusted. Such terms as reliability and validity are replaced instead with facts that some histories will have to be trusted because they have existed through time and space and that their "rigour" is based on their resiliency and existence even after violent colonial erasure. To that end, African knowledge making becomes a process of identifying ways in which subjugated knowledge continues to exist and resist colonialism. Rather than research being a fact-finding practice, it becomes a process of a genealogical ethical responsibility of identifying points of epistemological resistance of African knowledges.

The question of "reliability" speaks of the ways in which African-based knowledge continues to exist and serve communities through time and space. In a nutshell, "reliability" becomes a question of ethics where knowledge is not just about markets and truth making but also about service to community needs, desires, and aspirations. Reliability is a question of ways in which benefits return to the community. To be reliable is to look at the place of research in solving communities' problems even in their complex context and times. As such, Black communities have long relied on these African-based methodologies to answer their everyday challenges. The question of knowledge validations is philosophical, in that the "how" of knowledge (whose realities, knowledge, and values count) becomes the framework of Afrocentric knowledge creation. Afrocentric canons or principles define the "how" of doing research among communities of Black and African.

In a nutshell, research among African communities should be contextual to African values, realities, and histories. Researchers must appreciate African ways of life as an imperative. For example, in African communities, knowledge production is part of living and being African. What this means is that in everyday life, an African person is creating knowledge consciously and unconsciously. Having grown in a rural place in Kenya with my grandparents, I can attest to the fact that even when cooking food with my grandmother, the kitchen was also an educational centre where I learned a lot and came to appreciate African values and culture. This was done through story telling which would be told in a very cinematographic way (read research as art). Such spaces can easily be reduced or normally seen as "just cooking spaces" but in the African context they happen to be spaces where knowledge is also produced and disseminated. In Western thought, the kitchen is identified as a place of emotions and yet in an African context it is both the place of emotions and rationality. This mean that to be an Afrocentric researcher is to recognize the place of community (read emotions) in the research process. In Afrocentric research, knowledge is produced by the community and the role of the researcher is to guide such a production. Any Afrocentric research should pay attention to its purpose. This means that research should bring change and transformation within such societies (Mazama, 2003). Beyond that, an Afrocentric research should be a process of bringing people together for a cause (Asante, 2009). This means that research should not be about self-exultation but rather a process of bringing social change to Black communities.

5   Afrocentric Methods and Methodologies

According to Asante (2009), there are five general characteristics to Afrocentric research methods. One is that every phenomenon that is to be studied must be located. This speaks to context as a fundamental aspect of Afrocentric research methodology. The second Afrocentric research method looks at diversities and multiplicities of realities and phenomenon and the place of the researcher in these fluctuations. This speaks of the reflexive self as a necessity in research that is steeped in African values and realities. The third method looks at the use of words and language in our everyday research process. I would add that this point is also necessary to open discussion of how dominant discourse determines how we undertake research process. At this point, we seek to deconstruct how we term and divide research between they who know and subsequently termed as expert versus those who do not know and need to be introspected to correct their brokenness. This speaks to the dyadic colonial place in scientific research, for which Afrocentric research seeks to decolonize and blur how we look at researcher–participant relationships to start a different special conception of what really counts as knowledge.

An Afrocentric research method therefore deconstructs the use of language as a place of decolonizing the how of research process. According to Asante (2009), the question of power, prestige, and privilege is a fundamental place for critical reflection when doing an Afrocentric study. To add to this aspect is to ask how researcher and community exercise power and how knowledge so produced operates within power modalities that seek to affirm the place of market in the research process. To speak of critical reflection/reflexivity as fundamental in research is to identify and unravel colonial trails of our place of implication as researchers. Such a process of reflexivity calls for the centralization of difficult histories of slavery and colonialism in the how we come to know who we are and our place in this social world. Research therefore is an expression of those historical "ghosts" in the present operation of how we create knowledge without necessarily trying to run away from such uncomfortable discussions. The final part of Afrocentric research is to remember that we operate within political, social, institutional, and economic rationalities that do not work for us. Knowing our place in research and our implication in these rationalities while not forgetting their historical place of tormenting Black bodies is fundamental in every research process.

6   On Being Black in Research

To be Black and undertake research within and without the Black community entails more than White thinking (Speight Vaughn, 2019). Black and Blackness is a movement from colonial fixation of what is Black towards experiencing Blackness (Mercer, 1994; Walcott, 2003). Subsequently, Black research is an experience and an encounter—a violent encounter (Mendonca & Russell, 2017; Speight Vaughn, 2019). Blackness and Black research as a violent encounter (movement) means a revolution—a breaking of the "eggshell" from colonial fundamentalism of knowable Black other versus the ever-knowing White expert (Mbembe, 2016). To break the shell is to recognize that the current Black research logic sustains life within an embryonic place of being that denied Black communities from breaking away from those colonial borders. To claim such a denial to Black being and becoming is not to preclude the fact that Black skin has always resisted colonial production brought about by the White mask. The place between the White mask and the Black skin has always been a contested one, and as such a violent encounter. This chapter is framed around such a context of violence as fundamental in knowledge production.

To claim a breaking away is to rapture anti-Black sentiment prevailing in research. To break away is to verb Black and Blackness (Walcott, 2003), which mean a process of returning to the "source." This "return to the source" has for a while been a process of colonial disciplinary power of fixing Black problem. Central to this assertion is Blackening research as a process through which a Black researcher returns to the borderland without such return being dictated by the colonial other. The process of returning to the violent Borland is a self-implicating process of deciding to come to terms with the self in ways that inform social research differently. To return as coming to terms with the self speaks of modalities of sitting in discomfort on prevailing colonial histories of racial erasure and oppression of the Black that continue to affect how we come to know what we know.

The return to the "source" is a coming to terms with the psychic "death" of the self or what I may refer a return to the "territory/country" as a form of self-resurrection. For a while now, I keep asking what education (read also research) means to Black researchers. My take is that research should break away from the dominant ways of knowing as dictated by the White academy. To know is to return, and as such research should be a conduit of facilitating self-return through self-cannibalization. It is a "rage to kill" the I for the sake of sustaining the subjugated "me" (Butler, 2001, 2005). To return is to give accounts of lives that have never been accounted for or have been deemed lost, unintelligible, or forgotten. This means Black research should be a way through which we return home (read the kitchen) to give account of the discounted lives. It is a celebration between the Black researcher and the Black community.

Black research should not be colour coated but rather an engagement with the difference. My wager is that Black research is more than Black. It breaks away from the normalized sense of what Black should be and instead engages with the beyondness and betweenness of Blackness. Blackness is boundless and cannot be contained or conserved (Walcott, 2003). It calls for a breaking away from the "usual and known" colonial reference to Blackness (read Black as irrational, bleak, broke) and engaging with "greying" Blackness with emotions as a definition of knowing. To imagine Black emotions as central to knowledge creation is to "invite" body into the process of knowledge production. To invite is political because Black bodies are samples of accommodation but rather should be accorded their respect. It is not a passive form of accommodation but rather a form that understands the histories of atrocities meted on Black communities. It is a form of accommodation that understands that Black life is gendered, classed, raced, accented, transgendered (Nyaga, 2019) and as a researcher, one has to work with these interlocking socio-political and economic complexities and contradictions. Failure to recognize such interlocking identities (becoming charitable to one identity and discounting others) in research implicates a Black researcher to epistemological violence and imperialism (Butler, 1990; 2005; Spivak, 1998, 2003; Trowler, 2014).This does not mean an eradication of the mind from the process of knowledge production, but rather an acknowledgement that the mind has historically been positioned as fundamental rational complex of the "how" of the knowledge creation (Bereiter, 2002).

Black research is a blurring of the split between the mind and the body in ways that break research from colonial and dominant imprisonment of the mind as the container (Bereiter, 2002) of knowledge assemblages and affirmation of emotions as relevant spaces of knowledge production. It is uncoupling the fundamentals of knowledge production in ways that the mind and the body account for their place in knowledge production. My take on accountability is framed on the psychic process of retrieving the Black self from hidden places of the mind in ways that come to account for the accumulated losses and damages meted on the Black body through colonial atrocities expressed in self-hate and denial that the body is also central in producing knowledge. It is having a mind and body intercourse rather than mind/body break. It is a re-territorialization of the Black psychic land in ways that affirm Black as knowledgeable and affirming its ontological place of being as a requisite in knowledge production.

I want to argue that Black research goes beyond identity politics of who is Black and who is not (Walcott, 2003). It is a breaking away from colour-coated knowing of the other and discolouring (read unmarking) knowledge production. This call for a redefinition of research terms to refer Black research as a process of alliance between and beyond those engaged in research (read as participants and researchers). To that end, Black research is a social action and transformative project rather than a fact-finding event. Black research is a process of coalition building—a process of coming together.

If Blackness is a movement, then Black research should be a process of un-mapping colonial "land" demarcation. Black research should be opening hidden histories and making them move from their place of pastness (read

Foucault (1980) and genealogies of knowledge). It is not a return/movement to the past for its own sake but a recovering of those histories as fundamental to understanding contemporary atrocities meted on Black bodies. Such a movement requires the support of others. It should be a recognition that we are Black and that we need others for us to be Black. It is a move through which the other so referred as "not Black" dissolves and disappears from the "self" to come to a place where they become Black in their deeds, values, feelings, and thoughts. Blackening research should be coalitional and an acknowledgement that others have a place to play in the making of who we are. Of course, I assume that the first take to this claim would be: Can a White undertake Black research? This question has varied sentiments that evoke emotional responses as well as rage. I argue that such emotions are a necessary place of research. Black research is not a comfortable practice. It is a violent encounter with the self and others (Malpass et al., 2016). Black research is not about burying such encounters by a coming to terms with them. I refer to these encounters as inconsolable mourning and making Black and Blackness grievable (Alves, 2014). I look at this as rage framed around the fact that colonialism stole and continues to steal from Black communities. The systemic atrocities within Black communities deserves a place of Black rage.

My wager is that Black communities must realize that while White and Whiteness is out there and has been implicated in colonizing the Black community, its presence continues to define the "how" of our realities. Denying the "I" (which is White in values) in you is rather simplistic and plays within the colonial logic of the others versus us. In a nutshell, one may be Black but White in one's values and realities. To fail to account for our "Whiteness" in our Blackness is to sit on a time bomb that may explode on us and not them (those we refer to as enemies because they look White). To call for a Black research methodology is to identify ways in which we are implicated in self-violence and hate (read lateral violence). I would refer us back to Black rage in terms of coming to terms with our own implicit implication on colonial violence in our Black communities. It is easy for a Black researcher (read within the current identificatory politics of who really is Black) to find as his right to research Black community. Notice that such research has taken a gendered formulation-telling of the ways in which Black men attain direct licence to do research among the Black community. This returns us to the very original claim that while identity politics may play a role on who is to do research among the Black communities, it is equally important to identify the ways in which identity/ies in research are complex and interlocked in terms of how they are raced, gendered, and classed and as such we should pay attention to how they implicate us in epistemological violence and imperialism.

I argue that Black is interlocked and a ground of alliance. Black research should not be reduced to the question of "I am Black" but extend beyond "foundational construction of who is Black." This wager calls for a reformulation of identity politics to a point where Black research becomes an interlocking process of doing research. It brings sense that such an interlocking process of Blackening research identifies ways in which race, gender, class, and other social constructions are fundamental places in research process and alliance. It is an acknowledgement that the colonial process of knowledge production continues to play a role even within the Black community and as such our role is to find ways in which we can decolonize our psychic self through others. If we are to argue that a "White cannot work within a Black community" then we play within the colonial regime of "us versus them." Black research breaks away from coloniality by recognizing it as a process of engaging with past and present atrocities without necessarily replicating their effect through reducing others. To decide that the White has no place to undertake research within Black communities is to "label" them as unworthy to the becoming of us when we need them to become.

Black research is a form of being transparent and accountable with each other and the self (Reich et al., 2017). To map the other as placeless in Black research freezes us and the role of Blackening research. I argue that while colonization continues to inflict pain and atrocities in Black communities, it is equally an art of colonialism when we deny the fact that we have ethical duties and responsibilities to treat them differently (Butler, 2013). To treat the other differently means a revolution from colonial form of erasure to a form that recognizes the other as human with rights. Such a philosophical research orientation means re-organization of what we term as human and rights. As a Black researcher, one has to think of the precarious position one occupies within the right and human narrative. There is a sense in which being Black in research is being homeless; and yet this chapter claims that to be homeless is a powerful position of reorienting research among Black communities. To think of right and human as fundamental in research means breaking away from White formations of rights and human and enjoining our place of humanity that seek to affirm that research as human process of coming to know is also equally a process of becoming human as a praxis. To become human therefore will be acknowledging our place in the street and knowing our place of homelessness is an essential point of decolonizing our ways of knowing.

To be homeless is emotional yet a necessary point of decolonizing our minds. To break away and celebrate "being homeless as a research practice" means unwrapping our body and recognizing that the skin is prison misguided as our home. The body as an emotional place of knowledge identifies and connects community as fundamental place of knowledge creation, which is contradictory to the normalized way of knowing which seeks to place the individual above others. In a nutshell, to be a Black researcher within and without Black community is a journey of returning to our communities and acknowledging that as a researcher you are implicated in colonialism of Black communities and as such a necessity to be critically reflexive and decolonial.

7   Towards a Black Afrocentric Methodology

While I do concur with above assumptions on Afrocentric methods, my wager is that we need to reorient our view of Black research to what Emmanuel Levinas sought to affirm: that to know the other is to come to terms with the fact that the other is prior to us. As researchers, we have been operated to believe that we know the other and subsequently reduce the other to objects of introspection or what Foucault calls templates of knowledge production. To Levinas, ethics comes before knowledge. This means that knowledge will have to learn through and between what is ethical. To be ethical is to sit comfortable with what has never been said. This means bringing the unsaid to the foreground in ways that complicate how we come to know. To speak of this within and without research process is to claim that historical messiness must become central in our knowing. Knowledge without such return to history shall then become unethical and an exercise of simplification and reductionism, to which populations of Black continue to suffer and disappear. This means that Black research will have to find peace with that history in ways that call into question the role of colonialism in the maiming of these communities. To undertake Black research will mean to become Black. This means that one will have to relate with Black culture and ways of being without necessary centering themselves as the expert of that community. This is a psychic process of self-production that supersedes the self in ways that are ethical and political and meant to bring change to society.

To speak of Black research means that Black become an ethical imperative for every researcher planning to undertake research within Black communities. Black as an ethical place of becoming will first mean that as a researcher, one will have to find peace with the histories of colonialism. This will mean that as a researcher, one must die and find a place to become a ghost to be able to have a negotiation with that harsh reality of Black erasure. Key to Black research is to find comfort in a very uncomfortable process of knowing. Secondly, to be a Black researcher is to become Black again. This wager is necessary so that Black can be seen beyond the liturgy of colour. Black is a verb that cannot be nouned (Walcott, 2003). If Black research is to make any sense and contribute

to Black community, we must work with it variously and in its complex formations. This will mean that we look at Black as evolving and defying colonial
time and space. To be Black in research should not necessarily mean because
you are Black then consequently you have a ticket to undertake research in
Black community. This is reductionist and simplistic in nature and lies within
colonial logic of affirmative action that tokenizes and instrumentalizes politics
of social justice. What this means is that as a person who identifies as Black,
I happens to have lived within a very colonial academy that has diluted my
Blackness and as such I will have to return to my Blackness for me to be able
to undertake research that brings change to Black community. To claim that
return is to find a place where the self-formation finds peace with historical
injustices among this community while claiming my place of research in the
academy is implicated in this form of colonialism. To return is to realize that
I walk a precarious point of ethical imperative that may help me or deny my
place of being. This is an ethical liminality that may provide a resurrection
of the self to understand the other without necessarily being objective and
final. It is a shedding of the self to find the repressed me, who has historically
be suppressed, and making the candid decision to centralize Blackness as an
important ethical place of research process.

This return or ethical process of Black research is psychic in nature and
seeks to blur the divide between what is normal research and what is abnormal
knowledge. In a sense, to return to the self is a reflexive process of actioning
Blackness rather than containing its potential. It is a call for imagining Black
potential and strength in ways that bring social action informed by histories
of injustices. This form of research seeks to blur Black between and beyond
the normalized sense of knowledge production. My wager is that the ethical
responsibility of any researcher who wants to undertake research among the
Black community should be conscious of their implications and be ready to
emancipate themselves from their mental slavery. The process is psychic in
nature and entails recognizing that what they know about Black community
must be placed within a framework of understanding that ethics come prior
to knowledge. According to Adital Ben-ari and Roni Strier (2010), who discuss
cultural competence and understanding of the other,

> By emphasising the primacy of ethics to knowledge, Levinas creates a
> new framework for working across differences. It highlights the signif-
> icance and implications of the connection between knowledge of the
> other and dominating the other. The complex process of othering and
> debates about cultural differences and otherness raise fundamental
> questions with regard to the nature of social knowledge. It requires us to

reconsider our accumulated knowledge about the "Other" and to review its implications for limiting our openness in the encounter with the "Other." (p. 2159)

To take such a Levinasian philosophical research tangent will not mean a denial of the self but a coming to terms with the violent formation of self and the replication of that self on others. It means that research will have to define a new channel of knowledge formation that is critically reflexive and that acknowledges we are implicated in the violence meted on our Black community. To that end, one may ask, who has the right to do research among Black community if not people who identify as Black? My wager to this is to follow that question with: Who identifies as Black? Could such a question lead us to a finite discussion of Blackness to such an extent where Black ceases to be "Black" and becomes a psychic process of becoming? I return to the very question of just because I am Black does that mean I have the right to undertake research among "my people" (notice and read the ownership)? And when we talk of right, which right comes to define this ownership? As Black researchers, do we necessarily need to collapse Black communities to property of ownership for us to call such a process Black enough? My wager to these assumptions is to call for openness to others who are ready to form coalitions with Black communities to join hand in hand with Black research. This will mean a renewal of who we see as enemies. Sometimes the enemy is within us.

It is important to recognize our implication to the harsh realities that our Black communities face. To speak of open doors is to remind our conscious and unconscious self that change is necessary and that we will need to go beyond our current construction of colour to open up spaces of alliance with those we may normally see as enemies. To deny such a reality of breaking social construction is to be embroidered with the same colonial master. In a nutshell, we need our enemy for two things: they created the problem and as such they have every responsibility to clean it. Our role at this point is to facilitate the process of bringing that change. The enemy in us already understands the game of repression and as such they are the ones we are going to use to open the gate of freedom. Such a freedom shall be dictated by our histories.

References

Alves, J. A. (2014). From necropolis to blackpolis: Necropolitical governance and Black spatial praxis in São Paulo, Brazil. *Antipode* 46 (2): 323–339. https://doi.org/10.1111/anti.12055.

Asante, M. K. (2009, April 13). *Afrocentricity*. http://www.asante.net/articles/1/afrocentricity/.

Ben-Ari, A., & Strier, R. (2010). Rethinking cultural competence: What can we learn from Levinas? *The British Journal of Social Work* 40 (7): 2155–2167. doi:10.1093/bjsw/bcp153.

Bereiter, C. (2002). *Education and mind in the knowledge age*. Mahwah, NJ: Erlbaum.

Butler, J. (1990). *Gender trouble: Feminism and the subversion of identity*. Milton Park, Abingdon, UK: Routledge.

Butler, J. (2001). Giving an account of oneself. *Diacritics* 31 (4): 22–40.

Butler, J. (2005). *Giving an account of oneself*. New York: Fordham University Press.

Danso, R. (2015). An integrated framework of critical cultural competence and anti-oppressive practice for social justice social work research. *Qualitative Social Work* 14 (4): 572–588. https://doi.org/10.1177%2F1473325014558664.

Dei, G. J. S. (2018). "Black like me": Reframing Blackness for decolonial politics. *Educational Studies* 54 (2): 117–142. https://doi.org/10.1080/00131946.2018.1427586.

Foucault, M. (1980). *Power/knowledge: Selected interviews and other writings, 1972–1977*. New York: Pantheon.

George, P. (2017). Critical arts-based research: An effective strategy for knowledge mobilization and community activism. In H. Parada & S. Wehbi (Eds.), *Reimagining anti-oppression social work research* (pp. 29–38). Toronto, ON: Canadian Scholars' Press.

Gilroy, P. (1993). *The Black Atlantic: Modernity and double consciousness*. Cambridge, MA: Harvard University Press.

Gilroy, P. (2004a). *After empire: Melancholia or convivial culture?* Milton Park, Abingdon, UK: Routledge.

Gilroy, P. (2004b). *Between camps: Nations, cultures and the allure of race*. Milton Park, Abingdon, UK: Taylor & Francis.

Gilroy, P. (2010). *Darker than blue: On the moral economies of Black Atlantic culture*. Cambridge, MA: Harvard University Press.

Hall, S., & Ghazoul, F. (2012). Cultural identity and diaspora. *Alif: Journal of Comparative Poetics* 32: 257.

Hlela, Z. (2018). Learning through the action of research: Reflections on an Afrocentric research design. *Community Development Journal* 53 (2): 375–392. https://doi.org/10.1093/cdj/bsw033.

Liu, W. M., Sheu, H., & Williams, K. (2004). Multicultural competency in research: Examining the relationships among multicultural competencies, research training and self-efficacy, and the multicultural environment. *Cultural Diversity and Ethnic Minority Psychology* 10 (4): 324–339. https://doi.org/10.1037/1099-9809.10.4.324.

Malpass, A., Sales, K., & Feder, G. (2016). Reducing symbolic-violence in the research encounter: Collaborating with a survivor of domestic abuse in a qualitative study in UK primary care. *Sociology of Health & Illness* 38 (3): 442–458. https://doi.org/10.1111/1467-9566.12352.

Mazama, A. (2003). *The Afrocentric paradigm*. Trenton, NJ: Africa World Press.

Mbembe, A. (2016). Africa in the new century. *The Massachusetts Review* 57 (1): 91–104.

McKittrick, K. (2006). *Demonic grounds: Black women and the cartographies of struggle*. Minneapolis, MN: University of Minnesota Press.

Mendonca, K. J., & Russell, M. (2017). Threeing: Incorporating "relational circuits" into the research encounter. *The Design Journal* 20 (Suppl. 1): S4794–S4795. https://doi.org/10.1080/14606925.2017.1352996.

Mercer, K. (1994). *Welcome to the jungle: New positions in Black cultural studies*. Milton Park, Abingdon, UK: Routledge.

Nyaga, D. (2019). *Re-imagining Black masculinity: Praxis of Kenyan men in Toronto* (Doctoral dissertation, University of Toronto). TSpace. https://tspace.library.utoronto.ca/handle/1807/97580.

Padgett, D. K. (2017). Choosing the right qualitative approach(es). *In Qualitative methods in social work research* (3rd ed., pp. 31–56). Thousand Oaks, CA: Sage.

Pon, G. (2009). Cultural competency as new racism: An ontology of forgetting. *Journal of Progressive Human Services* 20 (1): 59–71. https://doi.org/10.1080/10428230902871173.

Reich, J., Liebenberg, L., Denny, M., Battiste, H., Bernard, A., Christmas, K., Dennis, R., Denny, D., Knockwood, I., Nicholas, R., & Paul, H. (2017). In this together: Relational accountability and meaningful research and dissemination with youth. *International Journal of Qualitative Methods* 16 (1). https://doi.org/10.1177%2F1609406917717345.

Reviere, R. (2001). Toward an Afrocentric research methodology. *Journal of Black Studies* 31 (6): 709–728. https://doi.org/10.1177%2F002193470103100601.

Rusert, B. (2009). "A study in nature": The Tuskegee experiments and the new south plantation. *Journal of Medical Humanities* 30 (3): 155–171. https://doi.org/10.1007/s10912-009-9086-4.

Sharma, A. (2010). Diseased race, racialized disease: The story of the Negro Project of American Social Hygiene Association against the backdrop of the Tuskegee syphilis experiment. *Journal of African American Studies* 14 (2): 247–262. https://doi.org/10.1007/s12111-009-9099-0.

Shipley, J. W., Comaroff, J., & Mbembe, A. (2010). Africa in theory: A conversation between Jean Comaroff and Achille Mbembe. *Anthropological Quarterly* 83 (3): 653–678. https://doi.org/10.1353/anq.2010.0010.

Smith, L. T. (2012). Colonizing knowledges. In *Decolonizing methodologies: Research and indigenous peoples* (2nd ed., pp. 61–80). London: Zed Books.

Speight Vaughn, M. (2019). Black epistemologies and blues methodology: Engaging liminal ontological space in qualitative research. *Qualitative Inquiry* 26 (8–9): 1090–1101. https://doi.org/10.1177%2F1077800419883307.

Spivak, G. S. (1988). Can the subaltern speak? In C. Nelson & L. Grossberg (Eds.), *Marxism and the interpretation of culture* (pp. 271–315). Champaign, IL: University of Illinois Press.

Spivak, G. C. (2003). Can the subaltern speak? *Die Philosophin* 14 (27): 42–58. https://doi.org/10.5840/philosophin200314275.

Thomas, G. (2008). *Counselling and reflexive research in healthcare: Working therapeutically with clients with inflammatory bowel disease.* London: Jessica Kingsley.

Trowler, V. (2014). May the subaltern speak? Researching the invisible "other" in higher education. *European Journal of Higher Education* 4 (1): 42–54. https://doi.org/10.1080/21568235.2013.851614.

Walcott, R. (2003). *Black like who? Writing Black Canada* (2nd rev. ed.). London, ON: Insomniac Press.

Washington, H. A. (2006). *Medical apartheid: The dark history of medical experimentation on Black Americans from colonial times to the present.* New York: Doubleday.

Wehbi, S. (2017). The use of photography in anti-oppressive research. In H. Parada & S. Wehbi (Eds.), *Reimagining anti-oppression social work research* (pp. 39–46). Toronto, ON: Canadian Scholars' Press.

Worthington, R. L., Soth-McNett, A. M., & Moreno, M. V. (2007). Multicultural counseling competencies research: A 20-year content analysis. *Journal of Counseling Psychology* 54 (4): 351–361. https://doi.org/10.1037/0022-0167.54.4.351.

Afterword

Using Critical Research Methodologies: The Significance of Reflexivity, Resistance, and Response

Rose Ann Torres and Dionisio Nyaga

This book attempts to reimagine the research process from critical, performative, transformative, and reflexive ways that help center communities' needs and aspirations as fundamental in meaning making and knowledge production. For a while, research has been and continues to be an ivory tower out of the community's reach. Production of knowledge has become a neoliberal process that alienates community members from the very knowledge that is supposed to emancipate them. Knowledge production is an industrial process that squeezes blood from communities without giving back. In this, we are reminded of the grinding meat machine that takes away blood from meat only to leave dry mincemeat that is then sold in the market. Key to this book is to engage with the process of removing blood from meat as market rationality that never pays attention to the life that is intrinsically connected to the blood that is shed.

The book engages with the ways in which research has and continues to be implicated in policing and taking life from communities. To speak of policing is to imagine how research has had the passport to walk in the marginalized territories and wreak havoc. This aspect of penetrating communities' spaces has been discussed previously as violent and as a means to imprint colonial power. Research is therefore implicated in the terrorization of communities in ways that are brutal and in disregard of law. In this way, research actions within and without communities have come to affirm what Foucault (1980) refers to as power becoming illegal in local spaces. To speak of research as policing is also to imagine the ways in which research has broken knowledge boundaries in ways never seek to ally with communities but instead that divide and rule over them. To break such a boundary is an exercise of power and privilege and we argue in this book that such a practice is steeped in Whiteness and coloniality.

To think of research as policing is to simultaneously imagine a biopolitical mechanism in terms of the ways in which research continues to be used as a process of surveying communities to determine who lives and who dies (Foucault, 1997). To speak of biopolitics in research, one needs to look at which values and ways of knowing are validated and which are supposedly eliminated.

For a while, Black and Indigenous ways of knowing have been referred to as emotional and broke and, as such, not rational enough. In this book, such emotional knowledges have been identified as the life of any research and our argument is to apply such subjugated knowledges as fundamental in production of knowledge. We argue that such broken or so-called mistaken knowledge are the lifeline of communities, hence if knowledge is to serve the needs of communities, we will need to return the blood to the mincemeat so that societies can start to breathe again.

To speak of some knowledges as emotional while others are deemed to be rational is to imagine the ways in which knowledge is gendered and racialized. For a while, knowledge production (read rational science) has been a public discourse through which heterosexual able-bodied men continue to rule. It is also taken for granted that only White bodies can be trusted in the production of truth. This aspect has helped create the impression that White men are the pinnacle of knowledge production and as such the only bodies that can save humanity from its degeneracy and brokenness. Research has helped affirm this colonial mentality in ways that have led to the elimination of other knowledges that are viewed as unwanted and unnecessary. This has led to the belief that colonial White knowledge is the only one that can civilize and breathe life into the community. One wonders exactly how such dry mincemeat can provide life to the community. How can knowledge from the center help give life to the margins? Our arguments in this book focus on the importance of working with communities in the margins (McKittrick, 2006). We argue that research needs to be marginal for it to speak to the needs of the communities in ways that are authentic and reflexive.

This volume showcases contributors' understanding of research from different vantage points. It centers the contributors' ways of looking at research and how they use these approaches from a critical perspective. The volume has a mix of different research vantage points that help reimagine research as beyond and between rationality and emotionality. This book identifies critical reflexivity as necessary in the re-evaluation of research. To be critically reflexive is to understand that all are implicated in the production of knowledge that continues to erase communities we work with. Critical reflexivity is thereby a process of engaging with the discomfort of self-cannibalization in a way that displaces the will of the researcher and engages more with the community (George, 2017). We look at critical reflexivity as a process through which we imagine the self as the vehicle that helps structural power within and without structure come to life. We breathe life into the very colonial structures that continue to squeeze life from our communities.

Having come to terms with our point of implication, critical reflexivity calls us to engage with the fact that sometimes we have to philosophically die in order to become the graveyards of our community in ways that allow communities to be grieved (Butler, 2009) and transform our philosophical assumptions in research. Critical reflexivity calls for decoupling the ways in which we imagine research so that the participants (read communities) take a leading role in research. This means that researchers will take a back seat. But we also want to engage with this aspect of taking the back seat and communities taking the leading role (Tanabe et al., 2017) not as a colonially simplistic process but rather one that is critically reflected between the communities and the research. According to Deliovsky (2017), participants also exercise power and as such if our acts as researchers is to allow them to lead without necessarily engaging them into the reason behind that will be counterproductive and may result in us being implicated based on the fact of assuming that we cannot engage with them. We therefore call for an engaged process of engaging participants in research in ways that humanize and make them take control of their life through research (Wilson, 2008). This helps mark research as critically reflexive and ready to mix the blood and the mincemeat in ways that go beyond the normalized process of making knowledge.

Key to critical reflexive research is to imagine the mix between mincemeat and blood as a necessary combination/methodology that can help unlock the colonial process of knowledge production in ways that give life to the communities. The methodologies of research and practice help imagine communities beyond their everyday experiences and start acknowledging how such experiences both resist and uncouple colonial boundaries of knowledge production. Through a critically reflexive research process, research takes an ethical tangent in ways that identify everybody as having the power to produce knowledge. Ethical obligation is a fundamental necessity of any critically reflexive research. As Levinas would say, we come to engage with the face of the other in ways that mark us as late (Llewelyn, 1995; Perpich, 2008). This means that the role of the researcher as the knower of the other is flawed and contradictory and steals the life out of communities. For researchers to be ethically responsible, they will have to come to terms with the fact that they cannot understand the face of the other. Rather, they can only imagine and acknowledge the pain of the other. To do this, every researcher will have to "kill" (read necropolitics) the urge to be the expert of the other. This means the death of self for the resurrection of another self that imagines others and their point of need.

References

Butler, J. (2009). *Frames of war: When is life grievable?* London: Verso.

Deliovsky, K. (2017). Whiteness in the qualitative research setting: Critical skepticism, radical reflexivity and anti-racist feminism. *Journal of Critical Race Inquiry* 4 (1): 1–24. https://doi.org/10.24908/JCRI.V4I1.6369.

Foucault, M. (1980). *Power/knowledge: Selected interviews and other writings, 1972–1977.* New York, NY: Pantheon.

Foucault, M. (1997). *Society must be defended* (D. Macey, Trans.). London: Penguin.

George, P. (2017). Critical arts-based research: An effective strategy for knowledge mobilization and community activism. In H. Parada & S. Wehbi (Eds.), *Reimagining anti-oppression social work research* (pp. 29–38). Toronto, ON: Canadian Scholars' Press.

Llewelyn, J. (1995). *Emmanuel Levinas: The genealogy of ethics.* Milton Park, Abingdon, UK: Routledge.

McKittrick, K. (2006). *Demonic grounds: Black women and the cartographies of struggle.* Minneapolis, MN: University of Minnesota Press.

Perpich, D. (2008). *The ethics of Emmanuel Levinas.* Stanford, CA: Stanford University Press.

Tanabe, M., Pearce, E., & Krause, S. K. (2017). "Nothing about us, without us": Conducting participatory action research among and with persons with disabilities in humanitarian settings. *Action Research* 16 (3): 280–298. https://doi.org/10.1177%2F1476750316685878.

Wilson, S. (2008). *Research is ceremony: Indigenous research methods.* Black Point, Nova Scotia: Fernwood.

Name Index

Subject Index

www.ingramcontent.com/pod-product-compliance
Lightning Source LLC
Chambersburg PA
CBHW070927030426
42336CB00014BA/2569